D1390326

A REFLECTION
OF GREATNESS

The speeches in this book, specially
selected for Corgi Books, include all
Sir Winston Churchill's most famous
wartime sayings . . .

. . . blood, toil, tears and sweat . . .
. . . never in the field of human conflict . . .
. . . we shall fight on the beaches . . .
. . . some chicken – some neck! . . .

. . . they are all here in a highly readable
volume which provides, in effect, a
brief history of World War II.

It is an exciting and stirring book that
reflects the greatness of one of the most
outstanding figures of our time.

Other books about Sir Winston Churchill

THE VALIANT YEARS
THE FINEST HOURS

and published by Corgi Books

Sir Winston Churchill
K.G., O.M., C.H., M.P.

Great War Speeches

CORGI BOOKS
A DIVISION OF TRANSWORLD PUBLISHERS LTD

GREAT WAR SPEECHES
A CORGI BOOK 0 552 11002 7

The speeches in this book were specially selected for
Corgi Books from The War Speeches of the
Rt. Hon. Winston S. Churchill, O.M., C.H., P.C., M.P.,
compiled by Charles Eade and published by
Cassell & Company Ltd., in three volumes.

PRINTING HISTORY
Corgi edition published 1957
Corgi edition reprinted 1958
Corgi edition reprinted 1959
Corgi edition reissued 1963
Corgi edition reprinted 1965 (twice)
Corgi edition reissued 1978

This book is set in 10/11pt Plantin

Corgi Books are published by Transworld Publishers Ltd.,
Century House, 61–63 Uxbridge Road,
Ealing, London, W.5.
Made and printed in Great Britain by
Hunt Barnard Printing Ltd., Aylesbury, Bucks.

Great War Speeches

CONTENTS

PRIME MINISTER

On May 10, 1940, Mr Neville Chamberlain resigned and Mr Winston Churchill became Prime Minister.

A SPEECH TO THE HOUSE OF COMMONS, MAY 13, 1940

On Friday evening last I received His Majesty's commission to form a new administration. It was the evident wish and will of Parliament and the nation that this should be conceived on the broadest possible basis and that it should include all parties, both those who supported the late Government and also the parties of the Opposition. I have completed the most important part of this task. A War Cabinet has been formed of five Members, representing, with the Opposition Liberals, the unity of the nation. The three party leaders have agreed to serve, either in the War Cabinet or in high executive office. The three fighting services have been filled. It was necessary that this should be done in one single day, on account of the extreme urgency and rigour of events. A number of other key positions were filled yesterday, and I am submitting a further list to His Majesty tonight. I hope to complete the appointment of the principal Ministers during tomorrow. The appointment of the other Ministers usually takes a little longer, but I trust that, when Parliament meets again, this part of my task will be completed, and that the administration will be complete in all respects.

I considered it in the public interest to suggest that the House should be summoned to meet today. Mr Speaker agreed, and took the necessary steps, in accordance with the powers conferred upon him by the Resolution of the House. At the end of the proceedings today, the adjournment of the House will be proposed until Tuesday, May 21, with, of course, provision for earlier meeting if need be. The business to be considered during that week will be notified to Members at the earliest opportunity. I now invite the House, by the Resolution which stands in my name, to record its approval of the steps taken and to declare its confidence in the new Government.

To form an administration of this scale and complexity is a serious undertaking in itself, but it must be remembered that we are in the preliminary stage of one of the greatest battles in history, that we are in action in many points in Norway and in Holland, that we have to be prepared in the Mediterranean, that the air battle is continuous and that many preparations have to be made here at home. In this crisis I hope I may be pardoned if I do not address the House at any length today. I hope that any of my friends and colleagues, or former colleagues, who are affected by the political reconstruction, will make all allowance for any lack of ceremony with which it has been necessary to act. I would say to the House, as I said to those who have joined this Government: 'I have nothing to offer but blood, toil, tears and sweat.'

We have before us an ordeal of the most grievous kind. We have before us many, many long months of struggle and of suffering. You ask what is our policy? I will say: It is to wage war, by sea, land and air, with all our might and with all the strength that God can give us: to wage war against a monstrous tyranny, never surpassed in the dark, lamentable catalogue of human crime. That is our policy. You ask, What is our aim? I can answer in one word: Victory – victory at all costs, victory in spite of all terror, victory, however long and hard the road may be; for without victory, there is no survival. Let that be realised; no survival for the British Empire; no survival for all that the British Empire has stood for, no survival for the urge and impulse of the ages, that mankind will move forward towards its goal. But I take up my task with buoyancy and hope. I feel sure that our cause will not be suffered to fail among men. At this time I feel entitled to claim the aid of all, and I say, 'Come, then, let us go forward together with our united strength.'

'BE YE MEN OF VALOUR'

A WORLD BROADCAST, MAY 19, 1940

I speak to you for the first time as Prime Minister in a solemn hour for the life of our country, of our Empire, of our allies, and, above all, of the cause of freedom. A tremendous battle is raging in France and Flanders. The Germans, by a remarkable combination of air bombing and heavily armoured tanks, have broken through the French defences north of the Maginot Line, and strong columns of their armoured vehicles are ravaging the open country, which for the first day or two was without defenders. They have penetrated deeply and spread alarm and confusion in their track. Behind them there are now appearing infantry in lorries, and behind them, again, the large masses are moving forward. The regroupment of the French armies to make head against, and also to strike at, this intruding wedge has been proceeding for several days, largely assisted by the magnificent efforts of the Royal Air Force.

We must not allow ourselves to be intimidated by the presence of these armoured vehicles in unexpected places behind our lines. If they are behind our front, the French are also at many points fighting actively behind theirs. Both sides are therefore in an extremely dangerous position. And if the French Army, and our own Army, are well handled, as I believe they will be; if the French retain that genius for recovery and counter-attack for which they have so long been famous; and if the British Army shows the dogged endurance and solid fighting power of which there have been so many examples in the past – then a sudden transformation of the scene might spring into being.

It would be foolish, however, to disguise the gravity of the hour. It would be still more foolish to lose heart and courage or to suppose that well-trained, well-equipped armies number-

13

ing three or four millions of men can be overcome in the space of a few weeks, or even months, by a scoop, or raid of mechanised vehicles, however formidable. We may look with confidence to the stabilisation of the front in France, and to the general engagement of the masses, which will enable the qualities of the French and British soldiers to be matched squarely against those of their adversaries. For myself, I have invincible confidence in the French Army and its leaders. Only a very small part of that splendid army has yet been heavily engaged; and only a very small part of France has yet been invaded. There is good evidence to show that practically the whole of the specialised and mechanised forces of the enemy have been already thrown into the battle; and we know that very heavy losses have been inflicted upon them. No officer or man, no brigade or division, which grapples at close quarters with the enemy, wherever encountered, can fail to make a worthy contribution to the general result. The armies must cast away the idea of resisting behind concrete lines or natural obstacles, and must realise that mastery can only be regained by furious and unrelenting assault. And this spirit must not only animate the High Command, but must inspire every fighting man.

In the air – often at serious odds – often at odds hitherto thought overwhelming – we have been clawing down three or four to one of our enemies; and the relative balance of the British and German Air Forces is now considerably more favourable to us than at the beginning of the battle. In cutting down the German bombers, we are fighting our own battle as well as that of France. My confidence in our ability to fight it out to the finish with the German Air Force has been strengthened by the fierce encounters which have taken place and are taking place. At the same time, our heavy bombers are striking nightly at the tap-root of German mechanised power, and have already inflicted serious damage upon the oil refineries on which the Nazi effort to dominate the world directly depends.

We must expect that as soon as stability is reached on the Western Front, the bulk of that hideous apparatus of aggression which gashed Holland into ruin and slavery in a few

14

days, will be turned upon us. I am sure I speak for all when I say we are ready to face it; to endure it; and to retaliate against it – to any extent that the unwritten laws of war permit. There will be many men, and many women, in this island who when the ordeal comes upon them, as come it will, will feel comfort, and even a pride – that they are sharing the perils of our lads at the front – soldiers, sailors and airmen, God bless them – and are drawing away from them a part at least of the onslaught they have to bear. Is not this the appointed time for all to make the utmost exertions in their power? If the battle is to be won, we must provide our men with ever-increasing quantities of the weapons and ammunition they need. We must have, and have quickly, more aeroplanes, more tanks, more shells, more guns. There is imperious need for these vital munitions. They increase our strength against the powerfully armed enemy. They replace the wastage of the obstinate struggle; and the knowledge that wastage will speedily be replaced enables us to draw more readily upon our reserves and throw them in now that everything counts so much.

Our task is not only to win the battle – but to win the war. After this battle in France abates its force, there will come the battle for our island – for all that Britain is, and all that Britain means. That will be the struggle. In that supreme emergency we shall not hesitate to take every step, even the most drastic, to call forth from our people the last ounce and the last inch of effort of which they are capable. The interests of property, the hours of labour, are nothing compared with the struggle for life and honour, for right and freedom, to which we have vowed ourselves.

I have received from the Chiefs of the French Republic, and in particular from its indomitable Prime Minister, M. Reynaud, the most sacred pledges that whatever happens they will fight to the end, be it bitter or be it glorious. Nay, if we fight to the end, it can only be glorious.

Having received His Majesty's commission, I have formed an administration of men and women of every party and of almost every point of view. We have differed and quarrelled in the past; but now one bond unites us all – to wage war until victory is won, and never to surrender ourselves to servitude and shame, whatever the cost and the agony may be. This is one of the most awe-striking periods in the long history of France and Britain. It is also beyond doubt the most sublime. Side by side, unaided except by their kith and kin in the great Dominions and by the wide Empires which rest beneath their shield – side by side, the British and French peoples have advanced to rescue not only Europe but mankind from the foulest and most soul-destroying tyranny which has ever darkened and stained the pages of history. Behind them – behind us – behind the armies and fleets of Britain and France – gather a group of shattered States and bludgeoned races: the Czechs, the Poles, the Norwegians, the Danes, the Dutch, the Belgians – upon all of whom the long night of barbarism will descend, unbroken even by a star of hope, unless we conquer, as conquer we must; as conquer we shall.

Today is Trinity Sunday. Centuries ago words were written to be a call and a spur to the faithful servants of truth and justice: 'Arm yourselves, and be ye men of valour, and be in readiness for the conflict; for it is better for us to perish in battle than to look upon the outrage of our nation and our altar. As the Will of God is in Heaven, even so let it be.'

'A COLOSSAL MILITARY DISASTER'

A SPEECH TO THE HOUSE OF COMMONS, JUNE 4, 1940

From the moment that the French defences at Sedan and on the Meuse were broken at the end of the second week of May, only a rapid retreat to Amiens and the south could have saved the British and French armies who had entered Belgium at the appeal of the Belgian King; but this strategic fact was not immediately realised. The French High Command hoped they would be able to close the gap, and the armies of the north were under their orders. Moreover, a retirement of this kind would have involved almost certainly the destruction of the fine Belgian Army of over twenty divisions and the abandonment of the whole of Belgium. Therefore, when the force and scope of the German penetration were realised and when a new French generalissimo, General Weygand, assumed command in place of General Gamelin, an effort was made by the French and British armies in Belgium to keep on holding the right hand of the Belgians and to give their own right hand to a newly created French army which was to have advanced across the Somme in great strength to grasp it.

However, the German eruption swept like a sharp scythe around the right and rear of the armies of the north. Eight or nine armoured divisions, each of about four hundred armoured vehicles of different kinds, but carefully assorted to be complementary and divisible into small self-contained units, cut off all communications between us and the main French armies. It severed our own communications for food and ammunition, which ran first to Amiens and afterwards through Abbeville, and it shore its way up the coast to Boulogne and Calais, and almost to Dunkirk. Behind this armoured and mechanised onslaught came a number of German divisions in lorries, and behind them again there plodded comparatively slowly the dull brute mass of the ordinary German Army and German people, always so ready to be led to the trampling down in other lands of liberties and comforts which they have never known in their own.

I have said this armoured scythe-stroke almost reached Dunkirk – almost but not quite. Boulogne and Calais were the scenes of desperate fighting. The Guards defended Boulogne for a while and were then withdrawn by orders from this country. The Rifle Brigade, the 60th Rifles, and the Queen Victoria's Rifles, with a battalion of British tanks and 1,000 Frenchmen, in all about 4,000 strong, defended Calais to the last. The British brigadier was given an hour to surrender. He spurned the offer, and four days of intense street fighting passed before silence reigned over Calais, which marked the end of a memorable resistance. Only thirty unwounded survivors were brought off by the Navy and we do not know the

17

fate of their comrades. Their sacrifice, however, was not in vain. At least two armoured divisions, which otherwise would have been turned against the British Expeditionary Force, had to be sent to overcome them. They have added another page to the glories of the light divisions, and the time gained enabled the Graveline waterlines to be flooded and to be held by the French troops.

Thus it was that the port of Dunkirk was kept open. When it was found impossible for the armies of the north to reopen their communications to Amiens with the main French armies, only one choice remained. It seemed, indeed, forlorn. The Belgian, British and French armies were almost surrounded. Their sole line of retreat was to a single port and to its neighbouring beaches. They were pressed on every side by heavy attacks and far outnumbered in the air.

When a week ago today I asked the House to fix this afternoon as the occasion for a statement, I feared it would be my hard lot to announce the greatest military disaster in our long history. I thought — and some good judges agreed with me — that perhaps 20,000 or 30,000 men might be re-embarked. But it certainly seemed that the whole of the French First Army and the whole of the British Expeditionary Force north of the Amiens–Abbeville gap, would be broken up in the open field or else would have to capitulate for lack of food and ammunition. These were the hard and heavy tidings for which I called upon the House and the nation to prepare themselves a week ago. The whole root and core and brain of the British Army, on which and around which we were to build, and are to build, the great British armies in the later years of the war, seemed about to perish upon the field or to be led into an ignominious and starving captivity.

That was the prospect a week ago. But another blow which might well have proved final was yet to fall upon us. The King of the Belgians had called upon us to come to his aid. Had not this ruler and his Government severed themselves from the Allies, who rescued their country from extinction in the late war, and had they not sought refuge in what has proved to be a fatal neutrality, the French and British Armies might well at the outset have saved not only Belgium but perhaps even Poland. Yet at the last moment when Belgium was already invaded, King Leopold called upon us to come to his aid, and even at the last moment we came. He and his brave, efficient army, nearly half a million strong, guarded our left flank and thus kept open our only line of retreat to the sea. Suddenly, without prior consultation, with the least possible notice, without the advice of his Ministers and upon his own personal act, he sent a plenipotentiary to the German Command, surrendered his army and exposed our whole flank and means of retreat.

I asked the House a week ago to suspend its judgement because the facts were not clear, but I do not feel that any reason now exists why we should not form our own opinions upon this pitiful episode. The surrender of the Belgian Army compelled the British at the shortest notice to cover a flank to the sea more than thirty miles in length. Otherwise all would have been cut off, and all would have shared the fate to which King Leopold had condemned the finest army his country had ever formed. So in doing this and in exposing this flank, as anyone who followed the operations on the map will see, contact was lost between the British and two out of the three corps forming the First French Army, who were still farther from the coast than we were, and it seemed impossible that any large number of Allied troops could reach the coast.

The enemy attacked on all sides with great strength and fierceness, and their main power, the power of their far more numerous air force, was thrown into the battle or else concentrated upon Dunkirk and the beaches. Pressing in upon the narrow exit, both from the east and from the west, the enemy began to fire with cannon upon the beaches by which alone the shipping could approach or depart. They sowed magnetic mines in the channels and seas; they sent repeated waves of hostile aircraft, sometimes more than a hundred strong in one formation, to cast their bombs upon the single pier that remained, and upon the sand dunes upon which the troops had their eyes for shelter. Their U-boats, one of which was sunk, and their motor launches took their toll of the vast traffic

19

which now began. For four or five days an intense struggle reigned. All their armoured divisions – or what was left of them – together with great masses of infantry and artillery, hurled themselves in vain upon the ever-narrowing, ever-contracting appendix within which the British and French armies fought.

Meanwhile, the Royal Navy, with the willing help of countless merchant seamen, strained every nerve to embark the British and Allied troops; 220 light warships and 650 other vessels were engaged. They had to operate upon the difficult coast, often in adverse weather, under an almost ceaseless hail of bombs and an increasing concentration of artillery fire. Nor were the seas, as I have said, themselves free from mines and torpedoes. It was in conditions such as these that our men carried on, with little or no rest, for days and nights on end, making trip after trip across the dangerous waters, bringing with them always men whom they had rescued. The numbers they have brought back are the measure of their devotion and their courage. The hospital ships, which brought off many thousands of British and French wounded, being so plainly marked were a special target for Nazi bombs; but the men and women on board them never faltered in their duty.

Meanwhile, the Royal Air Force, which had already been intervening in the battle, so far as its range would allow, from home bases, now used part of its main metropolitan fighter strength, and struck at the German bombers, and at the fighters which in large numbers protected them. This struggle was protracted and fierce. Suddenly the scene has cleared, the crash and thunder has for the moment – but only for the moment – died away. A miracle of deliverance, achieved by valour, by perserverance, by perfect discipline, by faultless service, by resource, by skill, by unconquerable fidelity, is manifest to us all. The enemy was hurled back by the retreating British and French troops. He was so roughly handled that he did not hurry their departure seriously. The Royal Air Force engaged the main strength of the German Air Force, and inflicted upon them losses of at least four to one; and the Navy, using nearly 1,000 ships of all kinds, carried over

335,000 men, French and British, out of the jaws of death and shame, to their native land and to the tasks which lie immediately ahead. We must be very careful not to assign to this deliverance the attributes of a victory. Wars are not won by evacuations. But there was a victory inside this deliverance, which should be noted. It was gained by the Air Force. Many of our soldiers coming back have not seen the Air Force at work; they saw only the bombers which escaped its protective attack. They underrate its achievements. I have heard much talk of this; that is why I go out of my way to say this. I will tell you about it.

This was a great trial of strength between the British and German Air Forces. Can you conceive a greater objective for the Germans in the air than to make evacuation from these beaches impossible, and to sink all these ships which were displayed, almost to the extent of thousands? Could there have been an objective of greater military importance and significance for the whole purpose of the war than this? They tried hard, and they were beaten back; they were frustrated in their task. We got the Army away; and they have paid four-fold for any losses which they have inflicted. Very large formations of German aeroplanes – and we know that they are a very brave race – have turned on several occasions from the attack of one-quarter of their number of the Royal Air Force, and have dispersed in different directions. Twelve aeroplanes have been hunted by two. One aeroplane was driven into the water and cast away, by the mere charge of a British aeroplane, which had no more ammunition. All of our types – the Hurricane, the Spitfire and the new Defiant – and all our pilots have been vindicated as superior to what they have at present to face.

When we consider how much greater would be our advantage in defending the air above this island against an overseas attack, I must say that I find in these facts a sure basis upon which practical and reassuring thoughts may rest. I will pay my tribute to these young airmen. The great French Army was very largely, for the time being, cast back and disturbed by the onrush of a few thousands of armoured vehicles. May it not also be that the cause of civilisation itself will be defended by

21

the skill and devotion of a few thousand airmen. There never had been, I suppose, in all the world, in all the history of war, such an opportunity for youth. The Knights of the Round Table, the Crusaders, all fall back into the past: not only distant but prosaic; these young men, going forth every morn to guard their native land and all that we stand for, holding in their hands these instruments of colossal and shattering power, of whom it may be said that

'Every morn brought forth a noble chance
And every chance brought forth a noble knight'

deserve our gratitude, as do all of the brave men who, in so many ways and on so many occasions, are ready, and continue ready, to give life and all for their native land.

I return to the Army. In the long series of very fierce battles, now on this front, now on that, fighting on three fronts at once, battles fought by two or three divisions against an equal or somewhat larger number of the enemy, and fought fiercely on some of the old grounds that so many of us knew so well, in these battles our losses in men have exceeded 30,000 killed, wounded and missing. I take occasion to express the sympathy of the House to all who have suffered bereavement or who are still anxious. The President of the Board of Trade* is not here today. His son has been killed, and many in the House have felt the pangs of affliction in the sharpest form. But I will say this about the missing. We have had a large number of wounded come home safely to this country, but I would say about the missing that there may be very many reported missing who will come back home, some day, in one way or another. In the confusion of this fight it is inevitable that many have been left in positions where honour required no further resistance from them.

Against this loss of over 30,000 men, we can set a far heavier loss certainly inflicted upon the enemy. But our losses in material are enormous. We have perhaps lost one-third of the men we lost in the opening days of the battle of March 21,

*Sir Andrew Duncan

22

1918, but we have lost nearly as many guns – nearly 1,000 – and all our transport, all the armoured vehicles that were with the Army in the north. This loss will impose a further delay on the expansion of our military strength. The expansion had not been proceeding as fast as we had hoped. The best of all we had to give had gone to the British Expeditionary Force, and although they had not the numbers of tanks and some articles of equipment which were desirable, they were a very well and finely equipped army. They had the first-fruits of all that our industry had to give, and that is gone. And now here is this further delay. How long it will be, how long it will last, depends upon the exertions which we make in this island. An effort the like of which has never been seen in our records is now being made. Work is proceeding everywhere, night and day, Sundays and weekdays. Capital and labour have cast aside their interests, rights and customs and put them into the common stock. Already the flow of munitions has leapt forward. There is no reason why we should not in a few months overtake the sudden and serious loss that has come upon us, without retarding the development of our general programme.

Nevertheless, our thankfulness at the escape of our Army and so many men, whose loved ones have passed through an agonising week, must not blind us to the fact that what has happened in France and Belgium is a colossal military disaster. The French Army has been weakened, the Belgian Army has been lost, a large part of those fortified lines upon which so much faith had been reposed is gone, many valuable mining districts and factories have passed into the enemy's possession, the whole of the Channel ports are in his hands, with all the tragic consequences that follow from that, and we must expect another blow to be struck almost immediately at us or at France. We are told that Herr Hitler has a plan for invading the British Isles. This has often been thought of before. When Napoleon lay at Boulogne for a year with his flat-bottomed boats and his Grand Army, he was told by someone, 'There are bitter weeds in England.' There are certainly a great many more of them since the British Expeditionary Force returned.

The whole question of home defence against invasion is, of

23

course, powerfully affected by the fact that we have for the time being in this island incomparably more powerful military forces than we have ever had at any moment in this war or the last. But this will not continue. We shall not be content with a defensive war. We have our duty to our ally. We have to reconstitute and build up the British Expeditionary Force once again, under its gallant Commander-in-Chief, Lord Gort. All this is in train; but in the interval we must put our defences in this island into such a high state of organisation that the fewest possible numbers will be required to give effective security and that the largest possible potential of offensive effort may be realised. On this we are now engaged. It will be very convenient, if it be the desire of the House, to enter upon this subject in a Secret Session. Not that the Government would necessarily be able to reveal in very great detail military secrets, but we like to have our discussions free, without the restraint imposed by the fact that they will be read the next day by the enemy; and the Government would benefit by views freely expressed in all parts of the House by Members with their knowledge of so many different parts of the country. I understand that some request is to be made upon this subject, which will be readily acceded to by His Majesty's Government.

We have found it necessary to take measures of increasing stringency, not only against enemy aliens and suspicious characters of other nationalities, but also against British subjects who may become a danger or a nuisance should the war be transported to the United Kingdom. I know there are a great many people affected by the orders which we have made who are the passionate enemies of Nazi Germany. I am very sorry for them, but we cannot, at the present time and under the present stress, draw all the distinctions which we should like to do. If parachute landings were attempted and fierce fighting attendant upon them followed, these unfortunate people would be far better out of the way, for their own sakes as well as for ours. There is, however, another class, for which I feel not the slightest sympathy. Parliament has given us the powers to put down Fifth Column activities with a strong hand, and we shall use those powers, subject to the supervision and correction of the House, without the slightest hesitation until we are satisfied, and more than satisfied, that this malignancy in our midst has been effectively stamped out.

Turning once again, and this time more generally, to the question of invasion, I would observe that there has never been a period in all these long centuries of which we boast when an absolute guarantee against invasion, still less against serious raids, could have been given to our people. In the days of Napoleon the same wind which would have carried his transports across the Channel might have driven away the blockading fleet. There was always the chance, and it is that chance which has excited and befooled the imaginations of many Continental tyrants. Many are the tales that are told. We are assured that novel methods will be adopted, and when we see the originality of malice, the ingenuity of aggression, which our enemy displays, we may certainly prepare ourselves for every kind of novel strategem and every kind of brutal and treacherous manoeuvre. I think that no idea is so outlandish that it should not be considered and viewed with a searching, but at the same time, I hope, with a steady eye. We must never forget the solid assurances of sea-power and those which belong to air-power if it can be locally exercised.

I have, myself, full confidence that if all do their duty, if nothing is neglected, and if the best arrangements are made, as they are being made, we shall prove ourselves once again able to defend our island home, to ride out the storm of war, and to outlive the menace of tyranny, if necessary for years, if necessary alone. At any rate, that is what we are going to try to do. That is the resolve of His Majesty's Government – every man of them. That is the will of Parliament and the nation. The British Empire and the French Republic, linked together in their cause and in their need, will defend to the death their native soil, aiding each other like good comrades to the utmost of their strength. Even though large tracts of Europe and many old and famous States have fallen or may fall into the grip of the Gestapo and all the odious apparatus of Nazi rule, we shall not flag or fail. We shall go on to the end, we shall fight in France, we shall fight on the seas and oceans, we shall fight with growing confidence and growing strength in the air, we shall defend our island, whatever the cost may be, we shall fight on the beaches, we shall fight on the landing grounds, we shall fight in the fields and in the streets, we shall fight in the hills; we shall never surrender, and even if, which I do not for a moment believe, this island or a large part of it were subjugated and starving, then our Empire beyond the seas, armed and guarded by the British Fleet, would carry on the struggle, until, in God's good time, the new world, with all its power and might, steps forth to the rescue and the liberation of the old.

THE FINEST HOUR

A SPEECH DELIVERED FIRST TO THE HOUSE OF COMMONS AND THEN BROADCAST, JUNE 18, 1940

I spoke the other day of the colossal military disaster which occurred when the French High Command failed to withdraw the northern armies from Belgium at the moment when they knew that the French front was decisively broken at Sedan and on the Meuse. This delay entailed the loss of fifteen or sixteen French divisions and threw out of action for the critical period the whole of the British Expeditionary Force. Our Army and 120,000 French troops were indeed rescued by the British Navy from Dunkirk but only with the loss of their cannon, vehicles and modern equipment. This loss inevitably took some weeks to repair, and in the first of those weeks the battle in France has been lost. When we consider the heroic resistance made by the French Army against heavy odds in this battle, the enormous losses inflicted upon the enemy and the evident exhaustion of the enemy, it may well be thought that these twenty-five divisions of the best-trained and best-equipped troops might have turned the scale. However, General Weygand had to fight without them. Only three

British divisions or their equivalent were able to stand in the line with their French comrades. They have suffered severely, but they have fought well. We sent every man we could to France as fast as we could re-equip and transport their formations.

I am not reciting these facts for the purpose of recrimination. That I judge to be utterly futile and even harmful. We cannot afford it. I recite them in order to explain why it was we did not have, as we could have had, between twelve and fourteen British divisions fighting in the line in this great battle instead of only three. Now I put all this aside. I put it on the shelf, from which the historians, when they have time, will select their documents to tell their stories. We have to think of the future and not of the past. This also applies in a small way to our own affairs at home. There are many who would hold an inquest in the House of Commons on the conduct of the Governments – and of Parliaments, for they are in it, too – during the years which led up to this catastrophe. They seek to indict those who were responsible for the guidance of our affairs. This also would be a foolish and pernicious process. There are too many in it. Let each man search his conscience and search his speeches. I frequently search mine.

Of this I am quite sure, that if we open a quarrel between the past and the present, we shall find that we have lost the future. Therefore, I cannot accept the drawing of any distinctions between Members of the present Government. It was formed at a moment of crisis in order to unite all the parties and all sections of opinion. It has received the almost unanimous support of both Houses of Parliament. Its Members are going to stand together, and, subject to the authority of the House of Commons, we are going to govern the country and fight the war. It is absolutely necessary at a time like this that every Minister who tries each day to do his duty shall be respected; and their subordinates must know that their chiefs are not threatened men, men who are here today and gone tomorrow, but that their directions must be punctually and faithfully obeyed. Without this concentrated power we cannot face what lies before us. I should not think it would be very advantageous for the House to prolong this Debate this afternoon under conditions of public stress. Many facts are not clear that will be clear in a short time. We are to have a Secret Session on Thursday, and I should think that would be a better opportunity for the many earnest expressions of opinion which Members will desire to make and for the House to discuss vital matters without having everything read the next morning by our dangerous foes.

The disastrous military events which have happened during the past fortnight have not come to me with any sense of surprise. Indeed, I indicated a fortnight ago as clearly as I could to the House that the worst possibilities were open: and I made it perfectly clear then that whatever happened in France would make no difference to the resolve of Britain and the British Empire to fight on, 'if necessary for years, if necessary alone'. During the last few days we have successfully brought off the great majority of the troops we had on the lines of communication in France; and seven-eighths of the troops we have sent to France since the beginning of the war – that is to say, about 350,000 out of 400,000 men – are safely back in this country. Others are still fighting with the French, and fighting with considerable success in their local encounters against the enemy. We have also brought back a great mass of stores, rifles and munitions of all kinds which had been accumulated in France during the last nine months.

We have, therefore, in this island today a very large and powerful military force. This force comprises all our best trained and our finest troops, including scores of thousands of those who have already measured their quality against the Germans and found themselves at no disadvantage. We have under arms at the present time in this island over a million and a quarter men. Behind these we have the Local Defence Volunteers, numbering half a million, only a portion of whom, however, are yet armed with rifles or other firearms. We have incorporated into our defence forces every man for whom we have a weapon. We expect very large additions to our weapons in the near future, and in preparation for this we intend forthwith to call up, drill and train further large numbers. Those who are not called up, or else are employed upon the vast business of munitions production in all its branches – and their ramifications are innumerable – will serve their country best by remaining at their ordinary work until they receive their summons. We have also over here Dominions armies. The Canadians had actually landed in France, but have now been safely withdrawn, much disappointed, but in perfect order, with all their artillery and equipment. And these very high-class forces from the Dominions will now take part in the defence of the Mother Country.

Lest the account which I have given of these large forces should raise the question: Why did they not take part in the great battle in France? I must make it clear that, apart from the divisions training and organising at home, only twelve divisions were equipped to fight upon a scale which justified their being sent abroad. And this was fully up to the number which the French had been led to expect would be available in France at the ninth month of the war. The rest of our forces at home have a fighting value for home defence which will, of course, steadily increase every week that passes. Thus, the invasion of Great Britain would at this time require the transportation across the sea of hostile armies on a very large scale, and after they had been so transported they would have to be continually maintained with all the masses of munitions and supplies which are required for continuous battle – as continuous battle it will surely be.

Here is where we come to the Navy – and after all, we have a Navy. Some people seem to forget that we have a Navy. We must remind them. For the last thirty years I have been concerned in discussions about the possibilities of oversea invasion, and I took the responsibility on behalf of the Admiralty, at the beginning of the last war, of allowing all regular troops to be sent out of the country. That was a very serious step to take, because our Territorials had only just been called up and were quite untrained. Therefore, this island was for several months practically denuded of fighting troops. The Admiralty had confidence at that time in their ability to prevent a mass invasion even though at that time the Germans had a magnificent battle fleet in the proportion of ten to sixteen, even though they were capable of fighting a general engagement every day and any day, whereas now they have only a couple of heavy ships worth speaking of – the *Scharnhorst* and the *Gneisenau*. We are also told that the Italian Navy is to come out and gain sea superiority in these waters. If they seriously intend it, I shall only say that we shall be delighted to offer Signor Mussolini a free and safeguarded passage through the Straits of Gibraltar in order that he may play the part to which he aspires. There is a general curiosity in the British Fleet to find out whether the Italians are up to the level they were at in the last war or whether they have fallen off at all.

Therefore, it seems to me that as far as seaborne invasion on a great scale is concerned, we are far more capable of meeting it today than we were at many periods in the last war and during the early months of this war, before our other troops were trained, and while the BEF had proceeded abroad. Now, the Navy have never pretended to be able to prevent raids by bodies of 5,000 or 10,000 men flung suddenly across and thrown ashore at several points on the coast some dark night or foggy morning. The efficiency of sea-power, especially under modern conditions, depends upon the invading force being of large size. It has to be of large size, in view of our military strength, to be of any use. If it is of large size, then the Navy have something they can find and meet and, as it were, bite on. Now we must remember that even five divisions, however lightly equipped, would require 200 to 250 ships, and with modern air reconnaissance and photography it would not be easy to collect such an armada, marshal it, and conduct it across the sea without any powerful naval forces to escort it; and there would be very great possibilities, to put it mildly, that this armada would be intercepted long before it reached the coast, and all the men drowned in the sea or, at the worst, blown to pieces with their equipment while they were trying to land. We also have a great system of minefields, recently strongly reinforced, through which we alone know the channels. If the enemy tries to sweep passages through these minefields, it will be the task of the Navy to destroy the minesweepers and any other forces employed to protect them. There should be no difficulty in this, owing to our great superiority at sea.

Those are the regular, well-tested, well-proved arguments on which we have relied during many years in peace and war. But the question is whether there are any new methods by which those solid assurances can be circumvented. Odd as it may seem, some attention has been given to this by the Admiralty, whose prime duty and responsibility it is to destroy any large seaborne expedition before it reaches, or at the moment when it reaches these shores. It would not be a good thing for me to go into details of this. It might suggest ideas to other people which they have not thought of, and they would not be likely to give us any of their ideas in exchange. All I will say is that untiring vigilance and mind-searching must be devoted to the subject, because the enemy is crafty and cunning and full of novel treacheries and stratagems. The House may be assured that the utmost ingenuity is being displayed and imagination is being evoked from large numbers of competent officers, well-trained in tactics and thoroughly up to date, to measure and counterwork novel possibilities. Untiring vigilance and untiring searching of the mind is being, and must be, devoted to the subject, because, remember, the enemy is crafty and there is no dirty trick he will not do.

Some people will ask why, then, was it that the British Navy was not able to prevent the movement of a large army from Germany into Norway across the Skagerrak? But the conditions in the Channel and in the North Sea are in no way like those which prevail in the Skagerrak. In the Skagerrak, because of the distance, we could give no air support to our surface ships, and consequently, lying as we did close to the enemy's main air power, we were compelled to use only our submarines. We could not enforce the decisive blockade or interruption which is possible from surface vessels. Our submarines took a heavy toll but could not, by themselves, prevent the invasion of Norway. In the Channel and in the North Sea, on the other hand, our superior naval surface forces, aided

31

by our submarines, will operate with close and effective air assistance.

This brings me, naturally, to the great question of invasion from the air, and of the impending struggle between the British and German Air Forces. It seems quite clear that no invasion on a scale beyond the capacity of our land forces to crush speedily is likely to take place from the air until our Air Force has been definitely overpowered. In the meantime, there may be raids by parachute troops and attempted descents of airborne soldiers. We should be able to give those gentry a warm reception, both in the air and on the ground, if they reach it in any condition to continue the dispute. But the great question is: Can we break Hitler's air weapon? Now, of course, it is a very great pity that we have not got an Air Force at least equal to that of the most powerful enemy within striking distance of these shores. But we have a very powerful Air Force which has proved itself far superior in quality, both in men and in many types of machines, to what we have met so far in the numerous and fierce air battles which have been fought with the Germans. In France, where we were at a considerable disadvantage and lost many machines on the ground when they were standing around the aerodromes, we were accustomed to inflict in the air losses of as much as two to two-and-a-half to one. In the fighting over Dunkirk, which was a sort of no-man's land, we undoubtedly beat the German Air Force, and gained the mastery of the local air, inflicting here a loss of three or four to one day after day. Anyone who looks at the photographs which were published a week or so ago of the re-embarkation, showing the masses of troops assembled on the beach and forming an ideal target for hours at a time, must realise that this re-embarkation would not have been possible unless the enemy had resigned all hope of recovering air superiority at that time and at that place.

In the defence of this island the advantages to the defenders will be much greater than they were in the fighting around Dunkirk. We hope to improve on the rate of three or four to one which was realised at Dunkirk; and in addition all our injured machines and their crews which get down safely – and, surprisingly, a very great many injured machines and men do get down safely in modern air fighting – all of these will fall, in an attack upon these islands, on friendly soil and live to fight another day; whereas all the injured enemy machines and their complements will be total losses as far as the war is concerned.

During the great battle in France, we gave very powerful and continuous aid to the French Army, both by fighters and bombers; but in spite of every kind of pressure we never would allow the entire metropolitan fighter strength of the Air Force to be consumed. This decision was painful, but it was also right, because the fortunes of the battle in France could not have been decisively affected even if we had thrown in our entire fighter force. That battle was lost by the unfortunate strategical opening, by the extraordinary and unforseen power of the armoured columns and by the great preponderance of the German Army in numbers. Our fighter Air Force might easily have been exhausted as a mere accident in that great struggle, and then we should have found ourselves at the present time in a very serious plight. But as it is, I am happy to inform the House that our fighter strength is stronger at the present time relatively to the Germans, who have suffered terrible losses, than it has ever been; and consequently we believe ourselves possessed of the capacity to continue the war in the air under better conditions than we have ever experienced before. I look forward confidently to the exploits of our fighter pilots – these splendid men, this brilliant youth – who will have the glory of saving their native land, their island home, and all they love, from the most deadly of all attacks.

There remains, of course, the danger of bombing attacks, which will certainly be made very soon upon us by the bomber forces of the enemy. It is true that the German bomber force is superior in numbers to ours; but we have a very large bomber force also, which we shall use to strike at military targets in Germany without intermission. I do not at all underrate the severity of the ordeal which lies before us; but I believe our countrymen will show themselves capable of standing up to it, like the brave men of Barcelona, and will be able to stand up to it, and carry on in spite of it, at least as well as any other people in the world. Much will depend upon this; every man and every woman will have the chance to show the finest qualities of their race, and render the highest service to their cause. For all of us, at this time, whatever our sphere, our station, our occupation or our duties, it will be a help to remember the famous lines:

'He nothing common did or mean,
Upon that memorable scene.'

I have thought it right upon this occasion to give the House and the country some indication of the solid, practical grounds upon which we base our inflexible resolve to continue the war. There are a good many people who say, 'Never mind. Win or lose, sink or swim, better die than submit to tyranny – and such a tyranny.' And I do not dissociate myself from them. But I can assure them that our professional advisers of the three Services unitedly advise that we should carry on the war, and that there are good and reasonable hopes of final victory. We have fully informed and consulted all the self-governing Dominions, these great communities far beyond the oceans who have been built up on our laws and on our civilisation, and who are absolutely free to choose their course, but are absolutely devoted to the ancient Motherland, and who feel themselves inspired by the same emotions which lead me to stake our all upon duty and honour. We have fully consulted them, and I have received from their Prime Ministers, Mr Mackenzie King of Canada, Mr Menzies of Australia, Mr Fraser of New Zealand and General Smuts of South Africa – that wonderful man, with his immense profound mind, and his eye watching from a distance the whole panorama of European affairs – I have received from all these eminent men, who all have Governments behind them elected on wide franchises, who are all there because they represent the will of their people, messages couched in the most moving terms in which they endorse our decision to fight on, and declare themselves ready to share our fortunes and to persevere to the end. That is what we are going to do.

We may now ask ourselves: In what way has our position worsened since the beginning of the war? It has worsened by the fact that the Germans have conquered a large part of the coastline of Western Europe, and many small countries have been overrun by them. This aggravates the possibilities of air attack and adds to our naval preoccupations. It in no way diminishes, but on the contrary definitely increases, the power of our long-distance blockade. Similarly, the entrance of Italy into the war increases the power of our long-distance blockade. We have stopped the worst leak by that. We do not know whether military resistance will come to an end in France or not, but should it do so, then of course the Germans will be able to concentrate their forces, both military and industrial, upon us. But for the reasons I have given to the House these will not be found so easy to apply. If invasion has become more imminent, as no doubt it has, we, being relieved from the task of maintaining a large army in France, have far larger and more efficient forces to meet it.

If Hitler can bring under his despotic control the industries of the countries he has conquered, this will add greatly to his already vast armament output. On the other hand, this will not happen immediately, and we are now assured of immense, continuous and increasing support in supplies and munitions of all kinds from the United States; and especially of aeroplanes and pilots from the Dominions and across the oceans, coming from regions which are beyond the reach of enemy bombers.

I do not see how any of these factors can operate to our detriment on balance before the winter comes; and the winter will impose a strain upon the Nazi regime, with almost all Europe writhing and starving under its cruel heel, which, for all their ruthlessness, will run them very hard. We must not forget that from the moment when we declared war on September 3 it was always possible for Germany to turn all her Air Force upon this country, together with any other devices of invasion she might conceive, and that France could have done little or nothing to prevent her doing so. We have, therefore, lived under this danger, in principle and in a slightly modified form, during all these months. In the meanwhile, however, we have enormously improved our methods of defence, and we have learned, what we had no right to assume at the beginning, namely, that the individual aircraft and the individual British pilot have a sure and definite superiority. Therefore, in casting up this dread balance-sheet and contemplating our dangers with a disillusioned eye, I see great reason for intense vigilance and exertion, but none whatever for panic or despair.

During the first four years of the last war the Allies experienced nothing but disaster and disappointment. That was our constant fear: one blow after another, terrible losses, frightful dangers. Everything miscarried. And yet at the end of those four years the morale of the Allies was higher than that of the Germans, who had moved from one aggressive triumph to another, and who stood everywhere triumphant invaders of the lands into which they had broken. During that war we repeatedly asked ourselves the question: How are we going to win? and no one was able ever to answer it with much precision, until at the end, quite suddenly, quite unexpectedly, our terrible foe collapsed before us, and we were so glutted with victory that in our folly we threw it away.

We do not know yet what will happen in France or whether the French resistance will be prolonged, both in France and in the French Empire overseas. The French Government will be throwing away great opportunities and casting adrift their future if they do not continue the war in accordance with their treaty obligations, from which we have not felt able to release them. The House will have read the historic declaration in which, at the desire of many Frenchmen – and of our own hearts – we have proclaimed our willingness at the darkest hour in French history to conclude a union of common citizenship in this struggle. However matters may go in France or with the French Government, or other French Governments, we in this island and in the British Empire will never lose our sense of comradeship with the French people. If we are now called upon to endure what they have been suffering, we shall emulate their courage, and if final victory rewards our toils

36

they shall share the gains, aye, and freedom shall be restored to all. We abate nothing of our just demands; not one jot or tittle do we recede. Czechs, Poles, Norwegians, Dutch, Belgians have joined their causes to our own. All these shall be restored.

What General Weygand called the Battle of France is over. I expect that the battle of Britain is about to begin. Upon this battle depends the survival of Christian civilisation. Upon it depends our own British life, and the long continuity of our institutions and our Empire. The whole fury and might of the enemy must very soon be turned on us. Hitler knows that he will have to break us in this island or lose the war. If we can stand up to him, all Europe may be free and the life of the world may move forward into broad, sunlit uplands. But if we fail, then the whole world, including the United States, including all that we have known and cared for, will sink into the abyss of a new dark age made more sinister, and perhaps more protracted, by the lights of perverted science. Let us therefore brace ourselves to our duties, and so bear ourselves that, if the British Empire and its Commonwealth last for a thousand years, men will still say, 'This was their finest hour.'

BRITAIN FIGHTS ALONE

On June 20, 1940, the House of Commons went into Secret Session to hear from Mr Churchill a statement on the war situation following the French debacle. In accordance with Parliamentary custom this speech was not recorded even for official and historical purposes and there is no full account of what he said. His speeches in subsequent Secret Sessions were written out and carefully checked before delivery, but on this occasion the Prime Minister spoke from nine pages of brief, typewritten notes to which he had added a few sentences and alterations in his own handwriting. Photographs of these notes appear in the following pages.

NOTES OF A SPEECH MADE IN SECRET SESSION OF THE HOUSE OF COMMONS, JUNE 20, 1940

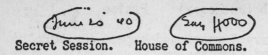

(June 20 '40) *(Say Hood)*

Secret Session. House of Commons.

My reliance on it as an instrument for waging
war.

More active and direct part for its Members
L.D.V.

All this in accordance with past history.

This S.S. a model of discretion.

My view always Govt. strengthened by S.S.

~~Quite ready to have others~~

Agree with idea S.S. shd be quite a normal part
        of our procedure,
            not associated with any crisis.

Relief to be able to talk without enemy reading.

Quite ready to have other S.Ss.,
        especially on precise subjects.

But I hope not press Ministers engaged in
        conduct of war too hard.
                                    this week !

⸺ refreshed by
Mood of the House.
            Cool and robust.

Speeches most informative.   *confidence of army*
    Difficult to betray any secrets disclosed
                                    today.

38

Moore-Brab (Wallesey)   Praise.

He was sorry I mentioned expert advisers
    favoured fighting on.

Politicians and Generals, -

In last war and this.

Not put too much on the politicians:
    even they may err.

Goering.   How do you class him?
    He was an airman turned politician.

I like him better as an airman.
    Not very much anyway.

Moore-Brab tells us of his wonderful brain,
        and the vast dictatorial powers and plans

Anyhow he did not produce the best pilots
        or the best machines,
            or perhaps, as we may see presently,
                the best Science.

M.B. said 250 nights in the year
    when no defence against night bombing.

~~I hope it is not so~~

This is one of those things you can only tell
                by finding out.

We have had a couple of nights of bombing,
    evidently much worse than that.

Folly underrate gravity attack impending.

But if 100 to 150 bombers employed
    entitled to remark:

Not very cleverly employed.

Hardly paid expenses.

Learn to get used to it.
    Eels get used to skinning.

Steady continuous bombing,
        probably rising to great intensity
                            occasionally,
            must be regular condition of our life.

The utmost importance preserve morale of
                                people,
        especially in the night work of factories.

A test of our nerve against theirs.

Our bombing incomparably superior.
    More precise, and so far more effective.

Ꞩ Indiscriminate bombing v. selected targets.

Enemy have a great preponderance numbers.
        but their industry
Oꞧ   much more concentrated.

No one can tell result.

This supreme battle depends upon
    the courage of the ordinary man and woman.

Whatever happens, keep a stiff upper lip.

Duty of all M.Ps. to uphold confidence
    and speed production.
=
Bellenger's speech.

Failure of French war conception.

The Maginot line. The defensive theory.
    Brilliant military achievement of Hitler.
      Triumph of the offensive spirit.

Triumph of long-prepared machinery.

Original strategic failure
      advance into Belgium
          without making sure of the sub-
                Maginot line,

    and without having a strategic reserve
          to plug a gap.

Fate of Northern Armies sealed when
    the G. armoured Divisions curled round
      their whole communication.
          Abbeville, Boulogne, Calais.

Not 2 days' food.
    only ammunition one battle.

Question of forming Torres-Vedras line.

Quite impossible with Air attack on ports.
  One in three supply ships sunk.
All experience thus turns of detachments
Situation looked terrible,
    especially when Belgium gave in.

Give all credit to all three Forces.

Army fought its way back;
  Navy showed its wonderful reserve power;
      Air Force rendered naval work possible.

B.E.F. a fine Army. Only 10 Divisions

Without proper armoured Divisions
    ~~or a~~ well-equipped,
            but placed in a hopeless
                strategic situation.

Much to be thankful for.

Melancholy position of the French Govt.

We have to make the best of them.

No criticisms, no recriminations.
      We cannot afford it, in public.

Petain.   Reynaud.   Darlan.

5 precious days largely wasted.

Surprise if mercy shown by Germany.

The French Fleet.   The French Empire.
    Our policy.

Urge them to continue
    but all depends upon the battle of Britain

I have good confidence.

Some remarks about <u>Home Defence</u>.

Belisha spoke of 'man the defences
    and resist the enemy.'

That will play its part;
    but essence of defence of Britain
        is to attack the landed enemy at once,

    leap at his throat
        and keep the grip until the life is out
                                of him.

We have a powerful Army
    growing in strength and equipment
                            every day.

Many very fine Divisions.
    Mobile-Brigades

Vigilant coast watch. Strong defence of
        ports and inlets.
Mobile Brigades acting on interior lines
    Good prospects of winning a victory

        radial lines

Quantities not qualities   commandos

43

If Hitler fails to invade
  or destroy Britain
      he has lost the war.

I do not consider only the severities
  of the winter in Europe.

I look to superiority in Air power
                    in the future.

Transatlantic reinforcements.

If get through next 3 months
  get through next 3 years.

It may well be our fine Armies
  have not said goodbye to the Continent
                        of Europe.

If enemy coastline extends from the Arctic
  to the Mediterranean

    and we retain sea-power
      and a growing Air power

    it is evident that Hitler
      master of a starving, agonized and
        surging Europe;

    will have his dangers as well as we.

But all depends upon winning this battle
        here in Britain, now this summer.

If we do, the prospects of the future
                                will expand,
        and we may look forward
        and make our plans for 1941 and 1942

        and that is what we are doing.

Attitude of United States.
        Nothing will stir them like fighting
                                in England.
                    to know
No good suggesting we are down and out.

The heroic struggle of Britain
        best chance of bringing them in.

Anyhow they have promised fullest aid
        in materials, munitions.

A tribute to Roosevelt.
                    Knox + Stimson
All depends upon our resolute bearing
        and holding out until Election issues
                are settled there.

If we can do so, I cannot doubt
    the whole English-speaking world
        will be in line together

        ~~and with all the Continents except Europe~~
        and with the Oceans and with the Air
                and all the Continents except Europe
                                (RUSSIA)

45

I do not see why we should not find our way
through
this time, as we did last.

:

Question of Ireland.
Greatly influenced by a great Army
developing here.

Germans would fight in Ireland
under great disadvantages.

Much rather they break Irish neutrality
than we.

:

Lastly, say a word about ourselves.

How the new Govt. was formed.

Tell the story Chamberlain's actions.

Imperative there should be loyalty, union
among men who have joined hands.

Otherwise no means of standing
the shocks and strains which are coming.

I have a right to depend loyalty
to the administration
and feel we have only one enemy to face,
the foul foe who menace/ threatens
our freedom and our life,
and bars the upward march of man.

THE WAR OF THE UNKNOWN WARRIORS

A WORLD BROADCAST, JULY 14, 1940

During the last fortnight the British Navy, in addition to blockading what is left of the German Fleet and chasing the Italian Fleet, has had imposed upon it the sad duty of putting effectually out of action for the duration of the war the capital ships of the French Navy. These, under the armistice terms, signed in the railway coach at Compiègne, would have been placed within the power of Nazi Germany. The transference of these ships to Hitler would have endangered the security of both Great Britain and the United States. We therefore had no choice but to act as we did, and to act forthwith. Our painful task is now complete. Although the unfinished battleship the *Jean Bart* still rests in a Moroccan harbour and there are a number of French warships at Toulon and in various French ports all over the world, these are not in a condition or of a character to derange our preponderance of naval power. As long, therefore, as they make no attempt to return to ports controlled by Germany or Italy, we shall not molest them in any way. That melancholy phase in our relations with France has, so far as we are concerned, come to an end.

Let us think rather of the future. Today is the fourteenth of July, the national festival of France. A year ago in Paris I watched the stately parade down the Champs Elysées of the French Army and the French Empire. Who can foresee what the course of other years will bring? Faith is given to us, to help and comfort us when we stand in awe before the unfurling scroll of human destiny. And I proclaim my faith that some of us will live to see a fourteenth of July when a liberated France will once again rejoice in her greatness and in her glory, and once again stand forward as the champion of the freedom and the rights of man. When the day dawns, as dawn it will, the soul of France will turn with comprehension and with kindness to those Frenchmen and Frenchwomen wherever they may be, who in the darkest hour did not despair of the Republic.

In the meantime, we shall not waste our breath nor cumber our thought with reproaches. When you have a friend and comrade at whose side you have faced tremendous struggles, and your friend is smitten down by a stunning blow, it may be necessary to make sure that the weapon that has fallen from his hands shall not be added to the resources of your common enemy. But you need not bear malice because of your friend's cries of delirium and gestures of agony. You must not add to his pain; you must work for his recovery. The association of interest between Britain and France remains. The cause remains. Duty inescapable remains. So long as our pathway to victory is not impeded, we are ready to discharge such offices of good will towards the French Government as may be possible, and to foster the trade and help the administration of those parts of the great French Empire which are now cut off from captive France, but which maintain their freedom. Subject to the iron demands of the war which we are waging against Hitler and all his works, we shall try so to conduct ourselves that every true French heart will beat and glow at the way we carry on the struggle; and that not only France, but all the oppressed countries in Europe may feel that each British victory is a step towards the liberation of the Continent from the foulest thraldom into which it has ever been cast.

All goes to show that the war will be long and hard. No one can tell where it will spread. One thing is certain: the peoples of Europe will not be ruled for long by the Nazi Gestapo, nor will the world yield itself to Hitler's gospel of hatred, appetite and domination.

And now it has come to us to stand alone in the breach, and face the worst that the tyrant's might and enmity can do. Bearing ourselves humbly before God, but conscious that we serve an unfolding purpose, we are ready to defend our native land against the invasion by which it is threatened. We are fighting *by* ourselves alone; but we are not fighting *for* ourselves alone. Here is this strong City of Refuge which enshrines the title-deeds of human progress and is of deep consequence to Christian civilisation; here girt about by the seas and oceans where the Navy reigns; shielded from above by the prowess and devotion of our airmen – we await undismayed the impending assault. Perhaps it will come tonight. Perhaps it will come next week. Perhaps it will never come. We must show ourselves equally capable of meeting a sudden violent shock, or what is perhaps a harder test, a prolonged vigil. But be the ordeal sharp or long, or both, we shall seek no terms, we shall tolerate no parley; we may show mercy – we shall ask for none.

I can easily understand how sympathetic onlookers across the Atlantic, or anxious friends in the yet unravished countries of Europe, who cannot measure our resources or our resolve, may have feared for our survival when they saw so many States and kingdoms torn to pieces in a few weeks or even days by the monstrous force of the Nazi war machine. But Hitler has not yet been withstood by a great nation with a will-power the equal of his own. Many of these countries have been poisoned by intrigue before they were struck down by violence. They have been rotted from within before they were smitten from without. How else can you explain what has happened to France? – to the French Army, to the French people, to the leaders of the French people?

But here, in our island, we are in good health, and in good heart. We have seen how Hitler prepared in scientific detail the plans for destroying the neighbour countries of Germany. He had his plans for Poland and his plans for Norway. He had his plans for Denmark. He had his plans all worked out for the doom of the peaceful, trustful Dutch; and, of course, for the Belgians. We have seen how the French were undermined and overthrown. We may therefore be sure that this *is* a plan – perhaps built up over years – for destroying Great Britain, which after all has the honour to be his main and foremost enemy. All I can say is that any plan for invading Britain which Hitler made two months ago must have had to be entirely recast in order to meet our new position. Two

4

months ago – nay, one month ago – our first and main effort was to keep our best army in France. All our regular troops, all our output of munitions, and a very large part of our Air Force, had to be sent to France and maintained in action there. But now we have it all at home. Never before in the last war – or in this – have we had in this island an Army comparable in quality, equipment or numbers to that which stands here on guard tonight. We have a million and a half men in the British Army under arms tonight, and every week of June and July has seen their organisation, their defences and their striking power advance by leaps and bounds. No praise is too high for the officers and men – aye, and civilians – who have made this immense transformation in so short a time. Behind these soldiers of the Regular Army, as a means of destruction for parachutists, airborne invaders, and any traitors that may be found in our midst (but I do not believe there are many – woe betide them, they will get short shrift), behind the Regular Army we have more than a million of the Local Defence Volunteers, or, as they are much better called, the 'Home Guard'. These officers and men, a large proportion of whom have been through the last war, have the strongest desire to attack and come to close quarters with the enemy wherever he may appear. Should the invader come to Britain, there will be no placid lying down of the people in submission before him as we have seen, alas, in other countries. We shall defend every village, every town, and every city. The vast mass of London itself, fought street by street, could easily devour an entire hostile army; and we would rather see London laid in ruins and ashes that it should be tamely and abjectly enslaved. I am bound to state these facts, because it is necessary to inform our people of our intentions, and thus to reassure them.

This has been a great week for the Royal Air Force, and for the Fighter Command. They have shot down more than five to one of the German aircraft which have tried to molest our convoys in the Channel, or have ventured to cross the British coast-line. These are, of course, only the preliminary encounters to the great air battles which lie ahead. But I know of no reason why we should be discontented with the results so far achieved; although, of course, we hope to improve upon them as the fighting becomes more widespread and comes more inland. Around all lies the power of the Royal Navy. With over a thousand armed ships under the White Ensign, patrolling the seas, the Navy, which is capable of transferring its force very readily to the protection of any part of the British Empire which may be threatened, is capable also of keeping open communications with the New World, from whom, as the struggle deepens, increasing aid will come. Is it not remarkable that after ten months of unlimited U-boat and air attack upon our commerce, our food reserves are higher than they have ever been, and we have a substantially larger tonnage under our own flag, apart from great numbers of foreign ships in our control, than we had at the beginning of the war?

Why do I dwell on all this? Not, surely, to induce any slackening of effort or vigilance. On the contrary. These must be redoubled, and we must prepare not only for the summer, but for the winter; not only for 1941, but for 1942; when the war will, I trust, take a different form from the defensive, in which it has hitherto been bound. I dwell on these elements in our strength – on these resources which we have mobilised and control – I dwell on them because it is right to show that the good cause *can* command the means of survival; and that while we toil through the dark valley we can see the sunlight on the uplands beyond.

I stand at the head of a Government representing all parties in the State – all creeds, all classes, every recognisable section of opinion. We are ranged beneath the Crown of our ancient monarchy. We are supported by a free Parliament and a free Press; but there is one bond which unites us all and sustains us in the public regard – namely (as is increasingly becoming known), that we are prepared to proceed to all extremities, to endure them and to enforce them; *that* is our bond of union in His Majesty's Government tonight. Thus only, in times like these, can nations preserve their freedom; and thus only can they uphold the cause entrusted to their care.

But all depends now upon the whole life-strength of the British race in every part of the world and of all our associated peoples and of all our well-wishers in every land, doing their utmost night and day, giving all, daring all, enduring all – to the utmost – to the end. This is no war of chieftains or of princes, of dynasties or national ambition; it is a war of peoples and of causes. There are vast numbers not only in this island but in every land, who will render faithful service in this war, but whose names will never be known, whose deeds will never be recorded. This is a war of the unknown warriors; but let us all strive without failing in faith or in duty, and the dark curse of Hitler will be lifted from our age.

THE FIRST YEAR

A SPEECH TO THE HOUSE OF COMMONS,
AUGUST 20, 1940

Almost a year has passed since the war began, and it is natural for us, I think, to pause on our journey at this milestone and survey the dark, wide field. It is also useful to compare the first year of this second war against German aggression with its forerunner a quarter of a century ago. Although this war is in fact only a continuation of the last, very great differences in its character are apparent. In the last war millions of men fought by hurling enormous masses of steel at one another. 'Men and shells' was the cry, and prodigious slaughter was the consequence. In this war nothing of this kind has yet appeared. It is a conflict of strategy, of organisation, of technical apparatus, of science, mechanics and morale. The British casualties in the first twelve months of the Great War amounted to 365,000. In this war, I am thankful to say, British killed, wounded, prisoners and missing, including civilians, do not exceed 92,000 and of these a large proportion are alive as prisoners of war. Looking more widely around, one may say that throughout all Europe for one man killed or wounded in the first year perhaps five were killed or wounded in 1914–15.

The slaughter is only a small fraction, but the consequences to the belligerents have been even more deadly. We have seen great countries with powerful armies dashed out of coherent existence in a few weeks. We have seen the French Republic and the renowned French Army beaten into complete and total submission with less than the casualties which they suffered in any one of half a dozen of the battles of 1914–18. The entire body – it might almost seem at times the soul – of France has succumbed to physical effects incomparably less terrible than those which were sustained with fortitude and undaunted will-power twenty-five years ago. Although up to the present the loss of life has been mercifully diminished, the decisions reached in the course of the struggle are even more profound upon the fate of nations than anything that has ever happened since barbaric times. Moves are made upon the scientific and strategic boards, advantages are gained by mechanical means, as a result of which scores of millions of men become incapable of further resistance, or judge themselves incapable of further resistance, and a fearful game of chess proceeds from check to mate by which the unhappy players seem to be inexorably bound.

There is another more obvious difference from 1914. The whole of the warring nations are engaged, not only soldiers, but the entire population, men, women and children. The fronts are everywhere. The trenches are dug in the towns and streets. Every village is fortified. Every road is barred. The front line runs through the factories. The workmen are soldiers with different weapons but the same courage. These are great and distinctive changes from what many of us saw in the struggle of a quarter of a century ago. There seems to be every reason to believe that this new kind of war is well suited to the genius and the resources of the British nation and the British Empire and that, once we get properly equipped and properly started, a war of this kind will be more favourable to us than the sombre mass slaughters of the Somme and Passchendaele. If it is a case of the whole nation fighting and suffering together, that ought to suit us, because we are the most united of all the nations, because we entered the war upon the national will and with our eyes open, and because we have been nurtured in freedom and individual responsibility and are the products, not of totalitarian uniformity but of tolerance and variety. If all these qualities are turned, as they are being turned, to the arts of war, we may be able to show the enemy quite a lot of things that they have not thought of yet. Since the Germans drove the Jews out and lowered their technical standards, our science is definitely ahead of theirs. Our geographical position, the command of the sea, and the friendship of the United States enables us to draw resources from the whole world and to manufacture weapons of war of every kind, but especially of the superfine kinds, on a scale hitherto practised only in Nazi Germany.

Hitler is now sprawled over Europe. Our offensive springs are being slowly compressed, and we must resolutely and methodically prepare ourselves for the campaigns of 1941 and 1942. Two or three years are not a long time, even in our short, precarious lives. They are nothing in the history of the nation, and when we are doing the finest thing in the world, and have the honour to be the sole champion of the liberties of all Europe, we must not grudge these years or weary as we toil and struggle through them. It does not follow that our energies in future years will be exclusively confined to defending ourselves and our possessions. Many opportunities may lie open to amphibious power, and we must be ready to take advantage of them. One of the ways to bring this war to a speedy end is to convince the enemy, not by words, but by deeds, that we have both the will and the means, not only to go on indefinitely but to strike heavy and unexpected blows. The road to victory may not be so long as we expect. But we have no right to count upon this. Be it long or short, rough or smooth, we mean to reach our journey's end.

It is our intention to maintain and enforce a strict blockade not only of Germany but of Italy, France, and all of the other countries that have fallen into the German power. I read in the papers that Herr Hitler has also proclaimed a strict blockade

54

of the British islands. No one can complain of that. I remember the Kaiser doing it in the last war. What indeed would be a matter of general complaint would be if we were to prolong the agony of all Europe by allowing food to come in to nourish the Nazis and aid their war effort, or to allow food to go in to the subjugated peoples, which certainly would be pillaged off them by their Nazi conquerors.

There have been many proposals, founded on the highest motives, that food should be allowed to pass the blockade for the relief of these populations. I regret that we must refuse these requests. The Nazis declare that they have created a new unified economy in Europe. They have repeatedly stated that they possess ample reserves of food and that they can feed their captive peoples. In a German broadcast of June 27 it was said that while Mr Hoover's plan for relieving France, Belgium and Holland deserved commendation, the German forces had already taken the necessary steps. We know that in Norway when the German troops went in, there were food supplies to last for a year. We know that Poland, though not a rich country, usually produces sufficient food for her people. Moreover, the other countries which Herr Hitler has invaded all held considerable stocks when the Germans entered and are themselves, in many cases, very substantial food producers. If all this food is not available now, it can only be because it has been removed to feed the people of Germany and to give them increased rations – for a change – during the last few months. At this season of the year and for some months to come, there is the least chance of scarcity as the harvest has just been gathered in. The only agencies which can create famine in any part of Europe now and during the coming winter, will be German exactions or German failure to distribute the supplies which they command.

There is another aspect. Many of the most valuable foods are essential to the manufacture of vital war material. Fats are used to make explosives. Potatoes make the alcohol for motor spirit. The plastic materials now so largely used in the construction of aircraft are made of milk. If the Germans use these commodities to help them to bomb our women and

55

children, rather than to feed the populations who produce them, we may be sure that imported foods would go the same way, directly or indirectly, or be employed to relieve the enemy of the responsibilities he has so wantonly assumed. Let Hitler bear his responsibilities to the full and let the peoples of Europe who groan beneath his yoke aid in every way the coming of the day when that yoke will be broken. Meanwhile, we can and we will arrange in advance for the speedy entry of food into any part of the enslaved area, when this part has been wholly cleared of German forces, and has genuinely regained its freedom. We shall do our best to encourage the building up of reserves of food all over the world, so that there will always be held up before the eyes of the peoples of Europe, including – I say deliberately – the German and Austrian peoples, the certainty that the shattering of the Nazi power will bring to them all immediate food, freedom and peace.

Rather more than a quarter of a year has passed since the new Government came into power in this country. What a cataract of disaster has poured out upon us since then. The trustful Dutch overwhelmed; their beloved and respected sovereign driven into exile; the peaceful city of Rotterdam the scene of a massacre as hideous and brutal as anything in the Thirty Years War. Belgium invaded and beaten down; our own fine Expeditionary Force, which King Leopold called to his rescue, cut off and almost captured, escaping as it seemed only by a miracle and with the loss of all its equipment; our ally, France, out; Italy in against us; all France in the power of the enemy, all its arsenals and vast masses of military material converted or convertible to the enemy's use; a puppet government set up at Vichy which may at any moment be forced to become our foe; the whole western seaboard of Europe from the North Cape to the Spanish frontier in German hands; all the ports, all the airfields on this immense front, employed against us as potential springboards of invasion. Moreover, the German air-power, numerically so far outstripping ours, has been brought so close to our island that what we used to dread greatly has come to pass and the hostile bombers not only reach our shores in a few minutes and from many directions, but can be escorted by their fighting aircraft. Why, sir, if we had been confronted at the beginning of May with such a prospect, it would have seemed incredible that at the end of a period of horror and disaster, or at this point in a period of horror and disaster, we should stand erect, sure of ourselves, masters of our fate and with the conviction of final victory burning unquenchable in our hearts. Few would have believed we could survive; none would have believed that we should today not only feel stronger but should actually be stronger than we have ever been before.

Let us see what has happened on the other side of the scales. The British nation and the British Empire finding themselves alone, stood undismayed against disaster. No one flinched or wavered; nay, some who formerly thought of peace, now think only of war. Our people are united and resolved, as they have never been before. Death and ruin have become small things compared with the shame of defeat or failure in duty. We cannot tell what lies ahead. It may be that even greater ordeals lie before us. We shall face whatever is coming to us. We are sure of ourselves and of our cause and that is the supreme fact which has emerged in these months of trial.

Meanwhile, we have not only fortified our hearts but our island. We have rearmed and rebuilt our armies in a degree which would have been deemed impossible a few months ago. We have ferried across the Atlantic, in the month of July, thanks to our friends over there, an immense mass of munitions of all kinds, cannon, rifles, machine-guns, cartridges and shell, all safely landed without the loss of a gun or a round. The output of our own factories, working as they have never worked before, has poured forth to the troops. The whole British Army is at home. More than 2,000,000 determined men have rifles and bayonets in their hands tonight and three-quarters of them are in regular military formations. We have never had armies like this in our island in time of war. The whole island bristles against invaders, from the sea or from the air. As I explained to the House in the middle of June, the stronger our Army at home, the larger must the invading expedition be, and the larger the invading expedition, the less difficult will be the task of the Navy in detecting its assembly and in intercepting and destroying it on passage; and the greater also would be the difficulty of feeding and supplying the invaders if ever they landed, in the teeth of continuous naval and air attack on their communications. All this is classical and venerable doctrine. As in Nelson's day, the maxim holds, 'Our first line of defence is the enemy's ports.' Now air reconnaissance and photography have brought to an old principle a new and potent aid.

Our Navy is far stronger than it was at the beginning of the war. The great flow of new construction set on foot at the outbreak is now beginning to come in. We hope our friends across the ocean will send us a timely reinforcement to bridge the gap between the peace flotillas of 1939 and the war flotillas of 1941. There is no difficulty in sending such aid. The seas and oceans are open. The U-boats are contained. The magnetic mine is, up to the present time, effectively mastered. The merchant tonnage under the British flag, after a year of unlimited U-boat war, after eight months of intensive mining attack, is larger than when we began. We have in addition, under our control, at least 4,000,000 tons of shipping from the captive countries which has taken refuge here or in the harbours of the Empire. Our stocks of food of all kinds are far more abundant than in the days of peace and a large and growing programme of food production is on foot.

Why do I say all this? Not assuredly to boast; not assuredly to give the slightest countenance to complacency. The dangers we face are still enormous, but so are our advantages and resources. I recount them because the people have a right to know that there are solid grounds for the confidence which we feel, and that we have good reason to believe ourselves capable, as I said in a very dark hour two months ago, of continuing the war 'if necessary alone, if necessary for years'. I say it also because the fact that the British Empire stands invincible, and that Nazidom is still being resisted, will kindle again the spark of hope in the breasts of hundreds of millions of downtrodden or despairing men and women throughout Europe, and far beyond its bounds, and that from these sparks there will presently come cleansing and devouring flame.

The great air battle which has been in progress over this island for the last few weeks has recently attained a high intensity. It is too soon to attempt to assign limits either to its scale or to its duration. We must certainly expect that greater efforts will be made by the enemy than any he has so far put forth. Hostile airfields are still being developed in France and the Low Countries, and the movement of squadrons and material for attacking us is still proceeding. It is quite plain that Herr Hitler could not admit defeat in his air attack on Great Britain without sustaining most serious injury. If, after all his boastings and blood-curdling threats and lurid accounts trumpeted around the world of the damage he has inflicted, of the vast numbers of our Air Force he has shot down, so he says, with so little loss to himself; if after tales of the panic-stricken British crushed in their holes cursing the plutocratic Parliament which has led them to such a plight; if after all this his whole air onslaught were forced after a while tamely to peter out, the Führer's reputation for veracity of statement might be seriously impugned. We may be sure, therefore, that he will continue as long as he has the strength to do so, and as long as any preoccupations he may have in respect of the Russian Air Force allow him to do so.

On the other hand, the conditions and course of the fighting have so far been favourable to us. I told the House two months ago that whereas in France our fighter aircraft were wont to inflict a loss of two or three to one upon the Germans, and in the fighting at Dunkirk, which was a kind of no-man's-land, a loss of about three or four to one, we expected that in an attack on this island we should achieve a larger ratio. This has certainly come true. It must also be remembered that all the enemy machines and pilots which are shot down over our island, or over the seas which surround it, are either destroyed or captured; whereas a considerable proportion of our machines, and also of our pilots, are saved, and soon again in many cases come into action.

A vast and admirable system of salvage, directed by the

Ministry of Aircraft Production, ensures the speediest return to the fighting line of damaged machines, and the most provident and speedy use of all the spare parts and material. At the same time the splendid, nay, astounding increase in the output and repair of British aircraft and engines which Lord Beaverbrook has achieved by a genius of organisation and drive, which looks like magic, has given us overflowing reserves of every type of aircraft, and an ever-mounting stream of production both in quantity and quality. The enemy is, of course, far more numerous than we are. But our new production already, as I am advised, largely exceeds his, and the American production is only just beginning to flow in. It is a fact, as I see from my daily returns, that our bomber and fighter strength now, after all this fighting, are larger than they have ever been. We believe that we shall be able to continue the air struggle indefinitely and as long as the enemy pleases, and the longer it continues the more rapid will be our approach, first towards that parity, and then into that superiority in the air, upon which in a large measure the decision of the war depends.

The gratitude of every home in our island, in our Empire, and indeed throughout the world, except in the abodes of the guilty, goes out to the British airmen who, undaunted by odds, unwearied in their constant challenge and mortal danger, are turning the tide of the world war by their prowess and by their devotion. Never in the field of human conflict was so much owed by so many to so few. All hearts go out to the fighter pilots, whose brilliant actions we see with our own eyes day after day; but we must never forget that all the time, night after night, month after month, our bomber squadrons travel far into Germany, find their targets in the darkness by the highest navigational skill, aim their attacks, often under the heaviest fire, often with serious loss, with deliberate careful discrimination, and inflict shattering blows upon the whole of the technical and war-making structure of the Nazi power. On no part of the Royal Air Force does the weight of the war fall more heavily than on the daylight bombers who will play an invaluable part in the case of invasion and whose unflinching zeal it has been necessary in the meanwhile on numerous occasions to restrain.

We are able to verify the results of bombing military targets in Germany, not only by reports which reach us through many sources, but also, of course, by photography. I have no hesitation in saying that this process of bombing the military industries and communications of Germany and the air bases and storage depots from which we are attacked, which process will continue upon an ever-increasing scale until the end of the war, and may in another year attain dimensions hitherto undreamed of, affords one at least of the most certain, if not the shortest of all the roads to victory. Even if the Nazi legions stood triumphant on the Black Sea, or indeed upon the Caspian, even if Hitler were at the gates of India, it would profit him nothing if at the same time the entire economic and scientific apparatus of German war-power lay shattered and pulverised at home.

The fact that the invasion of this island upon a large scale has become a far more difficult operation with every week that has passed since we saved our Army at Dunkirk, and our very great preponderance of sea-power enable us to turn our eyes and to turn our strength increasingly towards the Mediterranean and against that other enemy who, without the slightest provocation, coldly and deliberately, for greed and gain, stabbed France in the back at the moment of her agony, and is now marching against us in Africa. The defection of France has, of course, been deeply damaging to our position in what is called, somewhat oddly, the Middle East. In the defence of Somaliland, for instance, we had counted upon strong French forces attacking the Italians from Jibuti. We had counted also upon the use of the French naval and air bases in the Mediterranean, and particularly upon the North African shore. We had counted upon the French Fleet. Even though metropolitan France was temporarily overrun, there was no reason why the French Navy, substantial parts of the French Army, the French Air Force and the French Empire overseas should not have continued the struggle at our side.

Shielded by overwhelming sea-power, possessed of invaluable strategic bases and of ample funds, France might have remained one of the great combatants in the struggle. By so doing, France would have preserved the continuity of her life, and the French Empire might have advanced with the British Empire to the rescue of the independence and integrity of the French Motherland. In our own case, if we had been put in the terrible position of France, a contingency now happily impossible, although, of course, it would have been the duty of all war leaders to fight on here to the end, it would also have been their duty, as I indicated in my speech of June 4, to provide as far as possible for the naval security of Canada and our Dominions and to make sure they had the means to carry on the struggle from beyond the oceans. Most of the other countries that have been overrun by Germany for the time being have persevered valiantly and faithfully. The Czechs, Poles, the Norwegians, the Dutch, the Belgians are still in the field, sword in hand, recognised by Great Britain and the United States as the sole representative authorities and lawful Governments of their respective States.

That France alone should lie prostrate at this moment, is the crime, not of a great and noble nation, but of what are called 'the men of Vichy'. We have profound sympathy with the French people. Our old comradeship with France is not dead. In General de Gaulle and his gallant band, that comradeship takes an effective form. These free Frenchmen have been condemned to death by Vichy, but the day will come, as surely as the sun will rise tomorrow, when their names will be held in honour, and their names will be graven in stone in the streets and villages of a France restored in a liberated Europe to its full freedom and its ancient fame. But this conviction which I feel of the future cannot affect the immediate problems which confront us in the Mediterranean and in Africa. It had been decided some time before the beginning of the war not to defend the Protectorate of Somaliland. That policy was changed in the early months of the war. When the French gave in, and when our small forces there, a few battalions, a few guns, were attacked by all the Italian troops, nearly two divisions, which had formerly faced the French at Jibuti, it was right to withdraw our detachments, virtually intact, for action elsewhere. Far larger operations no doubt impend in the Middle East theatre, and I shall certainly not attempt to discuss or prophesy about their probable course. We have large armies and many means of reinforcing them. We have the complete sea command of the Eastern Mediterranean. We intend to do our best to give a good account of ourselves, and to discharge faithfully and resolutely all our obligations and duties in that quarter of the world. More than that I do not think the House would wish me to say at the present time.

A good many people have written to me to ask me to make on this occasion a fuller statement of our war aims, and of the kind of peace we wish to make after the war, than is contained in the very considerable declaration which was made early in the autumn. Since then we have made common cause with Norway, Holland and Belgium. We have recognised the Czech Government of Dr Benes, and we have told General de Gaulle that our success will carry with it the restoration of France. I do not think it would be wise at this moment, while the battle rages and the war is still perhaps only in its earlier stage, to embark upon elaborate speculations about the future shape which should be given to Europe or the new securities which must be arranged to spare mankind the miseries of a third world war. The ground is not new, it has been frequently traversed and explored, and many ideas are held about it in common by all good men, and all free men. But before we can undertake the task of rebuilding we have not only to be convinced ourselves, but we have to convince all other countries that the Nazi tyranny is going to be finally broken. The right to guide the course of world history is the noblest prize of victory. We are still toiling up the hill; we have not yet reached the crest-line of it; we cannot survey the landscape or even imagine what its condition will be when that longed-for morning comes. The task which lies before us immediately is at once more practical, more simple and more stern. I hope – indeed I pray – that we shall not be found unworthy of our victory if after toil and tribulation it is granted to us. For the rest, we have to gain the victory. That is our task.

There is, however, one direction in which we can see a little more clearly ahead. We have to think not only for ourselves but for the lasting security of the cause and principles for which we are fighting and of the long future of the British Commonwealth of Nations. Some months ago we came to the conclusion that the interests of the United States and of the British Empire both required that the United States should have facilities for the naval and air defence of the Western hemisphere against the attack of a Nazi Power which might have acquired temporary but lengthy control of a large part of Western Europe and its formidable resources. We had therefore decided spontaneously, and without being asked or offered any inducement, to inform the Government of the United States that we would be glad to place such defence facilities at their disposal by leasing suitable sites in our transatlantic possessions for their greater security against the unmeasured dangers of the future. The principle of association of interests for common purposes between Great Britain and the United States had developed even before the war. Various agreements had been reached about certain small islands in the Pacific Ocean which had become important as air fuelling points. In all this line of thought we found ourselves in very close harmony with the Government of Canada.

Presently we learned that anxiety was also felt in the United States about the air and naval defence of their Atlantic seaboard, and President Roosevelt has recently made it clear that he would like to discuss with us, and with the Dominion of Canada and with Newfoundland, the development of American naval and air facilities in Newfoundland and in the West Indies. There is, of course, no question of any transference of sovereignty – that has never been suggested – or of any action being taken, without the consent or against the wishes of the various colonies concerned, but for our part, His Majesty's Government are entirely willing to accord defence facilities to the United States on a 99 years' leasehold basis, and we feel sure that our interests no less than theirs, and the interests of the colonies themselves and of Canada and Newfoundland will be served thereby. These are important steps. Undoubtedly this process means that these two great organisations of the English-speaking democracies, the British Empire and the United States, will have to be somewhat mixed up together in some of their affairs for mutual and general advantage. For my own part, looking out upon the future, I do not view the process with any misgivings. I could not stop it if I wished; no one can stop it. Like the Mississippi, it just keeps rolling along. Let it roll. Let it roll on full flood, inexorable, irresistible, benignant, to broader lands and better days.

'THE CRUX OF THE WHOLE WAR'

A BROADCAST SPEECH, SEPTEMBER 11, 1940

When I said in the House of Commons the other day that I thought it improbable that the enemy's air attack in September could be more than three times as great as it was in August, I was not, of course, referring to barbarous attacks upon the civil population, but on the great air battle which is being fought out between our fighters and the German Air Force.

You will understand that whenever the weather is favourable waves of German bombers, protected by fighters often 300 or 400 at a time, surge over this island, especially the promontory of Kent, in the hope of attacking military and other objectives by daylight. However, they are met by our fighter squadrons and nearly always broken up; and their losses average three to one in machines and six to one in pilots.

This effort of the Germans to secure daylight mastery of the air over England is, of course, the crux of the whole war. So far it has failed conspicuously. It has cost them very dear, and we have felt stronger and actually are relatively a good deal stronger, than when the hard fighting began in July. There is no doubt that Herr Hitler is using up his fighter force at a very high rate, and that if he goes on for many more weeks he will wear down and ruin this vital part of his Air Force. That will give us a very great advantage.

On the other hand, for him to try to invade this country without having secured mastery in the air would be a very hazardous undertaking. Nevertheless, all his preparations for invasion on a great scale are steadily going forward. Several hundreds of self-propelled barges are moving down the coasts of Europe, from the German and Dutch harbours to the ports of northern France; from Dunkirk to Brest; and beyond Brest to the French harbours in the Bay of Biscay.

Besides this, convoys of merchant ships in tens of dozens are being moved through the Straits of Dover into the Channel, dodging along from port to port under the protection of the new batteries which the Germans have built on the French shore. There are now considerable gatherings of shipping in the German, Dutch, Belgian and French harbours – all the way from Hamburg to Brest. Finally, there are some preparations made of ships to carry an invading force from the Norwegian harbours.

Behind these clusters of ships or barges, there stand very large numbers of German troops, awaiting the order to go on board and set out on their very dangerous and uncertain voyage across the seas. We cannot tell when they will try to come; we cannot be sure that in fact they will try at all; but no one should blind himself to the fact that a heavy, full-scale invasion of this island is being prepared with all the usual German thoroughness and method, and that it may be launched now – upon England, upon Scotland, or upon Ireland, or upon all three.

If this invasion is going to be tried at all, it does not seem that it can be long delayed. The weather may break at any time. Besides this, it is difficult for the enemy to keep these gatherings of ships waiting about indefinitely, while they are bombed every night by our bombers, and very often shelled by our warships which are waiting for them outside.

Therefore, we must regard the next week or so as a very important period in our history. It ranks with the days when the Spanish Armada was approaching the Channel, and Drake

66

was finishing his game of bowls; or when Nelson stood between us and Napoleon's Grand Army at Boulogne. We have read all about this in the history books; but what is happening now is on a far greater scale and of far more consequence to the life and future of the world and its civilisation than these brave old days of the past.

Every man and woman will therefore prepare himself to do his duty, whatever it may be, with special pride and care. Our fleets and flotillas are very powerful and numerous; our Air Force is at the highest strength it has ever reached, and it is conscious of its proved superiority, not indeed in numbers, but in men and machines. Our shores are well fortified and strongly manned, and behind them, ready to attack the invaders, we have a far larger and better-equipped mobile Army than we have ever had before.

Besides this, we have more than a million and a half men of the Home Guard, who are just as much soldiers of the Regular Army as the Grenadier Guards, and who are determined to fight for every inch of the ground in every village and in every street.

It is with devout but sure confidence that I say: Let God defend the Right.

These cruel, wanton, indiscriminate bombings of London are, of course, a part of Hitler's invasion plans. He hopes, by killing large numbers of civilians, and women and children, that he will terrorise and cow the people of this mighty imperial city, and make them a burden and an anxiety to the Government and thus distract our attention unduly from the ferocious onslaught he is preparing. Little does he know the spirit of the British nation, or the tough fibres of the Londoners, whose forebears played a leading part in the establishment of Parliamentary institutions and who have been bred to value freedom far above their lives. This wicked man, the repository and embodiment of many forms of soul-destroying hatred, this monstrous product of former wrongs and shame, has now resolved to try to break our famous island race by a process of indiscriminate slaughter and destruction. What he has done is to kindle a fire in British hearts, here and all over the world, which will glow long after all traces of the conflagration he has caused in London have been removed. He has lighted a fire which will burn with a steady and consuming flame until the last vestiges of Nazi tyranny have been burnt out of Europe, and until the Old World – and the New – can join hands to rebuild the temples of man's freedom and man's honour, upon foundations which will not soon or easily be overthrown.

This is a time for everyone to stand together, and hold firm, as they are doing. I express my admiration for the exemplary manner in which all the Air Raid Precautions services of London are being discharged, especially the Fire Brigade, whose work has been so heavy and also dangerous. All the world that is still free marvels at the composure and fortitude with which the citizens of London are facing and surmounting the great ordeal to which they are subjected, the end of which or the severity of which cannot yet be foreseen.

It is a message of good cheer to our fighting forces on the seas, in the air, and in our waiting armies in all their posts and stations, that we send them from this capital city. They know that they have behind them a people who will not flinch or weary of the struggle – hard and protracted though it will be; but that we shall rather draw from the heart of suffering itself the means of inspiration and survival, and of a victory won not only for our own time, but for the long and better days that are to come.

THE AIR RAIDS ON LONDON

A SPEECH TO THE HOUSE OF COMMONS, OCTOBER 8, 1940

A month has passed since Herr Hitler turned his rage and malice on to the civil population of our great cities and particularly of London. He declared in his speech of September

4 that he would raze our cities to the ground, and since then he has been trying to carry out his fell purpose. Naturally, the first question we should ask is to what extent the full strength of the German bombing force has been deployed. I will give the House the best opinion I have been able to form on what is necessarily to some extent a matter of speculation. After their very severe mauling on August 15, the German short-range dive bombers, of which there are several hundred, have been kept carefully out of the air fighting. This may be, of course, because they are being held in reserve so that they may play their part in a general plan of invasion or reappear in some other theatre of war. We have, therefore, had to deal with the long-range German bombers alone.

It would seem that, taking day and night together, nearly 400 of these machines have, on the average, visited our shores every twenty-four hours. We are doubtful whether this rate of sustained attack could be greatly exceeded; no doubt a concentrated effort could be made for a few days at a time, but this would not sensibly affect the monthly average. Certainly there has been a considerable tailing off in the last ten days, and all through the month that has passed since the heavy raids began on September 7, we have had a steady decline in casualties and damage to so-called vulnerable points. We know, of course, exactly what we are doing in reply, and the size of our own bombing force, and from the many sources which are open to us we believe that the German heavy bomber pilots are being worked at least as hard as, and maybe a great deal harder than, our own. The strain upon them is, therefore, very considerable. The bulk of them do not seem capable of anything beyond blind bombing. I always hesitate to say anything of an optimistic nature, because our people do not mind being told the worst. They resent anything in the nature of soothing statements which are not borne out by later events, and, after all, war is full of unpleasant surprises.

On the whole, however, we may, I think, under all reserve reach, provisionally, the conclusion that the German average effort against this country absorbs a very considerable part of their potential strength. I should not like to say that we have the measure of their power, but we feel more confident about it than we have ever done before.

Let us now proceed to examine the effect of this ruthless and indiscriminate attack upon the easiest of all targets, namely, the great built-up areas of this land. The Germans have recently volunteered some statements of a boastful nature about the weight of explosives which they have discharged upon us during the whole war, and also on some particular occasions. These statements are not necessarily untrue, and they do not appear unreasonable to us. We were told on September 23 that 22,000 tons of explosives had been discharged upon Great Britain since the beginning of the war. No doubt this included the mines on the coast. We were told also, on last Thursday week, that 251 tons were thrown upon London in a single night, that is to say, only a few tons less than the total dropped on the whole country throughout the last war. Now, we know exactly what our casualties have been. On that particular Thursday night 180 persons were killed in London as a result of 251 tons of bombs. That is to say, it took one ton of bombs to kill three-quarters of a person. We know, of course, exactly the ratio of loss in the last war, because all the facts were ascertained after it was over. In that war the small bombs of early patterns which were used killed ten persons for every ton discharged in the built-up areas. Therefore, the deadliness of the attack in this war appears to be only one-thirteenth of that of 1914–18. Let us say 'less than one-tenth', so as to be on the safe side. That is, the mortality is less than one-tenth of the mortality attaching to the German bombing attacks in the last war. This is a very remarkable fact, deserving of profound consideration. I adduce it, because it is the foundation of some further statements, which I propose to make later on.

What is the explanation? There can only be one, namely, the vastly improved methods of shelter which have been adopted. In the last war there were hardly any air-raid shelters, and very few basements had been strengthened. Now we have this ever-growing system of shelters, among which the Anderson shelter justly deserves its fame, and the mortality has been reduced to one-thirteenth, or, say, at least one-tenth. This appears, as I say, not only to be remarkable, but also reassuring. It has altered, of course, the whole of the estimates we had made of the severity of the attacks to which we should be exposed. Whereas, when we entered the war at the call of duty and honour, we expected to sustain losses which might amount to 3,000 killed in a single night and 12,000 wounded, night after night, and made hospital arrangements on the basis of 250,000 casualties merely as a first provision – whereas that is what we did at the beginning of the war, we have actually had since it began, up to last Saturday, as a result of air bombing, about 8,500 killed and 13,000 wounded. This shows that things do not always turn out as badly as one expects. Also, it shows that one should never hesitate, as a nation or as an individual, to face dangers because they appear to the imagination to be so formidable. Since the heavy raiding began on September 7, the figures of killed and seriously wounded have declined steadily week by week, from over 6,000 in the first week to just under 5,000 in the second, and from about 4,000 in the third week to under 3,000 in the last of the four weeks.

The destruction of property has, however, been very considerable. Most painful is the number of small houses inhabited by working folk which has been destroyed, but the loss has also fallen heavily upon the West End, and all classes have suffered evenly, as they would desire to do. I do not propose to give exact figures of the houses which have been destroyed or seriously damaged. That is our affair. We will rebuild them, more to our credit than some of them were before. London, Liverpool, Manchester, Birmingham may have much more to suffer, but they will rise from their ruins, more healthy and, I hope, more beautiful. We must not exaggerate the material damage which has been done. The papers are full of pictures of demolished houses, but naturally they do not fill their restricted space with the numbers that are left standing. If you go, I am told, to the top of Primrose Hill or any of the other eminences of London and look around, you would not know that any harm has been done to our city.

Statisticians may amuse themselves by calculating that after making allowances for the working of the law of diminishing returns, through the same house being struck twice or three times over, it would take ten years at the present rate, for half the houses of London to be demolished. After that, of course, progress would be much slower. Quite a lot of things are going to happen to Herr Hitler and the Nazi regime before ten years are up, and even Signor Mussolini has some experiences ahead of him which he had not foreseen at the time when he thought it safe and profitable to stab the stricken and prostrate French Republic in the back. Neither by material damage nor by slaughter will the people of the British Empire be turned from their solemn and inexorable purpose. It is the practice and in some cases the duty of many of my colleagues and many Members of the House to visit the scenes of destruction as promptly as possible, and I go myself from time to time. In all my life, I have never been treated with so much kindness as by the people who have suffered most. One would think one had brought some great benefit to them, instead of the blood and tears, the toil and sweat which is all I have ever promised. On every side, there is the cry, 'We can take it,' but with it, there is also the cry, 'Give it 'em back.'

The question of reprisals is being discussed in some quarters as if it were a moral issue. What are reprisals? What we are doing now is to batter continuously, with forces which steadily increase in power, each one of those points in Germany which we believe will do the Germans most injury and will most speedily lessen their power to strike at us. Is that a reprisal? It seems to me very like one. At any rate, it is all we have time for now. We should be foolish to shift off those military targets which the skill of our navigators enables us to find with a very great measure of success, to any other targets at the present stage. Although the bombing force that we are able as yet to employ is, as I have told the House on several occasions, much less numerous than that of which the enemy disposes, I believe it to be true that we have done a great deal more harm to the war-making capacity of Germany than they have done to us. Do not let us get into a sterile controversy as to what are and what are not reprisals. Our object must be to inflict the maximum harm on the enemy's war-making capacity. That is the only object that we shall pursue.

It must not be thought that the mists and storms which enshroud our island in the winter months will by themselves prevent the German bombers from the crude, indiscriminate bombing by night of our built-up areas into which they have relapsed. No one must look forward to any relief merely from the winter weather. We have, however, been thinking about the subject for some time, and it may be that new methods will be devised to make the wholesale bombing of the civilian population by night and in fog more exciting to the enemy than it is at present. The House will not expect me to indicate or foreshadow any of these methods. It would be much better for us to allow our visitors to find them out for themselves in due course by practical experience. I think that is much the best way to handle that particular matter.

Meanwhile, upon the basis that this will continue and that our methods will also be improving, we have to organise our lives and the life of our cities on the basis of dwelling under fire and of having always this additional – not a very serious chance – of death, added to the ordinary precarious character of human existence. This great sphere of domestic organisation becomes the counterpart of our military war effort. The utmost drive and capacity of which we are capable as a Government and as a people will be thrown into this task. Nothing but the needs of the Fighting Services can stand in the way. We must try to have shelters with sleeping bunks for everyone in the areas which are liable to constant attack, and this must be achieved in the shortest possible time. As soon as it is accomplished, and in proportion as it is accomplished, people will have to go to their proper places, and above all, we must prevent large gatherings of people in any shelters which only gives illusory protection against a direct hit. People must be taught not to despise the small shelter. Dispersal is the sovereign remedy against heavy casualties. In my right hon Friend the new Minister of Home Security,* we have a man of warm sympathy, of resource and energy, who is well known

*Mr Herbert Morrison

to Londoners and has their confidence, and who will equally look after the other cities which are assailed. But do not let it be thought that the work of his predecessor, now Lord President of the Council* has not been of a very high order. There is no better war horse in the Government. I am ashamed of the attacks which are made upon him in ignorant and spiteful quarters. Every one of his colleagues knows that he is a tower of strength and good sense, fearless and unflinching in storm and action. With my many burdens, I rely greatly upon him to take a part of the civil and domestic load from off my shoulders, setting me free for the more direct waging of the war. Large schemes are always on foot for providing food and hot drinks for those who sleep in shelters, and also for entertainment during the winter evenings. Far-reaching measures are being taken to safeguard the health of the people under these novel and primordial conditions. Widespread organisation and relief to those whose homes are smitten is already in being and is expanding and improving every day. All these matters will be unfolded at length, some in public, some in private session, by the Ministers responsible for the various branches of action.

There is one scheme, however, upon which I must say a word today. The diminution of the damage done by blind bombing from what we had expected before the war, in the figures that I gave the House in the opening passage of my speech, enables us to take an enormous step forward in spreading the risk over the property of all classes, rich and poor. The Chancellor of the Exchequer, as I indicated a month ago, is preparing, and in fact has virtually completed the preparation of, a Bill for nation-wide compulsory insurance against damage to property from the enemy's fire. Immediate needs of food and shelter are already provided for, so is loss of life and limb as far as it is possible for human beings to be compensated for such calamities, but why should we have the whole value of the buildings of the country simultaneously and universally discounted and discredited by the shadow of a sporadic sky vulture? Such a course would be financially

*Sir John Anderson

improvident and also fiscally inane. An appropriate charge levied on the capital value of buildings and structures of all kinds will provide a fund from which, supplemented if need be by a State subvention, everyone can be made sure that compensation for his house and home and place of business will be paid to him in one form or another at the end of the war, if not sooner, and that, where necessity arises in the intervening period, means of carrying on will not be withheld. We also propose to provide insurance against the risk of war damage for all forms of movable property, such as industrial plant, machinery, household effects and other personal possessions which are not at present protected by insurance. This will also be retrospective.

As I see it, we must so arrange that, when any district is smitten by bombs which are flung about at utter random, strong, mobile forces will descend on the scene in power and mercy to conquer the flames, as they have done, to rescue sufferers, provide them with food and shelter, to whisk them away to places of rest and refuge, and to place in their hands leaflets which anyone can understand to reassure them that they have not lost all, because all will share their material loss, and in sharing it, sweep it away. These schemes and measures, pursued on the greatest scale and with fierce energy, will require the concentrated attention of the House in the weeks that lie before us. We have to make a job of this business of living and working under fire, and I have not the slightest doubt that when we have settled down to it, we shall establish conditions which will be a credit to our island society and to the whole British family, and will enable us to maintain the production of those weapons in good time upon which our whole safety and future depend. Thus we shall be able to prove to all our friends and sympathisers in every land, bound or free, that Hitler's act of mass terror against the British nation has failed as conspicuously as his magnetic mine and other attempts to strangle our seaborne trade.

Meanwhile, what has happened to the invasion which we have been promised every month and almost every week since the beginning of July? Do not let us be lured into supposing that the danger is past. On the contrary, unwearying vigilance and the swift and steady strengthening of our Forces by land, sea and air which is in progress must be at all costs maintained. Now that we are in October, however, the weather becomes very uncertain, and there are not many lucid intervals of two or three days together in which river barges can cross the narrow seas and land upon our beaches. Still, those intervals may occur. Fogs may aid the foe. Our armies, which are growing continually in numbers, equipment, mobility and training, must be maintained all through the winter, not only along the beaches but in reserve, as the majority are, like leopards crouching to spring at the invader's throat. The enemy has certainly got prepared enough shipping and barges to throw 500,000 men in a single night on to salt water – or into it. The Home Guard, which now amounts to 1,700,000 men, must nurse their weapons and sharpen their bayonets. [Interruption.] I have taken the trouble to find out very carefully how many hundred thousands of bayonets are at this time in their possession before I uttered such an adjuration; and for those who have not bayonets at the moment, I have provided for them by the phrase: 'They must nurse their weapons.' During the winter training must proceed, and the building of a great well-equipped army, not necessarily always to be confined to these islands, must go forward in a hardy and rigorous manner. My right hon Friend, the Secretary of State for War, will, in the course of the next few weeks, give a further account in Private Session of the tremendous strides which under his guidance our military organisation is making in all its branches. He will also announce in public the improvements which we have found it possible to make in the allowances for the dependants of the Fighting Services to meet the increased cost of living and to secure the proper nourishment and care of the wives and children of our fighting men. I shall not anticipate my right hon Friend this afternoon.

But, after all, the main reason why the invasion has not been attempted up to the present is, of course, the succession of brilliant victories gained by our fighter aircraft, and gained by them over the largely superior numbers which the enemy have launched against us. The three great days of August 15, September 15 and September 27 have proved to all the world that here at home over our own island we have the mastery of the air. That is a tremendous fact. It marks the laying down of the office * which he had held with so much distinction for the last three years by Sir Cyril Newall, and it enables us to record our admiration to him for the services he has rendered. It also marks the assumption of new and immense responsibilities by Sir Charles Portal, an officer who, I have heard from every source and every side, commands the enthusiastic support and confidence of the Royal Air Force. These victories of our Air Force enable the Navy, which is now receiving very great re-inforcements, apart altogether from the American destroyers now coming rapidly into service, to assert, on the basis of the air victories, its sure and well-tried power. It is satisfactory for me to be able to announce that both in fighters and in bombers we are at this moment and after all these months of battle substantially stronger actually and relatively than we were in May when the heavy fighting began, and also to announce that the pilot situation is rapidly improving and that in many weeks our repaired aircraft alone, such is the efficiency of this organisation for repair, exceed by themselves or make good the losses which are suffered; so that in many weeks the new construction is a clear gain. No one has ever pretended that we should overtake the Germans, with their immense lead, in the first year or so of war. We must give ourselves a chance. Perhaps it will be possible to make a more satisfactory statement on this subject this time next year. But do not forget that the resources of the enemy will also be substantially increased by their exploitation of the wealth, of the plants and to some extent of the skilled labour of captive countries. If it were not for the resources of the New World, which are becoming increasingly available, it would be a long time before we should be able to do much more than hold our own.

Although we have had to face this continual, imminent threat of invasion by a military Power which has stationed eighty of its best divisions in northern France, we have not

*Chief of the Air Staff

failed to reinforce our armies in the Middle East and elsewhere. All the while the great convoys have been passing steadily and safely on their course through the unknown wastes of the oceans, drawing from all parts of the Empire the forces which will, I trust, enable us to fill in time the terrible gap in our defences which was opened by the Vichy French desertion. I shall certainly not make any prophecies about what will happen when British, Australian, New Zealand, Indian and Egyptian troops come to close grips with the Italian invaders who are now making their way across the deserts towards them. All I will say is that we are doing our best and that there as here we feel a good deal better than we did some time ago.

I do not propose to give the House a detailed account of the episode at Dakar. I could easily do so in private, but it would be out of proportion to the scale of events. Moreover, I do not relish laying bare to the enemy all our internal processes. This operation was primarily French, and, although we were ready to give it a measure of support which in certain circumstances might have been decisive, we were no more anxious than was General de Gaulle to get involved in a lengthy or sanguinary conflict with the Vichy French. That General de Gaulle was right in believing that the majority of Frenchmen in Dakar was favourable to the Free French movement, I have no doubt; indeed, I think his judgement has been found extremely sure-footed, and our opinion of him has been enhanced by everything we have seen of his conduct in circumstances of peculiar and perplexing difficulty. His Majesty's Government have no intention whatever of abandoning the cause of General de Gaulle until it is merged, as merged it will be, in the larger cause of France.

There is, however, one part of this story on which I should like to reassure the House, as it concerns His Majesty's Government alone and does not affect those with whom we have been working. The whole situation at Dakar was transformed in a most unfavourable manner by the arrival there of three French cruisers and three destroyers which carried with them a number of Vichy partisans, evidently of a most bitter type. These partisans were sent to overawe the population, to grip the defences and to see to the efficient manning of the powerful shore batteries. The policy which His Majesty's Government had been pursuing towards the Vichy French warships was not to interfere with them unless they appeared to be proceeding to enemy-controlled ports. Obviously, however, while General de Gaulle's enterprise was proceeding it was specially important to prevent any of them reaching Dakar. By a series of accidents, and some errors which have been made the subject of disciplinary action or are now subject to formal inquiry, neither the First Sea Lord nor the Cabinet were informed of the approach of these ships to the Straits of Gibraltar until it was too late to stop them passing through. Orders were instantly given to stop them at Casablanca, or if that failed, to prevent them entering Dakar. If we could not cork them in, we could, at least, we hoped, have corked them out, but, although every effort was made to execute these orders, these efforts failed. The Vichy cruisers were, however, prevented from carrying out their further purpose of attacking the Free French Colony of Duala, and of the four French vessels concerned, two succeeded in regaining Dakar, while two were overtaken by our cruisers and were induced to return to Casablanca without any actual violence.

The House may therefore rest assured – indeed, it is the only point I am seeking to make today – that the mischievous arrival of these ships, and the men they carried, at Dakar arose in no way from any infirmity of purpose on the part of the Government; it was one of those mischances which often arise in war and especially in war at sea. The fighting which ensued between the shore batteries at Dakar, reinforced by the 16-inch guns of the damaged *Richelieu*, and the British squadron was pretty stiff. Two Vichy submarines which attacked the Fleet were sunk, the crew of one happily being saved. Two of the Vichy French destroyers were set on fire, one of the cruisers was heavily hit and the *Richelieu* herself suffered further damage. On our part we had two ships, one a battleship and the other a large cruiser, which suffered damage – damage which, although it does not prevent their steaming and fighting, will require considerable attention when convenient.

What an irony of fate it is that this fine French Navy, which Admiral Darlan shaped for so many years to fight in the common cause against German aggression, should now be the principal obstacle to the liberation of France and her Empire from the German yoke, and should be employed as the tools of German and Italian masters whose policy contemplates not merely the defeat and mutilation of France, but her final destruction as a great nation. The Dakar incident reminds us of what often happens when a drowning man casts his arms around the strong swimmer who comes to his rescue and seeks in his agony to drag him down into the depths. Force in these circumstances has to be used to save life as well as to take life. But we never thought that what happened or might happen at Dakar was likely to lead to a declaration of war by the Vichy Government, although evidently such a step might be imposed upon them at any time by their masters. Whatever happens it is the tide and not mere eddies of events which will dominate the French people. Nothing can prevent the increasing abhorrence with which they will regard their German conquerors or the growth of the new-born hope that Great Britain will be victorious, and that the British victory will carry with it, as it must, the deliverance and restoration of France and all other captive peoples.

That is all I think it is useful to say at the present time, either about the Dakar affair or our relations with the Vichy Government, except this. We must be very careful not to allow a failure of this kind to weaken or hamper our efforts to take positive action and regain the initiative. On the contrary, we must improve our methods and redouble our efforts. We must be baffled to fight better and not baffled to fight less. Here let me say that criticism which is well-meant and well-informed and searching is often helpful, but there is a tone in certain organs of the Press, happily not numerous, a tone not only upon the Dakar episode but in other and more important issues, that is so vicious and malignant that it would be almost indecent if applied to the enemy. I know that some people's nerves are frayed by the stresses of war, and they should be especially on their guard lest in giving vent to their own feelings they weaken the national resistance and blunt our sword.

I must now ask the House to extend its view more widely and to follow me if they can find the patience to the other side of the globe. Three months ago we were asked by the Japanese Government to close the Burma Road to certain supplies which might reach the Republic of China in its valiant struggle. We acceded to this demand because as we told both Houses of Parliament, we tried to give an opportunity to the Governments of Japan and China to reach what is called in diplomatic language 'a just and equitable settlement' of their long and deadly quarrel – there were no doubt some other reasons, but that one is enough for my argument. Unhappily this 'just and equitable settlement' has not been reached. On the contrary, the protracted struggle of Japan to subjugate the Chinese race is still proceeding with all its attendant miseries. We must regret that the opportunity has been lost. In the circumstances His Majesty's Government propose to allow the agreement about closing the Burma Road to run its course until October 17, but they do not see their way to renew it after that.

Instead of reaching an agreement with China, the Japanese Government have entered into a Three-Power Pact with Germany and Italy, a pact which, in many respects, is a revival of the Anti-Comintern Pact of a few years ago, but which binds Japan to attack the United States should the United States intervene in the war now proceeding between Great Britain and the two European dictators. This bargain appears so unfavourable to Japan that we wonder whether there are not some secret clauses. It is not easy now to see in what way Germany and Italy could come to the aid of Japan while the British and United States Navies remain in being, as they certainly do and as they certainly will. However, that is for the Japanese – with whom we have never wished to quarrel – to judge for themselves. Great services have been rendered to them by the peoples of the United States and Great Britain since their rise in the nineteenth century. This is a matter on which they must judge themselves. This Three-Power Pact is, of course, aimed primarily at the United States, but also in a secondary degree it is pointed against Russia. Neither of the branches of the English-speaking race is accustomed to react to threats of violence by submission, and certainly the reception of this strange, ill-balanced declaration in the United States has not been at all encouraging to those who are its authors. We hope, however, that all such dangers – and the dangers can plainly be seen – will be averted by the prudence and patience that Japan has so often shown in the gravest situations.

There is another country much nearer home which has for some months past seemed to hang in the balance between peace and war. We have always wished well to the Spanish people, and in a glorious period of our history we stood between the Spaniards and foreign domination. There is no country in Europe that has more need of peace and food and the opportunities of prosperous trade than Spain, which has been torn and tormented by the devastation of a civil war, into which the Spanish nation was drawn by a series of hideous accidents and misunderstandings, and from the ruins of which they must now rebuild their united national life of dignity, in mercy and in honour. Far be it from us to lap Spain and her own economic needs in the wide compass of our blockade. All we seek is that Spain will not become a channel of supply to our mortal foes. Subject to this essential condition, there is no problem of blockade that we will not study in the earnest desire to meet Spain's needs and aid her revival. Even less do we presume to intrude on the internal affairs of Spain or to stir the embers of what so lately were devouring fires. As in the days of the Peninsular War, British interests and policy are based on the independence and unity of Spain, and we look forward to seeing her take her rightful place both as a great Mediterranean Power and as a leading and famous member of the family of Europe and of Christendom, which, though now sundered by fearful quarrels and under the obsession of grievous tyrannies, constitutes the goal towards which we are marching and will march across the battlefields of the land, the sea, and the air.

Because we feel easier in ourselves and see our way more clearly through our difficulties and dangers than we did some months ago, because foreign countries, friends and foes, recognise the giant, enduring, resilient strength of Britain and the British Empire, do not let us dull for one moment the sense of the awful hazards in which we stand. Do not let us lose the conviction that it is only by supreme and superb exertions, unwearying and indomitable, that we shall save our souls alive. No one can predict, no one can even imagine, how this terrible war against German and Nazi aggression will run its course or how far it will spread or how long it will last. Long, dark months of trials and tribulations lie before us. Not only great dangers, but many more misfortunes, many shortcomings, many mistakes, many disappointments will surely be our lot. Death and sorrow will be the companions of our journey; hardship our garment; constancy and valour our only shield. We must be united, we must be undaunted, we must be inflexible. Our qualities and deeds must burn and glow through the gloom of Europe until they become the veritable beacon of its salvation.

TO THE FRENCH PEOPLE

Even in the darkest days of the war, Mr Winston Churchill never lost his faith in the power of the French people to rise superior to their temporary leaders and to join once more in the fight for freedom. It was in this mood that he made a broadcast call to the people of France in October.

AN ADDRESS BROADCAST IN FRENCH AND ENGLISH,
OCTOBER 21, 1940

Frenchmen! For more than thirty years in peace and war I have marched with you, and I am marching still along the same road. Tonight I speak to you at your firesides wherever you may be, or whatever your fortunes are. I repeat the prayer around the *louis d'or*, '*Dieu protège la France*'. Here at home in England, under the fire of the Boche, we do not forget the ties and links that unite us to France, and we are persevering steadfastly and in good heart in the cause of European freedom and fair dealing for the common people of all countries, for which, with you, we drew the sword. When good people get into trouble because they are attacked and heavily smitten by the vile and wicked, they must be very careful not to get at loggerheads with one another. The common enemy is always trying to bring this about, and, of course, in bad luck a lot of things happen which play into the hands of the enemy. We must just make the best of things as they come along.

Here in London, which Herr Hitler says he will reduce to ashes, and which his aeroplanes are now bombarding, our people are bearing up unflinchingly. Our Air Force has more than held its own. We are waiting for the long-promised invasion. So are the fishes. But, of course, this is for us only the beginning. Now in 1940, in spite of occasional losses, we have, as ever, command of the seas. In 1941 we shall have the command of the air. Remember what that means. Herr Hitler with his tanks and other mechanical weapons, and also by Fifth Column intrigue with traitors, has managed to subjugate for the time being most of the finest races in Europe, and his little Italian accomplice is trotting along hopefully and hungrily, but rather wearily and very timidly, at his side. They both wish to carve up France and her Empire as if it were a fowl: to one a leg, to another a wing or perhaps part of the breast. Not only the French Empire will be devoured by these two ugly customers, but Alsace-Lorraine will go once again under the German yoke, and Nice, Savoy and Corsica – Napoleon's Corsica – will be torn from the fair realm of France. But Herr Hitler is not thinking only of stealing other people's territories, or flinging gobbets of them to his little confederate. I tell you truly what you must believe when I say this evil man, this monstrous abortion of hatred and defeat, is resolved on nothing less than the complete wiping out of the French nation, and the disintegration of its whole life and future. By all kinds of sly and savage means, he is plotting and working to quench for ever the foundation of characteristic French culture and of French inspiration to the world. All Europe, if he has his way, will be reduced to one uniform Boche-land, to be exploited, pillaged, and bullied by his Nazi gangsters. You will excuse my speaking frankly because this is not a time to mince words. It is not defeat that France will now be made to suffer at German hands, but the doom of complete obliteration. Army, Navy, Air Force, religion, law, language, culture, institutions, literature, history, tradition, all are to be effaced by the brute strength of a triumphant army and the scientific low-cunning of a ruthless police force.

Frenchmen – re-arm your spirits before it is too late. Remember how Napoleon said before one of his battles: 'These same Prussians who are so boastful today were three to one at Jena, and six to one at Montmirail.' Never will I believe that the soul of France is dead. Never will I believe that her place amongst the greatest nations of the world has been lost for ever! All these schemes and crimes of Herr Hitler's are bringing upon him and upon all who belong to his system a retribution which many of us will live to see. The story is not yet finished, but it will not be so long. We are on his track, and so are our friends across the Atlantic Ocean, and your friends across the Atlantic Ocean. If he cannot destroy us, we will surely destroy him and all his gang, and all their works. Therefore, have hope and faith, for all will come right.

Now what is it we British ask of you in this present hard and bitter time? What we ask at this moment in our struggle to win the victory which we will share with you, is that if you cannot help us, at least you will not hinder us. Presently you will be able to weight the arm that strikes for you, and you ought to do so. But even now we believe that Frenchmen, wherever they may be, feel their hearts warm and a proud blood tingle in their veins when we have some success in the air or on the sea, or presently – for that will come – upon the land.

Remember we shall never stop, never weary, and never give

in, and that our whole people and Empire have vowed themselves to the task of cleansing Europe from the Nazi pestilence
and saving the world from the new Dark Ages. Do not imagine,
as the German-controlled wireless tells you, that we English
seek to take your ships and colonies. We seek to beat the life
and soul out of Hitler and Hitlerism. That alone, that all the
time, that to the end. We do not covet anything from any
nation except their respect. Those Frenchmen who are in the
French Empire, and those who are in so-called unoccupied
France, may see their way from time to time to useful action.
I will not go into details. Hostile ears are listening. As for
those, to whom English hearts go out in full, because they see
them under the sharp discipline, oppression and spying of the
Hun – as to those Frenchmen in the occupied regions, to them
I say, when they think of the future let them remember the
words which Gambetta, that great Frenchman, uttered after
1870 about the future of France and what was to come: 'Think
of it always: speak of it never.'

Good night then: sleep to gather strength for the morning.
For the morning will come. Brightly will it shine on the brave
and true, kindly upon all who suffer for the cause, glorious
upon the tombs of heroes. Thus will shine the dawn. *Vive la
France!* Long live also the forward march of the common
people in all the lands towards their just and true inheritance,
and towards the broader and fuller age.

'WE WILL NEVER CEASE TO STRIKE'

A SPEECH AT THE LORD MAYOR'S LUNCHEON AT THE
MANSION HOUSE, NOVEMBER 9, 1940

I thank you, my Lord Mayor, for the toast which you have
proposed to His Majesty's Government and for what you have
said about them and of the confidence felt in them. I thank you

also for your reference to Mr Chamberlain, who was so recently one of our most active colleagues, under whom so many of us have served, and whose illness causes us all the greatest sorrow today. Things happen so quickly nowadays and there are such a lot of them going on that one finds it somewhat difficult to measure evenly the march of time. For myself, I can say there are weeks which seem to pass in a flash and then again there are others which are unutterably long and slow. At times it is almost difficult to believe that so much has happened and at another that so little time has passed.

It is now six months since the King and Parliament confided to me and to my colleagues the very grave and heavy task to which we have devoted ourselves, as I can assure you, to the best of our abilities. It is lucky that we did not make any extravagant optimistic promises or predictions, because a succession of melancholy disasters and terrible assaults and perils have fallen upon us. We have had to face these great calamities; we have come through the disasters; we have surmounted the perils so far; but the fact remains that at the present time all we have got to show is survival and increasing strength and an inflexible will to win.

The outside world, which a little while ago took only a moderate view of our prospects, now believes that Britain will survive. But between immediate survival and lasting victory there is a long road to tread. In treading it, we shall show the world the perseverence and steadfastness of the British race and the glorious resilience and flexibility of our ancient institutions.

Let me remind you that in spite of all the blows we have endured and under all the burdens we bear, and amid so many deadly threats, we have not abandoned one jot of any of our obligations or undertakings towards the captive and enslaved countries of Europe or towards any of those countries which still act with us. On the contrary, since we have been left alone in this world struggle we have reaffirmed or defined more precisely all the causes of all the countries with whom or for whom we drew the sword – Austria, Czecho-slovakia, Poland, Norway, Holland, Belgium; greatest of all, France; latest of all, Greece. For all of these we will toil and strive, and our victory will supply the liberation of them all.

The week that has now ended has brought us a message from across the ocean, a message of the highest encouragement and good cheer during the protracted tumult and controversy of the Presidential Election. Everyone in this island – Parliament, Ministers, the Press, the public – discreetly abstained from the slightest expression of opinion about the domestic, political and party conflicts of the great democracy of the United States.

We are deeply touched by the words of kindness and good will and the promises of material aid which were uttered by Mr Willkie on behalf of the Republican Party, which he captained so ably. But I am sure it will give no offence, now that all is over, if I offer in the name of HM Government, and, if you will allow me, my Lord Mayor, in the name of the citizens of London, our most heart-felt congratulations to the illustrious American statesman who has never failed to give us a helping hand, and who now, in the supreme crisis, has achieved the unprecedented mark of American confidence of being chosen for the third time to lead his mighty people forward on their path.

The help that we have been promised by the United States takes the form at the present time of a most abundant sharing with us of the fruits of the gigantic munitions production which has now been set on foot throughout the matchless workshops, furnaces and foundries of the United States. This has no doubt been done primarily because our stubborn and unwavering resistance here will alone gain the time needed by the United States to convert its industry to a war basis and to build up the immense naval, military and air forces which they have set on foot for their own purposes and for their own protection.

Their interest in our successful resistance and final victory has been proclaimed by all parties in America. But no one over here has been left in any doubt that, beyond this strong material help and foundation of common interest, there flows a tide of comprehension, of sentiment and fierce, matchless sympathy for our cause which warms our hearts and strengthens our resolve.

People sometimes wonder why we are unable to take the offensive against the enemy, and always have to wait for some new blow which he will strike against us. The reason is that our production in munitions is now only in the early part of its second year, and that enormous factories and plants which we laid down on or shortly before the outbreak of war are only now beginning to come into production. The Germans, on the other hand, have long passed the culminating point of munitions production, which is reached usually about the fourth year.

We have, therefore, a long and arduous road to travel in which our war industries must grow up to their full stature, in which our Navy must receive the reinforcements of the hundreds of vessels which we began on the outbreak of war, and which are now coming continuously into service; in which our Army must be equipped, trained and perfected into a strong, keen offensive weapon; and, above all, our Air Force must add superiority of numbers to that superiority of quality which, in machines, and still more in manhood, they have so signally displayed. We are straining every nerve to accelerate our production, and with the ardent, resolute aid of British labour, guided by science and improving organisation, I do not doubt that we shall succeed.

But here is where the help from across the oceans is especially valuable, because in the United States, as in our great Dominions and in India, all the production of war materials and the training of pilots can proceed without any distraction or impediment. Therefore I welcome most cordially the aid which has been promised us from the United States as I do the important contributions which have already been received. There is one other point which must, however, be borne in mind in this survey. The enemy is naturally doing his utmost to cut us from these vital supplies and, therefore, the maintenance by sea-power of the ocean routes is an absolute necessity to our victory, and is of importance to all who need or who desire our victory.

It has been usual, on these occasions, for the Prime Minister to give a general survey of foreign policy and to refer to our relations with many countries in well-guarded, well-poised and happily balanced terms. Today I need not do that. It has been obvious to all that we are striving to the utmost of our strength for the freedom of nations against the oppressor, that we are striving for the progress of peoples through the process of self-government and for the creation of that wider brotherhood among men which alone will bring them back to prosperity and peace. We do not need to speak, therefore, of many of those nations.

But there is one small heroic country to whom our thoughts today go out in new sympathy and admiration. To the valiant Greek people and their armies – now defending their native soil from the latest Italian outrage, to them we send from the heart of old London our faithful promise that, amid all our burdens and anxieties, we will do our best to aid them in their struggle, and that we will never cease to strike at the foul aggressor in ever-increasing strength from this time forth until the crimes and treacheries which hang around the neck of Mussolini and disgrace the Italian name have been brought to condign and exemplary justice.

THE ATTACK ON THE ITALIAN FLEET AT TARANTO

A SPEECH TO THE HOUSE OF COMMONS, NOVEMBER 13, 1940

I have some news for the House. It is good news. The Royal Navy has struck a crippling blow at the Italian Fleet. The total strength of the Italian battle fleet was six battleships, two of them of the *Littorio* class, which have just been put into service and are, of course, among the most powerful vessels in the world, and four of the recently reconstructed *Cavour* class.

This fleet was, to be sure, considerably more powerful on paper than our Mediterranean Fleet, but it had consistently refused to accept battle. On the night of November 11–12, when the main units of the Italian Fleet were lying behind their shore defences in their naval base at Taranto, our aircraft of the Fleet Air Arm attacked them in their stronghold. Reports of our airmen have been confirmed by photographic reconnaissance. It is now established that one battleship of the *Littorio* class was badly down by the bows and that her forecastle is under water and she has a heavy list to starboard. One battleship of the *Cavour* class has been beached, and her stern, up to and including the after-turret, is under water. This ship is also heavily listed to starboard. It has not yet been possible to establish the fact with certainty, but it appears that a second battleship of the *Cavour* class has also been severely damaged and beached. In the inner harbour of Taranto two Italian cruisers are listed to starboard and are surrounded with fuel oil, and two fleet auxiliaries are lying with their sterns under water. The Italian communiqué of November 12, in admitting that one warship had been severely damaged, claimed that six of our aircraft had been shot down and three more probably. In fact, only two of our aircraft are missing, and it is noted that the enemy claimed that part of the crews had been taken prisoner.

I felt it my duty to bring this glorious episode to the immediate notice of the House. As the result of a determined and highly successful attack, which reflects the greatest honour on the Fleet Air Arm, only three Italian battleships now remain effective. This result, while it affects decisively the balance of naval power in the Mediterranean, also carries with it reactions upon the naval situation in every quarter of the globe. The spirit of the Royal Navy, as shown in this daring attack, is also exemplified in the forlorn and heroic action which has been fought by the captain, officers and ship's company of the *Jervis Bay* in giving battle against overwhelming odds in order to protect the merchant convoy which they were escorting, and thus securing the escape of by far the greater part of that convoy.

The Mediterranean Fleet has also continued to harass the Italian communications with their armies in Libya. On the night of November 9-10 a bombardment was carried out at Sidi Barrani, and, though the fire was returned by shore batteries, our ships sustained no damage and no casualties. Moreover, one of our submarines attacked a convoy of two Italian supply ships escorted by destroyers, with the result that one heavily-laden ship of 3,000 tons sank and a second ship was certainly damaged and probably sunk. I feel sure that the House will regard these results as highly satisfactory, and as reflecting the greatest credit upon the Admiralty and upon Admiral Cunningham, Commander-in-Chief in the Mediterranean, and, above all, on our pilots of the Fleet Air Arm, who, like their brothers in the Royal Air Force, continue to render the country services of the highest order.

VICTORY AT SIDI BARRANI

A STATEMENT TO THE HOUSE OF COMMONS, DECEMBER 12, 1940

The House evidently appreciated the full significance of the fact, which I announced, without commenting upon it, that a British column had reached the coast between Buq-Buq and Sidi Barrani. This, of course, cut the principal road by which the main body of the Italian army which had invaded Egypt could effect a retreat. The question then was whether the encircling positions which General Wilson's forces had captured after their brilliantly executed desert march could be effectively maintained, and whether the net so drawn could be forced at all points to the seashore. The strong position of Sidi Barrani and various fortified posts in this neighbourhood appeared to be a considerable obstacle. However, Sidi Barrani has been captured, and the whole coastal region with the exception of one or two points still holding out is in the hands of the British and Imperial troops. Seven thousand prisoners have already reached Mersa Matruh.

We do not yet know how many Italians were caught in the encirclement, but it would not be surprising if, at least, the best part of three Italian divisions, including numerous Black Shirt formations, have been either destroyed or captured. As Sidi Barrani was the advance base for all the Italian forces which had invaded Egypt and were preparing for a further inroad, it seems probable that considerable masses of material may be found there. The pursuit to the westward continues with the greatest vigour, the Air Force are now bombing and the Navy are shelling the principal road open to the retreating enemy, and considerable additional captures have already been reported besides those which fell within the original encirclement.

While it is too soon to measure the scale of these operations, it is clear that they constitute a victory which, in this African theatre of war, is of the first order, and reflects the highest credit upon Sir Archibald Wavell, Sir Maitland Wilson, the staff officers who planned this exceedingly complicated operation, and the troops who performed the remarkable feats of endurance and daring which accomplished it. The whole episode must be judged upon the background of the fact that it is only three or four months ago that our anxieties for the defence of Egypt were acute. Those anxieties are now removed, and the British guarantee and pledge that Egypt would be effectually defended against all comers has been, in every way, made good.

'GIVE US THE TOOLS AND WE WILL FINISH THE JOB'

A WORLD BROADCAST, FEBRUARY 9, 1941

Five months have passed since I spoke to the British nation and the Empire on the broadcast. In wartime there is a lot to be said for the motto: 'Deeds, not words.' All the same, it is a good thing to look around from time to time and take stock, and certainly our affairs have prospered in several directions during these last four or five months, far better than most of us would have ventured to hope.

We stood our ground and faced the two dictators in the hour of what seemed their overwhelming triumph, and we have shown ourselves capable, so far, of standing up against them alone. After the heavy defeats of the German Air Force by our fighters in August and September, Herr Hitler did not dare attempt the invasion of this island, although he had every need to do so and although he had made vast preparations. Baffled in this mighty project, he sought to break the spirit of the British nation by the bombing, first of London, and afterwards of our great cities. It has now been proved, to the admiration of the world, and of our friends in the United States, that this form of blackmail by murder and terrorism, so far from weakening the spirit of the British nation, has only roused it to a more intense and universal flame than was ever seen before in any modern community.

The whole British Empire has been proud of the Mother Country, and they long to be with us over here in even larger numbers. We have been deeply conscious of the love for us which has flowed from the Dominions of the Crown across the broad ocean spaces. *There* is the first of our war aims: to be worthy of that love, and to preserve it.

All through these dark winter months the enemy has had the power to drop three or four tons of bombs upon us for every ton we could send to Germany in return. We are arranging so that presently this will be rather the other way around; but meanwhile, London and our big cities have had to stand their pounding. They remind me of the British squares at Waterloo. They are not squares of soldiers; they do not wear scarlet coats. They are just ordinary English, Scottish and Welsh folk – men, women and children – standing steadfastly together. But their spirit is the same, their glory is the same; and, in the end, their victory will be greater than far-famed Waterloo.

All honour to the Civil Defence Services of all kinds – emergency and regular, volunteer and professional – who have helped our people through this formidable ordeal, the like of which no civilised community has ever been called upon to undergo. If I mention only one of these services here, namely the Police, it is because many tributes have been paid already to the others. But the Police have been in it everywhere, all the time, and, as a working woman wrote to me: 'What gentlemen they are!'

More than two-thirds of the winter has now gone, and so far we have had no serious epidemic; indeed, there is no increase of illness in spite of the improvised conditions of the shelters. That is most creditable to our local, medical and sanitary authorities, to our devoted nursing staff, and to the Ministry of Health, whose head, Mr Malcolm MacDonald, is now going to Canada in the important office of High Commissioner.

There is another thing which surprised me when I asked about it. In spite of all these new wartime offences and prosecutions of all kinds; in spite of all the opportunities for looting and disorder, there has been less crime this winter and there are now fewer prisoners in our gaols than in the years of peace.

We have broken the back of the winter. The daylight grows. The Royal Air Force grows, and is already certainly master of the daylight air. The attacks may be sharper, but they will be shorter; there will be more opportunities for work and service of all kinds; more opportunities for life. So, if our first victory was the repulse of the invader, our second was the frustration of his acts of terror and torture against our people at home.

Meanwhile, abroad, in October, a wonderful thing happened. One of the two dictators – the crafty, cold-blooded, black-hearted Italian, who had thought to gain an Empire on the cheap by stabbing fallen France in the back, got into trouble. Without the slightest provocation, spurred on by lust of power and brutish greed, Mussolini attacked and invaded Greece, only to be hurled back ignominiously by the heroic

Greek Army; who, I will say, with your consent, have revived before our eyes the glories which from the classic age gild their native land. While Signor Mussolini was writhing and smarting under the Greek lash in Albania, Generals Wavell and Wilson, who were charged with the defence of Egypt and of the Suez Canal in accordance with our treaty obligations, whose task seemed at one time so difficult, had received very powerful reinforcements of men, cannon, equipment and, above all, tanks, which we had sent from our island in spite of the invasion threat. Large numbers of troops from India, Australia and New Zealand had also reached them. Forthwith began that series of victories in Libya which have broken irretrievably the Italian military power on the African Continent. We have all been entertained, and I trust edified, by the exposure and humiliation of another of what Byron called.

> Those Pagod things of sabre sway,
> With fronts of brass, and feet of clay.

Here, then, in Libya, is the third considerable event upon which we may dwell with some satisfaction. It is just exactly two months ago, to a day, that I was waiting anxiously, but also eagerly, for the news of the great counter-stroke which had been planned against the Italian invaders of Egypt. The secret had been well kept. The preparations had been well made. But to leap across those seventy miles of desert, and attack an army of ten or eleven divisions, equipped with all the appliances of modern war, who had been fortifying themselves for three months, that was a most hazardous adventure.

When the brilliant decisive victory at Sidi Barrani, with its tens of thousands of prisoners, proved that we had quality, manoeuvring power and weapons superior to the enemy, who had boasted so much of his virility and his military virtues, it was evident that all the other Italian forces in Eastern Libya were in great danger. They could not easily beat a retreat along the coastal road without running the risk of being caught in the open by our armoured divisions and brigades ranging far out into the desert in tremendous swoops and scoops. They had to expose themselves to being attacked piecemeal.

General Wavell – nay, all our leaders, and all their lithe, active, ardent men, British, Australian, Indian, in the Imperial Army, saw their opportunity. At that time I ventured to draw General Wavell's attention to the seventh chapter of the Gospel of St Matthew, at the seventh verse, where, as you all know – or ought to know – it is written: 'Ask, and it shall be given; seek, and ye shall find; knock, and it shall be opened unto you.' The Army of the Nile has asked, and it was given; they sought, and they have found; they knocked, and it has been opened unto them. In barely eight weeks, by a campaign which will long be studied as a model of the military art, an advance of over 400 miles has been made. The whole Italian Army in the east of Libya, which was reputed to exceed 150,000 men, has been captured or destroyed. The entire province of Cyrenaica – nearly as big as England and Wales – has been conquered. The unhappy Arab tribes, who have for thirty years suffered from the cruelty of Italian rule, carried in some cases to the point of methodical extermination, these Bedouin survivors have at last seen their oppressors in disorderly flight, or led off in endless droves as prisoners of war.

Egypt and the Suez Canal are safe, and the port, the base and the airfields of Benghazi constitute a strategic point of high consequence to the whole of the war in the Eastern Mediterranean.

This is the time, I think, to speak of the leaders who, at the head of their brave troops, have rendered this distinguished service to the King. The first and foremost, General Wavell, Commander-in-Chief of all the armies of the Middle East, has proved himself a master of war, sage, painstaking, daring and tireless. But General Wavell has repeatedly asked that others should share his fame.

General Wilson, who actually commands the Army of the Nile, was reputed to be one of our finest tacticians – and few will now deny that quality. General O'Connor commanding the 13th Corps, with General Mackay commanding the splendid Australians, and General Creagh, who trained and commanded the various armoured divisions which were employed; these three men executed the complicated and astounding rapid movements which were made, and fought the action which occurred. I have just seen a telegram from General Wavell in which he says that the success at Benghazi was due to the outstanding leadership and resolution of O'Connor and Creagh, ably backed by Wilson.

I must not forget here to point out the amazing mechanical feats of the British tanks, whose design and workmanship have beaten all records and stood up to all trials; and show us how closely and directly the work in the factories at home is linked with the victories abroad.

Of course, none of our plans would have succeeded had not our pilots, under Air Chief Marshal Longmore, wrested the control of the air from a far more numerous enemy. Nor would the campaign itself have been possible if the British Mediterranean Fleet, under Admiral Cunningham, had not chased the Italian Navy into its harbours and sustained every forward surge of the Army with all the flexible resources of sea-power. How far-reaching these resources are we can see from what happened at dawn this morning, when our Western Mediterranean Fleet, under Admiral Somerville, entered the Gulf of Genoa and bombarded in a shattering manner the naval base from which perhaps a Nazi German expedition might soon have sailed to attack General Weygand in Algeria or Tunis. It is right that the Italian people should be made to feel the sorry plight into which they have been dragged by Dictator Mussolini; and if the cannonade of Genoa, rolling along the coast, reverberating in the mountains, reached the ears of our French comrades in their grief and misery, it might cheer them with the feeling that friends – active friends – are near, and that Britannia rules the waves.

The events in Libya are only part of the story: they are only part of the story of the decline and fall of the Italian Empire, that will not take a future Gibbon so long to write as the original work. Fifteen hundred miles away to the southward a strong British and Indian army, having driven the invaders out of the Sudan, is marching steadily forward through the

Italian colony of Eritrea, thus seeking to complete the isolation of all the Italian troops in Abyssinia. Other British forces are entering Abyssinia from the west, while the army gathered in Kenya – in the van of which we may discern the powerful forces of the Union of South Africa, organised by General Smuts – is striking northward along the whole enormous front. Lastly, the Ethopian patriots, whose independence was stolen five years ago, have risen in arms; and their Emperor, so recently an exile in England, is in their midst to fight for their freedom and his throne. Here, then, we see the beginnings of a process of reparation and of the chastisement of wrongdoing, which reminds us that though the mills of God grind slowly, they grind exceedingly small.

While these auspicious events have been carrying us stride by stride from what many people thought a forlorn position, and was certainly a very grave position in May and June, to one which permits us to speak with sober confidence of our power to discharge our duty, heavy though it be, in the future – while this has been happening, a mighty tide of sympathy, of good will and of effective aid, has begun to flow across the Atlantic in support of the world cause which is at stake. Distinguished Americans have come over to see things here at the front, and to find out how the United States can help us best and soonest. In Mr Hopkins, who has been my frequent companion during the last three weeks, we have the envoy of the President who has been newly re-elected to his august office. In Mr Wendell Willkie we have welcomed the champion of the great Republican Party. We may be sure that they will both tell the truth about what they have seen over here, and more than that we do not ask. The rest we leave with good confidence to the judgement of the President, the Congress and the people of the United States.

I have been so very careful, since I have been Prime Minister, not to encourage false hopes or prophesy smooth and easy things, and yet the tale that I have to tell today is one which must justly and rightly give us cause for deep thankfulness, and also, I think, for strong comfort and even rejoicing. But now I must dwell upon the more serious, darker and more dangerous aspects of the vast scene of the war. We must all of us have been asking ourselves: what has that wicked man whose crime-stained regime and system are at bay and in the toils – what has he been preparing during the winter months? What new devilry is he planning? What new small country will he overrun or strike down? What fresh form of assault will be made upon our island home and fortress; which – let there be no mistake about it – is all that stands between him and the dominion of the world?

We may be sure that the war is soon going to enter upon a phase of greater violence. Hitler's confederate, Mussolini, has reeled back in Albania; but the Nazis – having absorbed Hungary and driven Rumania into a frightful internal convulsion – are now already upon the Black Sea. A considerable Nazi German army and air force is being built up in Rumania, and its forward tentacles have already penetrated Bulgaria. With – we must suppose – the acquiescence of the Bulgarian Government, airfields are being occupied by German ground personnel numbering thousands, so as to enable the German air force to come into action from Bulgaria. Many preparations have been made for the movement of German troops into or through Bulgaria, and perhaps this southward movement has already begun.

We saw what happened last May in the Low Countries; how they hoped for the best; how they clung to their neutrality; how woefully they were deceived, overwhelmed, plundered, enslaved and since starved. We know how we and the French suffered when, at the last moment, at the urgent belated appeal of the King of the Belgians, we went to his aid. Of course, if all the Balkan peoples stood together and acted together, aided by Britain and Turkey, it would be many months before a German army and air force of sufficient strength to overcome them could be assembled in the southeast of Europe. And in those months much might happen. Much will certainly happen as American aid becomes effective, as our air-power grows, as we become a well-armed nation, and as our armies in the East increase in strength. But nothing is more certain than that, if the countries of south-eastern Europe allow themselves to be pulled to pieces one by one, they will share the fate of Denmark, Holland and Belgium. And none can tell how long it will be before the hour of their deliverance strikes.

One of our difficulties is to convince some of these neutral countries in Europe that we are going to win. We think it astonishing that they should be so dense as not to see it as clearly as we do ourselves. I remember in the last war, in July 1915, we began to think that Bulgaria was going wrong, so Mr Lloyd George, Mr Bonar Law, Sir F. E. Smith and I asked the Bulgarian Minister to dinner to explain to him what a fool King Ferdinand would make of himself if he were to go in on the losing side. It was no use. The poor man simply could not believe it, or could not make his Government believe it. So Bulgaria, against the wishes of her peasant population, against all her interests, fell in at the Kaiser's tail and got sadly carved up and punished when the victory was won. I trust that Bulgaria is not going to make the same mistake again. If they do, the Bulgarian peasantry and people, for whom there has been much regard, both in Great Britain and in the United States, will for the third time in thirty years have been made to embark upon a needless and disastrous war.

In the Central Mediterranean the Italian quisling, who is called Mussolini, and the French quisling, commonly called Laval, are both in their different ways trying to make their countries into doormats for Hitler and his New Order, in the hope of being able to keep, or get the Nazi Gestapo and Prussian bayonets to enforce, their rule upon their fellow-countrymen. I cannot tell how the matter will go, but at any rate we shall do our best to fight for the Central Mediterranean.

I dare say you will have noticed the very significant air action which was fought over Malta a fortnight ago. The Germans sent an entire *Geschwader* of dive-bombers to Sicily. They seriously injured our new aircraft-carrier *Illustrious*, and then, as this wounded ship was sheltering in Malta harbour, they concentrated upon her all their force so as to beat her to pieces. But they were met by the batteries of Malta, which is one of the strongest defended fortresses in the world against air attack; they were met by the Fleet Air Arm and by the Royal Air Force, and, in two or three days, they had lost, out of 150 dive-bombers, upwards of ninety, fifty of which were destroyed in the air and forty on the ground. Although the *Illustrious*, in her damaged condition, was one of the great prizes of the air and naval war, the German *Geschwader* accepted the defeat; they would not come any more. All the necessary repairs were made to the *Illustrious* in Malta harbour, and she steamed safely off to Alexandria under her own power at twenty-three knots. I dwell upon this incident, not at all because I think it disposes of the danger in the Central Mediterranean, but in order to show you that there, as elsewhere, we intend to give a good account of ourselves.

But after all, the fate of this war is going to be settled by what happens on the oceans, in the air and – above all – in this island. It seems now to be certain that the Government and people of the United States intend to supply us with all that is necessary for victory. In the last war the United States sent 2,000,000 men across the Atlantic. But this is not a war of vast armies, firing immense masses of shells at one another. We do not need the gallant armies which are forming throughout the American Union. We do not need them this year, nor next year; nor any years that I can foresee. But we do need most urgently an immense and continuous supply of war materials and technical apparatus of all kinds. We need them here and we need to bring them here. We shall need a great mass of shipping in 1942, far more than we can build ourselves, if we are to maintain and augment our war effort in the West and in the East.

These facts are, of course, all well known to the enemy, and we must therefore expect that Herr Hitler will do his utmost to prey upon our shipping and to reduce the volume of American supplies entering these islands. Having conquered France and Norway, his clutching fingers reach out on both sides of us into the ocean. I have never underrated this danger, and you know I have never concealed it from you. Therefore, I hope you will believe me when I say I have complete confidence in the Royal Navy, aided by the Air Force of

102

the Coastal Command, and that in one way or another I am sure they will be able to meet every changing phase of this truly mortal struggle, and that sustained by the courage of our merchant seamen, and the dockers and workmen of all our ports, we shall outwit, outmanoeuvre, outfight and outlast the worst that the enemy's malice and ingenuity can contrive.

I have left the greatest issue to the end. You will have seen that Sir John Dill, our principal military adviser, the Chief of the Imperial General Staff, has warned us all that Hitler may be forced by the strategic, economic and political stresses in Europe, to try to invade these islands in the near future. That is a warning which no one should disregard. Naturally, we are working night and day to have everything ready. Of course, we are far stronger than we ever were before, incomparably stronger than we were in July, August and September. Our Navy is more powerful, our flotillas are more numerous; we are far stronger, actually and relatively, in the air above these islands, than we were when our Fighter Command beat off and beat down the Nazi attack last autumn. Our Army is more numerous, more mobile and far better equipped and trained than in September, and still more than in July.

I have the greatest confidence in our Commander-in-Chief, General Brooke, and in the generals of proved ability who, under him, guard the different quarters of our land. But most of all I put my faith in the simple unaffected resolve to conquer or die which will animate and inspire nearly 4,000,000 Britons with serviceable weapons in their hands. It is not an easy military operation to invade an island like Great Britain, without the command of the sea and without the command of the air, and then to face what will be waiting for the invader here. But I must drop one word of caution; for next to cowardice and treachery, over-confidence, leading to neglect or slothfulness, is the worst of martial crimes. Therefore, I drop one word of caution. A Nazi invasion of Great Britain last autumn would have been a more or less improvised affair. Hitler took it for granted that when France gave in we should give in; but we did not give in. And he had to think again. An invasion now will be supported by a much more carefully prepared tackle and equipment of landing-craft and other apparatus, all of which will have been planned and manufactured in the winter months. We must all be prepared to meet gas attacks, parachute attacks and glider attacks, with constancy, forethought and practised skill.

I must again emphasise what General Dill has said, and what I pointed out myself last year. In order to win the war Hitler must destroy Great Britain. He may carry havoc into the Balkan States; he may tear great provinces out of Russia; he may march to the Caspian; he may march to the gates of India. All this will avail him nothing. He may spread his curse more widely throughout Europe and Asia, but it will not avert his doom. With every month that passes the many proud and once happy countries he is now holding down by brute force and vile intrigue are learning to hate the Prussian yoke and the Nazi name as nothing has ever been hated so fiercely and so widely among men before. And all the time, masters of the sea and air, the British Empire – nay, in a certain sense, the whole English-speaking world – will be on his track, bearing with them the swords of justice.

The other day, President Roosevelt gave his opponent in the late Presidential Election a letter of introduction to me, and in it he wrote out a verse, in his own handwriting, from Longfellow which, he said, 'applies to you people as it does to us.' Here is the verse:

> ... Sail on, O Ship of State!
> Sail on, O Union, strong and great!
> Humanity with all its fears,
> With all the hopes of future years,
> Is hanging breathless on thy fate!

What is the answer that I shall give, in your name, to this great man, the thrice-chosen head of a nation of 130,000,000? Here is the answer which I will give to President Roosevelt: Put your confidence in us. Give us your faith and your blessing, and, under Providence, all will be well.

We shall not fail or falter; we shall not weaken or tire.

Neither the sudden shock of battle, nor the long-drawn trials of vigilance and exertion will wear us down. Give us the tools, and we will finish the job.

'WESTWARD, LOOK, THE LAND IS BRIGHT'

A WORLD BROADCAST, APRIL 27, 1941

I was asked last week whether I was aware of some uneasiness which it was said existed in the country on account of the gravity, as it was described, of the war situation. So I thought it would be a good thing to go and see for myself what this 'uneasiness' amounted to, and I went to some of our great cities and seaports which had been most heavily bombed, and to some of the places where the poorest people had got it worst. I have come back not only reassured, but refreshed. To leave the offices in Whitehall with their ceaseless hum of activity and stress, and to go out to the front, by which I mean the streets and wharves of London or Liverpool, Manchester, Cardiff, Swansea or Bristol, is like going out of a hot-house on to the bridge of a fighting ship. It is a tonic which I should recommend any who are suffering from fretfulness to take in strong doses when they have need of it.

It is quite true that I have seen many painful scenes of havoc, and of fine buildings and acres of cottage homes blasted into rubble-heaps of ruin. But it is just in those very places where the malice of the savage enemy has done its worst, and where the ordeal of the men, women and children has been most severe, that I found their morale most high and splendid. Indeed, I felt encompassed by an exaltation of spirit in the people which seemed to lift mankind and its troubles above the level of material facts into that joyous serenity we think belongs to a better world than this.

Of their kindness to me I cannot speak, because I have never sought it or dreamed of it, and can never deserve it. I can only assure you that I and my colleagues, or comrades rather – for that is what they are – will toil with every scrap of life and strength, according to the lights that are granted to us, not to fail these people or be wholly unworthy of their faithful and generous regard. The British nation is stirred and moved as it has never been in any time in its long, eventful, famous history, and it is no hackneyed trope of speech to say that they mean to conquer or to die.

What a triumph the life of these battered cities is, over the worst that fire and bomb can do. What a vindication of the civilised and decent way of living we have been trying to work for and work towards in our island. What a proof of the virtues of free institutions. What a test of the quality of our local authorities, and of institutions and customs and societies so steadily built. This ordeal by fire has even in a certain sense exhilarated the manhood and womanhood of Britain. The sublime but also terrible and sombre experiences and emotions of the battlefield which for centuries has been reserved for the soldiers and sailors, are now shared, for good or ill, by the entire population. All are proud to be under the fire of the enemy. Old men, little children, the crippled veterans of former wars, aged women, the ordinary hard-pressed citizen or subject of the King, as he likes to call himself, the sturdy workmen who swing the hammers or load the ships; skilful craftsmen; the members of every kind of ARP service, are proud to feel that they stand in the line together with our fighting men, when one of the greatest of causes is being fought out, as fought out it will be, to the end. This is indeed the grand heroic period of our history, and the light of glory shines on all.

You may imagine how deeply I feel my own responsibility to all these people; my responsibility to bear my part in bringing them safely out of this long, stern, scowling valley through which we are marching, and not to demand from them their sacrifices and exertions in vain.

I have thought in this difficult period, when so much fighting and so many critical and complicated manoeuvres are going on, that it is above all things important that our policy and conduct should be upon the highest level, and that honour should be our guide. Very few people realise how small were the forces with which General Wavell, that fine commander whom we cheered in good days and will back through bad – how small were the forces which took the bulk of the Italian masses in Libya prisoners. In none of his successive victories could General Wavell maintain in the desert or bring into action more than two divisions, or about 30,000 men. When we reached Benghazi, and what was left of Mussolini's legions scurried back along the dusty road to Tripoli, a call was made upon us which we could not resist. Let me tell you about that call.

You will remember how in November the Italian dictator fell upon the unoffending Greeks, and without reason and without warning invaded their country, and how the Greek nation, reviving their classic fame, hurled his armies back at the double-quick. Meanwhile Hitler, who had been creeping and worming his way steadily forward, doping and poisoning and pinioning, one after the other, Hungary, Rumania and Bulgaria, suddenly made it clear that he would come to the rescue of his fellow-criminal. The lack of unity among the Balkan States had enabled him to build up a mighty army in their midst. While nearly all the Greek troops were busy beating the Italians, the tremendous German military machine suddenly towered up on their other frontier. In their mortal peril the Greeks turned to us for succour. Strained as were our own resources, we could not say them nay. By solemn guarantee given before the war, Great Britain had promised them her help. They declared they would fight for their native soil even if neither of their neighbours made common cause with them, and even if we left them to their fate. But we could not do that. There are rules against that kind of thing; and to break those rules would be fatal to the honour of the British Empire, without which we could neither hope nor deserve to win this hard war. Military defeat or miscalculation can be redeemed. The fortunes of war are fickle and changing. But an act of shame would deprive us of the respect which we now enjoy throughout the world, and this would sap the vitals of our strength.

During the last year we have gained by our bearing and conduct a potent hold upon the sentiments of the people of the United States. Never, never in our history, have we been held in such admiration and regard across the Atlantic Ocean. In that great Republic, now in much travail and stress of soul, it is customary to use all the many valid, solid arguments about American interests and American safety, which depend upon the destruction of Hitler and his foul gang and even fouler doctrines. But in the long run – believe me, for I know – the action of the United States will be dictated, not by methodical calculations of profit and loss, but by moral sentiment, and by that gleaming flash of resolve which lifts the hearts of men and nations, and springs from the spiritual foundations of human life itself.

We, for our part, were of course bound to hearken to the Greek appeal to the utmost limit of our strength. We put the case to the Dominions of Australia and New Zealand, and their Governments, without in any way ignoring the hazards, told us that they felt the same as we did. So an important part of the mobile portion of the Army of the Nile was sent to Greece in fulfilment of our pledge. It happened that the divisions available and best suited to this task were from New Zealand and Australia, and that only about half the troops who took part in this dangerous expedition came from the Mother Country. I see the German propaganda is trying to make bad blood between us and Australia by making out that we have used them to do what we would not have asked of the British Army. I shall leave it to Australia to deal with that taunt.

Let us see what has happened. We knew, of course, that the forces we could send to Greece would not by themselves alone be sufficient to stem the German tide of invasion. But there was a very real hope that the neighbours of Greece would by our intervention be drawn to stand in the line together with her while time remained. How nearly that came off will be known some day. The tragedy of Yugoslavia has been that these brave people had a Government who hoped to purchase an ignoble immunity by submission to the Nazi will. Thus when at last the people of Yugoslavia found out where they were being taken, and rose in one spontaneous surge of revolt, they saved the soul and future of their country; but it was already too late to save its territory. They had no time to mobilise their armies. They were struck down by the ruthless and highly mechanised Hun before they could even bring their armies into the field. Great disasters have occurred in the Balkans. Yugoslavia has been beaten down. Only in the mountains can she continue her resistance. The Greeks have been overwhelmed. Their victorious Albanian army has been cut off and forced to surrender, and it has been left to the Anzacs and their British comrades to fight their way back to the sea, leaving their mark on all who hindered them.

I turn aside from the stony path we have to tread, to indulge a moment of lighter relief. I dare say you have read in the newspapers that, by a special proclamation, the Italian Dictator has congratulated the Italian Army in Albania on the glorious laurels they have gained by their victory over the Greeks. Here surely is the world's record in the domain of the ridiculous and the contemptible. This whipped jackal, Mussolini, who to save his own skin has made all Italy a vassal state of Hitler's Empire, comes frisking up at the side of the German tiger with yelpings not only of appetite – that can be understood – but even of triumph. Different things strike different people in different ways. But I am sure that there are a great many millions in the British Empire and in the United States, who will find a new object in life in making sure that when we come to the final reckoning this absurd imposter will be abandoned to public justice and universal scorn.

While these grievous events were taking place in the Balkan Peninsula and in Greece, our forces in Libya have sustained a vexatious and damaging defeat. The Germans advanced sooner and in greater strength than we or our generals expected. The bulk of our armoured troops, which had played such a decisive part in beating the Italians, had to be refitted, and the single armoured brigade which had been judged sufficient to hold the frontier till about the middle of May was worsted and its vehicles largely destroyed by a somewhat stronger German armoured force. Our infantry, which had not exceeded one division, had to fall back upon the very large Imperial armies that have been assembled and can be nourished and maintained in the fertile delta of the Nile.

Tobruk – the fortress of Tobruk – which flanks any German advance on Egypt, we hold strongly. There we have repulsed many attacks, causing the enemy heavy losses and taking many prisoners. That is how the matters stand in Egypt and on the Libyan front.

We must now expect the war in the Mediterranean on the sea, in the desert, and above all in the air, to become very fierce, varied and widespread. We had cleaned the Italians out of Cyrenaica, and it now lies with us to purge that province of the Germans. That will be a harder task, and we cannot expect to do it at once. You know I never try to make out that defeats are victories. I have never underrated the German as a warrior. Indeed I told you a month ago that the swift, unbroken course of victories which we have gained over the Italians could not possibly continue, and that misfortunes must be expected. There is only one thing certain about war, that it is full of disappointments and also full of mistakes. It remains to be seen, however, whether it is the Germans who have made the mistake in trampling down the Balkan States and in making a river of blood and hate between themselves and the Greek and Yugoslav peoples. It remains also to be seen whether they have made a mistake in their attempt to invade Egypt with the forces and means of supply which they have now got. Taught by experience, I make it a rule not to prophesy about battles which have yet to be fought out. This, however, I will venture to say, that I should be very sorry to see the tasks of the combatants in the Middle East exchanged, and that General Wavell's armies should be in the position of the German invaders. That is only a personal opinion, and I can well understand you may take a different view. It is certain that fresh dangers besides those which threaten Egypt may come upon us in the Mediterranean. The war may spread to Spain and Morocco. It may spread eastward to Turkey and Russia. The Huns may lay their hands for a time upon the granaries of the Ukraine and the oil-wells of the Caucasus. They may dominate the Black Sea. They may dominate the Caspian. Who can tell? We shall do our best to meet them and fight them wherever they go. But there is one thing which is certain. There is one thing which rises out of the vast welter which is sure and solid, and which no one in his senses can mistake. Hitler cannot find safety from avenging justice in the East, in the Middle East or in the Far East. In order to win this war, he must either conquer this island by invasion, or he must cut the ocean life-line which joins us to the United States.

Let us look into these alternatives, if you will bear with me for a few minutes longer. When I spoke to you last, early in February, many people believed the Nazi boastings that the invasion of Britain was about to begin. It has not begun yet, and with every week that passes we grow stronger on the sea, in the air and in the numbers, quality, training and equipment of the great armies that now guard our island. When I compare the position at home as it is today with what it was in the summer of last year, even after making allowance for a much more elaborate mechanical preparation on the part of the enemy, I feel that we have very much to be thankful for, and I believe that provided our exertions and our vigilance are not relaxed even for a moment, we may be confident that we shall give a very good account of ourselves. More than that it would be boastful to say. Less than that it would be foolish to believe.

But how about our life-line across the Atlantic? What is to happen if so many of our merchant ships are sunk that we cannot bring in the food we need to nourish our brave people? What if the supplies of war materials and war weapons which the United States are seeking to send us in such enormous quantities should in large part be sunk on the way? What is to happen then? In February, as you may remember, that bad man in one of his raving outbursts threatened us with a terrifying increase in the numbers and activities of his U-boats and in his air attack – not only on our island but, thanks to his use of French and Norwegian harbours, and thanks to the denial to us of the Irish bases – upon our shipping far out into the

111

Atlantic. We have taken and are taking all possible measures to meet this deadly attack, and we are now fighting against it with might and main. That is what is called the Battle of the Atlantic, which in order to survive we have got to win on salt water just as decisively as we had to win the Battle of Britain last August and September in the air.

Wonderful exertions have been made by our Navy and Air Force; by the hundreds of mine-sweeping vessels which with their marvellous appliances keep our ports clear in spite of all the enemy can do; by the men who build and repair our immense fleets of merchant ships; by the men who load and unload them; and need I say by the officers and men of the Merchant Navy who go out in all weathers and in the teeth of all dangers to fight for the life of their native land and for a cause they comprehend and serve. Still, when you think how easy it is to sink ships at sea and how hard it is to build them and protect them, and when you remember that we have never less than 2,000 ships afloat and 300 or 400 in the danger zone; when you think of the great armies we are maintaining and reinforcing in the East, and of the world-wide-traffic we have to carry on – when you remember all this, can you wonder that it is the Battle of the Atlantic which holds the first place in the thought of those upon whom rests the responsibility for procuring the victory?

It was therefore with indescribable relief that I learned of the tremendous decisions lately taken by the President and people of the United States. The American Fleet and flying boats have been ordered to patrol the wide waters of the Western Hemisphere, and to warn the peaceful shipping of all nations outside the combat zone of the presence of lurking U-boats or raiding cruisers belonging to the two aggressor nations. We British shall therefore be able to concentrate our protecting forces far more upon the routes nearer home, and to take a far heavier toll of the U-boats there. I have felt for some time that something like this was bound to happen. The President and Congress of the United States, having newly fortified themselves by contact with their electors, have solemnly pledged their aid to Britain in this war because they deem our cause just, and because they know their own interests and safety would be endangered if we were destroyed. They are taxing themselves heavily. They have passed great legislation. They have turned a large part of their gigantic industry to making munitions which we need. They have even given us or lent us valuable weapons of their own. I could not believe that they would allow the high purposes to which they have set themselves to be frustrated and the products of their skill and labour sunk to the bottom of the sea. U-boat warfare as conducted by Germany is entirely contrary to international agreements freely subscribed to by Germany only a few years ago. There is no effective blockade, but only a merciless murder and marauding over wide, indiscriminate areas utterly beyond the control of the German sea-power. When I said ten weeks ago: 'Give us the tools and we will finish the job,' I meant, *give* them to us; put them within our reach – and that is what it now seems the Americans are going to do. And that is why I feel a very strong conviction that though the Battle of the Atlantic will be long and hard, and its issue is by no means yet determined, it has entered upon a more grim but at the same time a far more favourable phase. When you come to think of it, the United States are very closely bound up with us now, and have engaged themselves deeply in giving us moral, material and, within the limits I have mentioned, naval support.

It is worth while therefore to take a look on both sides of the ocean at the forces which are facing each other in this awful struggle, from which there can be no drawing back. No prudent and far-seeing man can doubt that the eventual and total defeat of Hitler and Mussolini is certain, in view of the respective declared resolves of the British and American democracies. There are less than 70,000,000 malignant Huns – some of whom are curable and others killable – many of whom are already engaged in holding down Austrians, Czechs, Poles, French, and the many other ancient races they now bully and pillage. The peoples of the British Empire and of the United States number nearly 200,000,000 in their homelands and in the British Dominions alone. They possess the unchallengeable command of the oceans, and will soon obtain decisive superiority in the air. They have more wealth, more technical resources, and they make more steel, than the whole of the rest of the world put together. They are determined that the cause of freedom shall not be trampled down, nor the tide of world progress turned backwards, by the criminal dictators.

While therefore we naturally view with sorrow and anxiety much that is happening in Europe and in Africa, and may happen in Asia, we must not lose our sense of proportion and thus become discouraged or alarmed. When we face with a steady eye the difficulties which lie before us, we may derive new confidence from remembering those we have already overcome. Nothing that is happening now is comparable in gravity with the dangers through which we passed last year. Nothing that can happen in the East is comparable with what is happening in the West.

Last time I spoke to you I quoted the lines of Longfellow which President Roosevelt had written out for me in his own hand. I have some other lines which are less well known but which seem apt and appropriate to our fortunes tonight, and I believe they will be so judged wherever the English language is spoken or the flag of freedom flies:

> For while the tired waves, vainly breaking,
>   Seem here no painful inch to gain,
> Far back, through creeks and inlets making,
>   Comes silent, flooding in, the main.
>
> And not by eastern windows only,
>   When daylight comes, comes in the light;
> In front the sun climbs slow, how slowly!
>   But westward, look, the land is bright.

DRAMA IN MEDITERRANEAN AND ATLANTIC

A SPEECH TO THE HOUSE OF COMMONS,
MAY 27, 1941

The battle in Crete has now lasted for a week. During the whole of this time our troops have been subjected to an intense and continuous scale of air attack, to which, owing to the geographical conditions, our Air Forces have been able to make only a very limited, though very gallant, counterblast. The fighting has been most bitter and severe, and the enemy's losses up to the present have been much heavier than ours. We have not, however, been able to prevent further descents of airborne German reinforcements, and the enemy's attack and the weight of this attack has grown from day to day. The battle has swayed backwards and forwards with indescribable fury at Canea, and equally fiercely, though on a smaller scale, at Retimo and Heraklion. Reinforcements of men and supplies have reached and are reaching General Freyberg's forces, and at the moment at which I am speaking the issue of their magnificent resistance hangs in the balance.

So far, the Royal Navy have prevented any landing of a seaborne expedition, although a few shiploads of troops in caiques may have slipped through. Very heavy losses have been inflicted by our submarines, cruisers and destroyers upon the transports and the small Greek ships. It is not possible to state with accuracy how many thousands of enemy troops have been drowned, but the losses have been very heavy. The services rendered by the Navy in the defence of Crete have not been discharged without heavy losses to them. Our Fleet has been compelled to operate constantly without air protection within effective range of the enemy airfields. Claims even more exaggerated than usual have been made by the German and Italian wireless, which it has hitherto not been thought expedient to contradict. I may state, however, that we have lost the cruisers *Gloucester* and *Fiji* and the destroyers *Juno*, *Greyhound*, *Kelly* and *Kashmir*, by far the greater part of their crews having been saved. Two battleships and several other cruisers have been damaged, though not seriously, either by hits or near misses, but all will soon be in action again, and some are already at sea. The Mediterranean Fleet is today relatively stronger, compared to the Italian Navy, than it was before the Battle of Cape Matapan. There is no question whatever of our naval position in the Eastern Mediterranean having been prejudicially affected. However the decision of the battle may go, the stubborn defence of Crete, one of the important outposts of Egypt, will always rank high in the military and naval annals of the British Empire.

In Iraq, our position has been largely re-established, and the prospects have greatly improved. There have been no further adverse developments in Syria. In Abyssinia, the daily Italian surrender continues, many thousands of prisoners and masses of equipment being taken.

While this drama has been enacted in the Eastern Mediterranean, another episode of an arresting character has been in progress in the northern waters of the Atlantic Ocean. On Wednesday of last week, May 21, the new German battleship, the *Bismarck*, accompanied by the new 8-in. gun cruiser *Prince Eugen*, was discovered by our air reconnaissance at Bergen, and on Thursday, May 22, it was known that they had left. Many arrangements were made to intercept them should they attempt, as seemed probable, to break out into the Atlantic Ocean with a view to striking at our convoys from the United States. During the night of 23rd to 24th our cruisers got into visual contact with them as they were passing through the Denmark Strait between Iceland and Greenland. At dawn on Saturday morning the *Prince of Wales* and the *Hood* intercepted the two enemy vessels. I have no detailed account of the action, because events have been moving so rapidly, but the *Hood* was struck at about 23,000 yards by a shell which penetrated into one of her magazines, and blew up, leaving

116

only very few survivors. This splendid vessel, designed twenty-three years ago, is a serious loss to the Royal Navy, and even more so are the men and officers who manned her.

During the whole of Saturday our ships remained in touch with the *Bismarck* and her consort. In the night aircraft of the Fleet Air Arm from the *Victorious* struck the *Bismarck* with a torpedo, and arrangements were made for effective battle at dawn yesterday morning; but as the night wore on the weather deteriorated, the visibility decreased, and the *Bismarck*, by making a sharp turn, shook off the pursuit. I do not know what has happened to the *Prince Eugen*, but measures are being taken in respect of her. Yesterday, shortly before midday, a Catalina aircraft – one of the considerable number of these very far-ranging scouting aeroplanes which have been sent to us by the United States – picked up the *Bismarck*, and it was seen that she was apparently making for the French ports – Brest or Saint Nazaire. On this, further rapid dispositions were made by the Admiralty and by the Commander-in-Chief, and, of course, I may say that the moment the *Bismarck* was known to be at sea the whole apparatus of our ocean control came into play, very far-reaching combinations began to work, and from yesterday afternoon – I have not had time to prepare a detailed statement – Fleet Air Arm torpedo-carrying sea-planes from the *Ark Royal* made a succession of attacks upon the *Bismarck*, which now appears to be alone and without her consort. About midnight we learned that the *Bismarck* had been struck by two torpedoes, one amidships and the other astern. This second torpedo apparently affected the steering of the ship, for not only was she reduced to a very slow speed, but she continued making uncontrollable circles in the sea. While in this condition she was attacked by one of our flotillas, and hit by two more torpedoes, which brought her virtually to a standstill, far from help and far outside the range at which the enemy bomber aircraft from the French coast could have come upon the scene. This morning, at daylight or shortly after daylight, the *Bismarck* was attacked by the British pursuing battleships. I do not know what were the results of the bombardment; it appears, however, that the

Bismarck was not sunk by gunfire, and she will now be dispatched by torpedo. It is thought that this is now proceeding, and it is also thought that there cannot be any lengthy delay in disposing of this vessel.

Great as is our loss in the *Hood*, the *Bismarck* must be regarded as the most powerful, as she is the newest, battleship in the world; and this striking of her from the German Navy is a very definite simplification of the task of maintaining the effective mastery of the northern seas and the maintenance of the northern blockade. I daresay that in a few days it will be possible to give a much more detailed account, but the essentials are before the House, and although there is shade as well as light in this picture, I feel that we have every reason to be satisfied with the outcome of this fierce and memorable naval encounter.

Later Mr Churchill rose again in the House of Commons to add:

I do not know whether I might venture, with great respect, to intervene for one moment. I have just received news that the *Bismarck* is sunk.

'THE FOURTH CLIMACTERIC'

A WORLD BROADCAST ON THE GERMAN INVASION OF RUSSIA, JUNE 22, 1941

I have taken occasion to speak to you tonight because we have reached one of the climacterics of the war. The first of these intense turning-points was a year ago when France fell prostrate under the German hammer, and when we had to face the storm alone. The second was when the Royal Air Force beat the Hun raiders out of the daylight air, and thus warded off the Nazi invasion of our island while we were still ill-armed and ill-prepared. The third turning-point was when the President and Congress of the United States passed the Lease-

and-Lend enactment, devoting nearly 2,000 millions sterling of the wealth of the New World to help us to defend our liberties and their own. Those were the three climacterics. The fourth is now upon us.

At four o'clock this morning Hitler attacked and invaded Russia. All his usual formalities of perfidy were observed with scrupulous technique. A non-aggression treaty had been solemnly signed and was in force between the two countries. No complaint had been made by Germany of its non-fulfilment. Under its cloak of false confidence, the German armies drew up in immense strength along a line which stretches from the White Sea to the Black Sea; and their air fleets and armoured divisions slowly and methodically took their stations. Then suddenly, without declaration of war, without even an ultimatum, German bombs rained down from the air upon the Russian cities, the German troops violated the frontiers; and an hour later the German Ambassador, who till the night before was lavishing his assurances of friendship, almost of alliance, upon the Russians, called upon the Russian Foreign Minister to tell him that a state of war existed between Germany and Russia.

Thus was repeated on a far larger scale the same kind of outrage against every form of signed compact and international faith which we have witnessed in Norway, Denmark, Holland and Belgium, and which Hitler's accomplice and jackal Mussolini so faithfully imitated in the case of Greece.

All this was no surprise to me. In fact I gave clear and precise warnings to Stalin of what was coming. I gave him warning as I have given warning to others before. I can only hope that this warning did not fall unheeded. All we know at present is that the Russian people are defending their native soil and that their leaders have called upon them to resist to the utmost.

Hitler is a monster of wickedness, insatiable in his lust for blood and plunder. Not content with having all Europe under his heel, or else terrorised into various forms of abject submission, he must now carry his work of butchery and desolation among the vast multitudes of Russia and of Asia. The terrible military machine, which we and the rest of the civilised world so foolishly, so supinely, so insensately allowed the Nazi gangsters to build up year by year from almost nothing, cannot stand idle lest it rust or fall to pieces. It must be in continual motion, grinding up human lives and trampling down the homes and the rights of hundreds of millions of men. Moreover it must be fed, not only with flesh but with oil.

So now this bloodthirsty guttersnipe must launch his mechanised armies upon new fields of slaughter, pillage and devastation. Poor as are the Russian peasants, workmen and soldiers, he must steal from them their daily bread; he must devour their harvests; he must rob them of the oil which drives their ploughs; and thus produce a famine without example in human history. And even the carnage and ruin which his victory, should he gain it – he has not gained it yet – will bring upon the Russian people, will itself be only a stepping-stone to the attempt to plunge the 400,000,000 or 500,000,000 who live in China, and the 350,000,000 who live in India, into that bottomless pit of human degradation over which the diabolic emblem of the Swastika flaunts itself. It is not too much to say here this summer evening that the lives and happiness of 1,000,000,000 additional people are now menaced with brutal Nazi violence. That is enough to make us hold our breath. But presently I shall show you something else that lies behind, and something that touches very nearly the life of Britain and of the United States.

The Nazi regime is indistinguishable from the worst features of Communism. It is devoid of all theme and principle except appetite and racial denomination. It excels all forms of human wickedness in the efficiency of its cruelty and ferocious aggression. No one has been a more consistent opponent of Communism than I have for the last twenty-five years. I will unsay no word that I have spoken about it. But all this fades away before the spectacle which is now unfolding. The past with its crimes, its follies and its tragedies, flashes away. I see the Russian soldiers standing on the threshold of their native land, guarding the fields which their fathers have tilled from time immemorial. I see them guarding their homes where mothers and wives pray – ah yes, for there are times when all pray – for the safety of their loved ones, the return of the bread-winner, of their champion, of their protector. I see the 10,000 villages of Russia, where the means of existence was wrung so hardly from the soil, but where there are still primordial human joys, where maidens laugh and children play. I see advancing upon all this in hideous onslaught the Nazi war machine, with its clanking, heel-clicking, dandified Prussian officers, its crafty expert agents fresh from the cowing and tying-down of a dozen countries. I see also the dull, drilled, docile, brutish masses of the Hun soldiery plodding on like a swarm of crawling locusts. I see the German bombers and fighters in the sky, still smarting from many a British whipping, delighted to find what they believe is an easier and a safer prey.

Behind all this glare, behind all this storm, I see that small group of villainous men who plan, organise and launch this cataract of horrors upon mankind. And then my mind goes back across the years to the days when the Russian armies were our allies against the same deadly foe; when they fought with so much valour and constancy, and helped to gain a victory from all share in which, alas, they were – through no fault of ours – utterly cut off. I have lived through all this, and you will pardon me if I express my feelings and the stir of old memories.

But now I have to declare the decision of His Majesty's Government – and I feel sure it is a decision in which the great Dominions will, in due course, concur – for we must speak out now at once, without a day's delay. I have to make the declaration, but can you doubt what our policy will be? We have but one aim and one single, irrevocable purpose. We are resolved to destroy Hitler and every vestige of the Nazi regime. From this nothing will turn us – nothing. We will never parley, we will never negotiate with Hitler or any of his gang. We shall fight him by land, we shall fight him by sea, we shall fight him in the air, until with God's help we have rid the earth of his shadow and liberated its peoples from his yoke. Any man or State who fights on against Nazidom will have our aid. Any man or State who marches with Hitler is our foe. This applies not only to organised States but to all representatives of that vile race of quislings who make themselves the tools and agents of the Nazi regime against their fellow-countrymen and the lands of their birth. They – these quislings – like the Nazi leaders themselves, if not disposed of by their fellow-countrymen, which would save trouble, will be delivered by us on the morrow of victory to the justice of the Allied tribunals. That is our policy and that is our declaration. It follows, therefore, that we shall give whatever help we can to Russia and the Russian people. We shall appeal to all our friends and allies in every part of the world to take the same course and pursue it, as we shall, faithfully and steadfastly to the end.

We have offered the Government of Soviet Russia any technical or economic assistance which is in our power, and which is likely to be of service to them. We shall bomb Germany by day as well as by night in ever-increasing measure, casting upon them month by month a heavier discharge of bombs, and making the German people taste and gulp each month a sharper dose of the miseries they have showered upon mankind. It is noteworthy that only yesterday the Royal Air Force, fighting inland over French territory, cut down with very small loss to themselves twenty-eight of the Hun fighting machines in the air above the French soil they have invaded, defiled and profess to hold. But this is only a beginning. From now forward the main expansion of our Air Force proceeds with gathering speed. In another six months the weight of the help we are receiving from the United States in war materials of all kinds, and especially in heavy bombers, will begin to tell.

This is no class war, but a war in which the whole British Empire and Commonwealth of Nations is engaged without distinction of race, creed or party. It is not for me to speak of the action of the United States, but this I will say: if Hitler imagines that his attack on Soviet Russia will cause the slightest division of aims or slackening of effort in the great democracies who are resolved upon his doom, he is woefully mistaken. On the contrary, we shall be fortified and encouraged in our efforts to rescue mankind from his tyranny. We shall be strengthened and not weakened in determination and in resources.

This is no time to moralise on the follies of countries and Governments which have allowed themselves to be struck down one by one, when by united action they could have saved themselves and saved the world from this catastrophe. But when I spoke a few minutes ago of Hitler's blood-lust and the hateful appetites which have impelled or lured him on his Russian adventure, I said there was one deeper motive behind his outrage. He wishes to destroy the Russian power because he hopes that if he succeeds in this, he will be able to bring back the main strength of his Army and Air Force from the East and hurl it upon this island, which he knows he must conquer or suffer the penalty of his crimes. His invasion of Russia is no more than a prelude to an attempted invasion of the British Isles. He hopes, no doubt, that all this may be accomplished before the winter comes, and that he can over-whelm Great Britain before the Fleet and air-power of the United States may intervene. He hopes that he may once again repeat, upon a greater scale than ever before, that process of destroying his enemies one by one, by which he has so long thrived and prospered, and that then the scene will be clear for the final act, without which all his conquests would be in vain – namely, the subjugation of the Western Hemisphere to his will and to his system.

The Russian danger is therefore our danger, and the danger of the United States, just as the cause of any Russian fighting for his hearth and home is the cause of free men and free peoples in every quarter of the globe. Let us learn the lessons already taught by such cruel experience. Let us redouble our exertions, and strike with united strength while life and power remain.

'DO YOUR WORST – AND WE WILL DO OUR BEST'

A SPEECH AT A LUNCHEON GIVEN BY THE LONDON COUNTY COUNCIL AFTER THE REVIEW OF THE CIVIL DEFENCE SERVICES IN HYDE PARK, JULY 14, 1941

It seems to me odd that it should have taken the stresses of a great world war to bring me for the first time to the County Hall, and I am very glad indeed to find that by the time the call came the hall had not already ceased to exist. You have taken in this building some of the blows and scars which have fallen upon London, but like the rest of London you carry on.

The impressive and inspiring spectacle we have witnessed in Hyde Park this morning displays the vigour and efficiency of the civil defence forces of London. They have grown up in the stress of emergency. They have been shaped and tempered by the fire of the enemy, and this morning we saw them all, in their many grades and classes – the wardens, the rescue and first-aid parties, the casualty services, the decontamination squads, the fire services, the report and control centre staffs, the highways and public utility services, the messengers, the police. All these we have seen on a lovely English summer morning, marching past, men and women in all the pomp and panoply – not of war, though it is war – but of their civic duties. There they marched, and as one saw them passing by no one could but feel how great a people, how great a nation we have the honour to belong to.

How complex, sensitive, resilient, is the society we have evolved over centuries, and how capable of withstanding the most unexpected strain! Those whom we saw this morning were the representatives of nearly a quarter of a million organised functionaries and servants in the defence of London, who,

124

in one way or another, stand to their posts or take an active part in the maintenance of the life of London and Greater London against an attack which, when it began and while it was at its pitch, was unexampled in history.

And what we saw today in Hyde Park was only symbolic of what can be produced, though on a smaller scale, throughout the length and breadth of this country – a competent and embattled island.

In September last, having been defeated in his invasion plans by the RAF, Hitler declared his intention to raze the cities of Britain to the ground, and in the early days of that month he set the whole fury of the Hun upon London.

None of us quite knew what would be the result of a concentrated and prolonged bombardment of this vast centre of population. Here in the Thames Valley, over 8,000,000 people are maintained at a very high level of modern civilisation. They are dependent from day to day upon light, heat, power, water, sewerage and communications on the most complicated scale.

The administration of London in all its branches was confronted with problems hitherto unknown and unmeasured in all the history of the past. Public order, public health, the maintenance of all the essential services, the handling of the millions of people who came in and out of London every day; the shelter – not indeed from the enemy's bombs, for that was beyond us, but from their blast and splinters – the shelter of millions of men and women, and the removal of the dead and wounded from the shattered buildings; the care of the wounded when hospitals were being ruthlessly bombed, and the provision for the homeless – sometimes amounting to many thousands in a single day, and accumulating to many more after three or four days of successive attacks – all these things, with the welfare and the education amid these scenes of our great numbers of children here – all these presented tasks which, viewed in cold blood beforehand, might well have seemed overwhelming.

Indeed, before the war, when the imagination painted pictures of what might happen in the great air raids on our cities,

125

plans were made to move the Government, to move all the great controlling services which are centred in London, and disperse them about the countryside, and also it was always considered a very great danger that a sudden wave of panic might send millions of people crowding out into the countryside along all the roads.

Well, when you are doing your duty and you are sure of that, you need not worry too much about the dangers or the consequences. We have not been moved in this war except by the promptings of duty and conscience, and therefore we do not need to be deterred from action by pictures which our imagination or careful forethought painted of what the consequences would be.

I must, however, admit that when the storm broke in September, I was for several weeks very anxious about the result. We were then not prepared as we are now. Our defences had not the advantages they have since attained, and again I must admit that I greatly feared injury to our public services, I feared the ravages of fire, I feared the dislocation of life and the stoppage of work. I feared epidemics of serious disease or even pestilence among the crowds who took refuge in our by no means completely constructed or well equipped shelters.

I remember one winter evening travelling to a railway station – which still worked – on my way north to visit troops. It was cold and raining. Darkness had almost fallen on the blacked-out streets. I saw everywhere long queues of people, among them hundreds of young girls in their silk stockings and high-heeled shoes, who had worked hard all day and were waiting for bus after bus, which came by already overcrowded, in the hope of reaching their homes for the night. When at that moment the doleful wail of the siren betokened the approach of the German bombers, I confess to you that my heart bled for London and the Londoners.

All this sort of thing went on for more than four months with hardly any intermission. I used to hold meetings of my Ministerial colleagues and members of the authorities concerned every week in Downing Street in order to check up and see how we stood. Sometimes the gas had failed over large areas – the only means of cooking for great numbers of people; sometimes the electricity. There were grievous complaints about the shelters and about conditions in them. Water was cut off, railways were cut or broken, large districts were destroyed by fire, 20,000 people were killed, and many more thousands were wounded.

But there was one thing about which there was never any doubt. The courage, the unconquerable grit and stamina of the Londoners showed itself from the very outset. Without that all would have failed. Upon that rock, all stood unshakable. All the public services were carried on, and all the intricate arrangements, far-reaching details, involving the daily lives of so many millions, were carried out, improvised, elaborated and perfected in the very teeth of the cruel and devastating storm.

I am very glad to come here today to pay my tribute and to record in the name of the Government our gratitude to all the civil authorities of London who, first under Sir John Anderson, and through the darkest moments under the courageous and resourceful leadership of Mr Herbert Morrison – so long master of the London County Council, and now acting in an even higher sphere – to all who carried out their duties faithfully, skilfully and devotedly, so that at last we made our way through the tempest, and came for the time being, at any rate, into a calm spell.

During her long ordeal London was upheld by the sympathy and admiration of the other great cities of our island – and let us not forget here loyal Belfast, in Northern Ireland – and when after the enemy wearied of his attack upon the capital and turned to other parts of the country, many of us in our hearts felt anxiety lest the weight of attack concentrated on those smaller organisms should prove more effective than when directed on London, which is so vast and strong that she is like a prehistoric monster into whose armoured hide showers of arrows can be shot in vain. But in the event, the staunchness and vigour of London were fully matched by the splendid behaviour of our ports and cities when they in turn received the full violence and frightful cruelty of the enemy's assault; and I say here that, while we are entitled to speak particularly of London, we honour them for their constancy in a comradeship of suffering, of endurance and triumph. That comradeship in this hideous, unprecedented, novel pressure has united us all, and it has proved to the world the quality of our island life.

I have no doubt whatever, as I said to the civil defence forces in Hyde Park this morning, that the behaviour of the British people in this trial gained them conquests in the mind and spirit and sympathy of the United States of America which swept into an ignominious corner all the vilest strokes of Goebbels' propaganda.

We have to ask ourselves this question: Will the bombing attacks of last autumn and winter come back again? We have proceeded on the assumption that they will. Some months ago I requested the Home Secretary and Minister of Home Security and his principal colleagues, the Minister of Health and others, to make every preparation for the autumn and winter war as if we should have to go through the same ordeal as last year, only rather worse. I am sure that everything is being done in accordance with those directions. The shelters are being strengthened, improved, lighted and warmed. All arrangements for fire-control and fire-watching are being perpetually improved.

Many new arrangements are being contrived as a result of the hard experience through which we have passed and the many mistakes which no doubt we have made — for success is the result of making many mistakes and learning from experience. If the lull is to end, if the storm is to renew itself, London will be ready, London will not flinch, London can take it again.

We ask no favours of the enemy. We seek from them no compunction. On the contrary, if tonight the people of London were asked to cast their vote whether a convention should be entered into to stop the bombing of all cities, the overwhelming majority would cry, 'No, we will mete out to the Germans the measure, and more than the measure, that they have meted out to us.' The people of London with one voice would say to Hitler: 'You have committed every crime under the sun. Where you have been the least resisted there you have been the most brutal. It was you who began the indiscriminate bombing. We remember Warsaw in the very first few days of the war. We remember Rotterdam. We have been newly reminded of your habits by the hideous massacre of Belgrade. We know too well the bestial assault you are making upon the Russian people, to whom our hearts go out in their valiant struggle. We will have no truce or parley with you, or the grisly gang who work your wicked will. You do your worst – and we will do our best.' Perhaps it may be our turn soon; perhaps it may be our turn now.

We live in a terrible epoch of the human story, but we believe there is a broad and sure justice running through its theme. It is time that the Germans should be made to suffer in their own homeland and cities something of the torment they have twice in our lifetime let loose upon their neighbours and upon the world.

We have now intensified for a month past our systematic, scientific, methodical bombing on a large scale of the German cities, seaports, industries and other military objectives. We believe it to be in our power to keep this process going, on a steadily rising tide, month after month, year after year, until the Nazi regime is either extirpated by us, or, better still, torn to pieces by the German people themselves.

Every month as the great bombers are finished in our factories or sweep hither across the Atlantic Ocean we shall continue the remorseless discharge of high explosives on Germany. Every month we will see the tonnage increase, and, as the nights lengthen and the range of our bombers also grows, that unhappy, abject, subject province of Germany which used to be called Italy will have its fair share too.

In the last few weeks alone we have thrown upon Germany about half the tonnage of bombs thrown by the Germans upon our cities during the whole course of the war. But this is only the beginning, and we hope by next July to multiply our deliveries manifold.

It is for this reason that I must ask you to be prepared for vehement counter-action by the enemy. Our methods of dealing with the German night raiders have steadily improved. They no longer relish their trips to our shores. It is not true to say they did not come this last moon because they were all engaged in Russia. They have a bombing force in the West quite capable of making very heavy attacks. I do not know why they did not come, but, as I mentioned in Hyde Park, it is certainly not because they have begun to love us more. It may be because they are saving up, but even if that be so, the very fact that they have to save up should give us confidence by revealing the truth of our steady advance from an almost unarmed position to a position at least of equality, and soon of superiority to them in the air.

But all engaged in our civil defence forces, whether in London or throughout the country, must prepare themselves for further heavy assaults. Your organisation, your vigilance, your devotion to duty, your zeal for the cause must be raised to the highest intensity.

We do not expect to hit without being hit back, and we intend with every week that passes to hit harder. Prepare yourselves, then, my friends and comrades in the Battle of London, for this renewal of your exertions. We shall never turn from our purpose, however sombre the road, however grievous the cost, because we know that out of this time of trial and tribulation will be born a new freedom and glory for all mankind.

ALLIANCE WITH RUSSIA

A STATEMENT TO THE HOUSE OF COMMONS, JULY 15, 1941

Towards the end of last week it became possible to make a solemn agreement between the British and Russian Governments, carrying with it the full assent of the British and Russian people and all the great Dominions of the Crown, for united action against the common foe. Both the British and

Russian Governments have undertaken to continue the war against Hitlerite Germany to the utmost of their strength, to help each other as much as possible in every way, and not to make peace separately. My right hon Friend the Foreign Secretary and the right hon Member for East Bristol (Sir Stafford Cripps), our Ambassador in Moscow, were indefatigable in carrying matters to a swift conclusion. The Agreement which has been signed, the text of which has been published, cannot fail to exercise a highly beneficial and potent influence on the future of the war. It is, of course, an alliance, and the Russian people are now our allies. General Smuts has, with his usual commanding wisdom, made a comment which, as it entirely represents the view of His Majesty's Government, I should like to repeat now. He says:

'Let no one say that we are now in league with Communists and are fighting the battle of Communism. More fitly can neutralists and fence-sitters be charged with fighting the battle of Nazism. If Hitler, in his insane megalomania, has driven Russia to fighting in self-defence, we bless her arms and wish her all success, without for a moment identifying ourselves with her Communistic creed. Hitler has made her his enemy and not us friendly to her creed, just as previously he treacherously made her his friend without embracing her Communism.'

My right hon Friend the Foreign Secretary, in these busy days, has also been instrumental in bringing about a very great measure of agreement between the Russian Soviet State and the Polish Republic. These negotiations have not yet reached their conclusion, but I am very hopeful that, aided by the statesmanship of General Sikorski, another important step will soon be taken in the marshalling of all the peoples of the world against the criminals who have darkened its life and menaced its future.

The House will also have read, I have no doubt, the good news from Syria. A military convention has been signed, in a cordial spirit on both sides, putting an end to a period of fratricidal strife between Frenchman and Frenchman, and also between Frenchmen and British, Australian and Indian soldiers, all of whom drew the sword of their own free will in defence of the soil of France. The fact that our relations, such as they are, with the Vichy Government have not been worsened during these weeks of distressing fighting, when the forces on both sides acquitted themselves with so much discipline, skill and gallantry, is a proof of the deep comprehension by the French people of the true issues at stake in the world. It is a manifestation of that same spirit which leads them to wave encouragement to our bombing aircraft, although the bombs have, in the hard fortune of war, to be cast on French territory because it is in enemy hands.

We seek no British advantage in Syria. Our only object in occupying the country has been to beat the Germans and help to win the war. We rejoice that with the aid of the forces of General de Gaulle, led by General Catroux and General Legentilhomme, we have been able to bring to the peoples of Syria and the Lebanon the restoration of their full sovereign independence. We have liberated the country from the thraldom exercised by the German Armistice Commission at Wiesbaden, and from the dangerous German intrigues and infiltrations which were in progress. The historic interests of France in Syria, and the primacy of those interests over the interests of other European nations, are preserved without prejudice to the rights and sovereignty of the Syrian races.

The conclusion of this brief Syrian campaign reflects credit upon all responsible – upon General Wavell, who was able to spare the force, first to put down the revolt in Iraq, and afterwards to act in Syria, while at the same time making vigorous head against the German and Italian army and its strong armoured elements which have for so many months been attempting unsuccessfully to invade the Nile Valley. The actual conduct of the campaign was in the hands of General Sir Maitland Wilson, who, it will be remembered, was the general who extricated our forces from the very great dangers by which they were encompassed in Greece. He did not tell us much about what was going on in either sphere, but in both his operations constitute an admirable example of military skill. I hope it will soon be possible to give fuller accounts to the public than they have yet received of the Syrian fighting, marked as it was by so many picturesque episodes, such as the arrival of His Majesty's Lifeguards and Royal Horse Guards, and the Essex Yeomanry, in armoured cars, across many hundreds of miles of desert, to surround and capture the oasis of Palmyra. There are many episodes of that kind, of great interest, which I trust may soon be made public.

We are entitled to say that the situation in the Nile Valley has for the time being, at any rate, been considerably improved. If any one had predicted two months ago, when Iraq was in revolt and our people were hanging on by their eyelids at Habbaniyah, and our ambassador was imprisoned in his embassy at Bagdad, and when all Syria and Iraq began to be overrun by German tourists and were in the hands of forces controlled indirectly but none the less powerfully by German authority – if anyone had predicted that we should already, by the middle of July, have cleaned up the whole of the Levant and re-established our authority there for the time being, such a prophet would have been considered most imprudent. The heavy and indecisive fighting at Sollum by our desert army, and the stubborn defence of Crete, in which such heavy losses were inflicted on the enemy's air power, must be judged to have played their part in arriving at the general result.

V FOR VICTORY

A MESSAGE TO THE PEOPLES OF EUROPE ON THE LAUNCHING OF THE 'V FOR VICTORY' PROPA- GANDA CAMPAIGN, JULY 20, 1941

The V sign is the symbol of the unconquerable will of the occupied territories, and a portent of the fate awaiting the Nazi tyranny. So long as the peoples of Europe continue to refuse all collaboration with the invader, it is sure that his cause will perish, and that Europe will be liberated.

THE ATLANTIC CHARTER

During the first half of August 1941 the Russians retreated steadily under the fierce German offensive. Smolensk fell and Odessa was encircled.

In the Far East, Japan announced general mobilisation and Britain strengthened Singapore with reinforcements of British and Indian troops.

But the most dramatic event of the month was the secret meeting of Mr Winston Churchill and President Roosevelt on board a warship off the coast of Newfoundland. The first announcement was made on August 14 when an Eight-Point Declaration, subsequently known to the world as the Atlantic Charter, was issued.

A JOINT DECLARATION BY MR WINSTON CHURCHILL AND PRESIDENT ROOSEVELT AT THEIR MEETING ON BOARD A WARSHIP OFF NEWFOUNDLAND AUGUST 14, 1941

The President of the United States and the Prime Minister, Mr Churchill, representing His Majesty's Government in the United Kingdom, being met together, deem it right to make known certain common principles in the national policies of their respective countries on which they base their hopes for a better future for the world.

FIRST, their countries seek no aggrandisement, territorial or other.

SECOND, they desire to see no territorial changes that do not accord with the freely expressed wishes of the peoples concerned.

THIRD, they respect the right of all peoples to choose the form of Government under which they will live; and they wish to see sovereign rights and self-government restored to those who have been forcibly deprived of them.

FOURTH, they will endeavour, with due respect for their existing obligations, to further enjoyment by all States, great or small, victor or vanquished, of access, on equal terms, to the trade and to the raw materials of the world which are needed for their economic prosperity.

FIFTH, they desire to bring about the fullest collaboration between all nations in the economic field, with the object of securing for all improved labour standards, economic advancement and social security.

SIXTH, after the final destruction of Nazi tyranny, they hope to see established a peace which will afford to all nations the means of dwelling in safety within their own boundaries, and which will afford assurance that all men in all the lands may live out their lives in freedom from fear and want.

SEVENTH, such a peace should enable all men to traverse the high seas and oceans without hindrances.

EIGHTH, they believe all of the nations of the world, for realistic as well as spiritual reasons, must come to the abandonment of the use of force. Since no further peace can be maintained if land, sea, or air armaments continue to be employed by nations which threaten, or may threaten, aggression outside of their frontiers, they believe, pending the establishment of a wider and permanent system of general security, that the disarmament of such nations is essential. They will likewise aid and encourage all other practicable measures which will lighten for peace-loving peoples the crushing burden of armament.

THE MEETING WITH
PRESIDENT ROOSEVELT

A WORLD BROADCAST, AUGUST 24, 1941

I thought you would like me to tell you something about the voyage which I made across the ocean to meet our great friend, the President of the United States. Exactly where we met is a secret, but I don't think I shall be indiscreet if I go so far as to say that it was 'somewhere in the Atlantic'.

In a spacious, landlocked bay which reminded me of the West Coast of Scotland, powerful American warships protected by strong flotillas and far-ranging aircraft awaited our arrival, and, as it were, stretched out a hand to help us in. Our party arrived in the newest, or almost the newest, British battleship, the *Prince of Wales*, with a modern escort of British and Canadian destroyers; and there for three days I spent my time in company, and I think I may say in comradeship, with Mr Roosevelt; while all the time the chiefs of the staff and the naval and military commanders both of the British Empire and of the United States sat together in continual council.

President Roosevelt is the thrice-chosen head of the most powerful state and community in the world. I am the servant of King and Parliament at present charged with the principal direction of our affairs in these fateful times, and it is my duty also to make sure, as I have made sure, that anything I say or do in the exercise of my office is approved and sustained by the whole British Commonwealth of Nations. Therefore this meeting was bound to be important, because of the enormous forces at present only partially mobilised but steadily mobilising which are at the disposal of these two major groupings of the human family; the British Empire and the United States, who, fortunately for the progress of mankind, happen to speak the same language, and very largely think the same thoughts, or anyhow think a lot of the same thoughts.

The meeting was therefore symbolic. That is its prime importance. It symbolises, in a form and manner which everyone can understand in every land and in every clime, the deep underlying unities which stir and at decisive moments rule the English-speaking peoples throughout the world. Would it be presumptuous for me to say that it symbolises something even more majestic – namely, the marshalling of the good forces of the world against the evil forces which are now so formidable and triumphant and which have cast their cruel spell over the whole of Europe and a large part of Asia?

This was a meeting which marks for ever in the pages of history the taking-up by the English-speaking nations, amid all this peril, tumult and confusion, of the guidance of the fortunes of the broad toiling masses in all the continents; and our loyal effort without any clog of selfish interest to lead them forward out of the miseries into which they have been plunged back to the broad highboard of freedom and justice. This is the highest honour and the most glorious opportunity which could ever have come to any branch of the human race.

When one beholds how many currents of extraordinary and terrible events have flowed together to make this harmony, even the most sceptical person must have the feeling that we all have the chance to play our part and do our duty in some great design, the end of which no mortal can foresee. Awful and horrible things are happening in these days. The whole of Europe has been wrecked and trampled down by the mechanical weapons and barbaric fury of the Nazis; the most deadly instruments of war-science have been joined to the extreme refinements of treachery and the most brutal exhibitions of ruthlessness, and thus have formed a combine of aggression the like of which has never been known, before which the rights, the traditions, the characteristics and the structure of many ancient honoured states and peoples have been laid prostrate and are now ground down under the heel and terror of a monster. The Austrians, the Czechs, the Poles, the Norwegians, the Danes, the Belgians, the Dutch, the

Greeks, the Croats and the Serbs, above all the great French nation, have been stunned and pinioned. Italy, Hungary, Rumania, Bulgaria have brought a shameful respite by becoming the jackals of the tiger, but their situation is very little different and will presently be indistinguishable from that of his victims. Sweden, Spain and Turkey stand appalled, wondering which will be struck down next.

Here, then, is the vast pit into which all the most famous states and races of Europe have been flung and from which unaided they can never climb. But all this did not satiate Adolf Hitler; he made a treaty of non-aggression with Soviet Russia, just as he made one with Turkey, in order to keep them quiet till he was ready to attack them, and then, nine weeks ago today, without a vestige of provocation, he hurled millions of soldiers, with all their apparatus, upon the neighbour he had called his friend, with the avowed object of destroying Russia and tearing her in pieces. This frightful business is now unfolding day by day before our eyes. Here is a devil who, in a mere spasm of his pride and lust for domination, can condemn two or three millions, perhaps it may be many more, of human beings, to speedy and violent death. 'Let Russia be blotted out – Let Russia be destroyed. Order the armies to advance.' Such were his decrees. Accordingly from the Arctic Ocean to the Black Sea, six or seven millions of soldiers are locked in mortal struggle. Ah, but this time it was not so easy.

This time it was not all one way. The Russian armies and all the peoples of the Russian Republic have rallied to the defence of their hearths and homes. For the first time Nazi blood has flowed in a fearful torrent. Certainly 1,500,000, perhaps 2,000,000 of Nazi cannon-fodder have bit the dust of the endless plains of Russia. The tremendous battle rages along nearly 2,000 miles of front. The Russians fight with magnificent devotion; not only that, our generals who have visited the Russian front line report with admiration the efficiency of their military organisation and the excellence of their equipment. The aggressor is surprised, startled, staggered. For the first time in his experience mass murder has become unprofitable. He retaliates by the most frightful cruelties. As his armies advance, whole districts are being exterminated. Scores of thousands – literally scores of thousands – of executions in cold blood are being perpetrated by the German police-troops upon the Russian patriots who defend their native soil. Since the Mongol invasions of Europe in the sixteenth century, there has never been methodical, merciless butchery on such a scale, or approaching such a scale. And this is but the beginning. Famine and pestilence have yet to follow in the bloody ruts of Hitler's tanks. We are in the presence of a crime without a name.

But Europe is not the only continent to be tormented and devastated by aggressions. For five long years the Japanese military factions, seeking to emulate the style of Hitler and Mussolini, taking all their posturing as if it were a new European revelation, have been invading and harrying the 50,000,000 inhabitants of China. Japanese armies have been wandering about that vast land in futile excursions, carrying with them carnage, ruin and corruption and calling it the 'Chinese Incident'. Now they stretched a grasping hand into the southern seas of China; they snatch Indo-China from the wretched Vichy French; they menace by their movements Siam; menace Singapore, the British link with Australasia; and menace the Philippine Islands under the protection of the United States. It is certain that this has got to stop. Every effort will be made to secure a peaceful settlement. The United States are labouring with infinite patience to arrive at a fair and amicable settlement which will give Japan the utmost reassurance for her legitimate interests. We earnestly hope these negotiations will succeed. But this I must say: that if these hopes should fail we shall of course range ourselves unhesitatingly at the side of the United States.

And thus we come back to the quiet bay somewhere in the Atlantic where misty sunshine plays on great ships which carry the White Ensign, or the Stars and Stripes. We had the idea, when we met there – the President and I – that without attempting to draw up final and formal peace aims, or war aims, it was necessary to give all peoples, especially the oppressed and conquered peoples, a simple, rough-and-ready

139

wartime statement of the goal towards which the British Commonwealth and the United States mean to make their way, and thus make a way for others to march with them upon a road which will certainly be painful, and may be long.

There are, however, two distinct and marked differences in this joint declaration from the attitude adopted by the Allies during the latter part of the last war; and no one should overlook them. The United States and Great Britain do not now assume that there will never be any more war again. On the contrary, we intend to take ample precautions to prevent its renewal in any period we can foresee by effectively disarming the guilty nations while remaining suitably protected ourselves.

The second difference is this: that instead of trying to ruin German trade by all kinds of additional trade barriers and hindrances as was the mood of 1917, we have definitely adopted the view that it is not in the interests of the world and of our two countries that any large nation should be unprosperous or shut out from the means of making a decent living for itself and its people by its industry and enterprise. These are far-reaching changes in principle upon which all countries should ponder. Above all, it was necessary to give hope and the assurance of final victory to those many scores of millions of men and women who are battling for life and freedom, or who are already bent down under the Nazi yoke. Hitler and his confederates have for some time past been adjuring, bullying and beseeching the populations whom they have wronged and injured, to bow to their fate, to resign themselves to their servitude, and for the sake of some mitigations and indulgences, to 'collaborate' – that is the word – in what is called the New Order in Europe.

What is this New Order which they seek to fasten first upon Europe and if possible – for their ambitions are boundless – upon all the continents of the globe? It is the rule of the *Herrenvolk* – the master-race – who are to put an end to democracy, to parliaments, to the fundamental freedoms and decencies of ordinary men and women, to the historic rights of nations; and give them in exchange the iron rule of Prussia, the universal goose-step, and a strict, efficient discipline enforced upon the working-class by the political police, with the German concentration camps and firing parties, now so busy in a dozen lands, always handy in the background. There is the New Order.

Napoleon in his glory and his genius spread his Empire far and wide. There was a time when only the snows of Russia and the white cliffs of Dover with their guardian fleets stood between him and the dominion of the world. Napoleon's armies had a theme: they carried with them the surges of the French Revolution. Liberty, Equality and Fraternity – that was the cry. There was a sweeping away of outworn medieval systems and aristocratic privilege. There was the land for the people, a new code of law. Nevertheless, Napoleon's Empire vanished like a dream. But Hitler, Hitler has no theme, naught but mania, appetite and exploitation. He has, however, weapons and machinery for grinding down and for holding down conquered countries which are the product, the sadly perverted product, of modern science.

The ordeals, therefore, of the conquered peoples will be hard. We must give them hope; we must give them the conviction that their sufferings and their resistances will not be in vain. The tunnel may be dark and long, but at the end there is light. That is the symbolism and that is the message of the Atlantic meeting. Do not despair, brave Norwegians: your land shall be cleansed not only from the invader but from the filthy quislings who are his tools. Be sure of yourselves, Czechs: your independence shall be restored. Poles, the heroism of your people standing up to cruel oppressors, the courage of your soldiers, sailors and airmen, shall not be forgotten: your country shall live again and resume its rightful part in the new organisation of Europe. Lift up your heads, gallant Frenchmen: not all the infamies of Darlan and of Laval shall stand between you and the restoration of your birthright. Tough, stout-hearted Dutch, Belgians, Luxembergers, tormented, mishandled, shamefully cast-away peoples of Yugoslavia, glorious Greece, now subjected to the crowning insult of the rule of the Italian jackanapes; yield not an inch! Keep your souls clean from all contact with the Nazis; make them feel even in their fleeting hour of brutish triumph that they are the moral outcasts of mankind. Help is coming; mighty forces are arming in your behalf. Have faith. Have hope. Deliverance is sure.

There is the signal which we have flashed across the water; and if it reaches the hearts of those to whom it is sent, they will endure with fortitude and tenacity their present misfortunes in the sure faith that they, too, are still serving the common cause, and that their efforts will not be in vain.

You will perhaps have noticed that the President of the United States and the British representative, in what is aptly called the 'Atlantic Charter', have jointly pledged their countries to the final destruction of the Nazi tyranny. That is a solemn and grave undertaking. It must be made good; it will be made good. And, of course, many practical arrangements to fulfil that purpose have been and are being organised and set in motion.

The question has been asked: how near is the United States to war? There is certainly one man who knows the answer to that question. If Hitler has not yet declared war upon the United States, it is surely not out of his love for American institutions; it is certainly not because he could not find a pretext. He has murdered half a dozen countries for far less. Fear of immediately redoubling the tremendous energies now being employed against him is no doubt a restraining influence. But the real reason is, I am sure, to be found in the method to which he has so faithfully adhered and by which he has gained so much.

What is that method? It is a very simple method. One by one: that is his plan; that is his guiding rule; that is the trick by which he has enslaved so large a portion of the world. Three and a half years ago I appealed to my fellow countrymen to take the lead in weaving together a strong defensive union within the principles of the League of Nations, a union of all the countries who felt themselves in ever-growing danger. But none would listen; all stood idle while Germany rearmed. Czechoslovakia was subjugated; a French Government deserted their faithful ally and broke a plighted word in that ally's hour of need. Russia was cajoled and deceived into a kind of neutrality or partnership, while the French Army was being annihilated. The Low Countries and the Scandinavian countries, acting with France and Great Britain in good time, even after the war had begun, might have altered its course, and would have had, at any rate, a fighting chance. The Balkan States had only to stand together to save themselves from the ruin by which they are now engulfed. But one by one they were undermined and overwhelmed. Never was the career of crime made more smooth.

Now Hitler is striking at Russia with all his might, well knowing the difficulties of geography which stand between Russia and the aid which the Western Democracies are trying to bring. We shall strive our utmost to overcome all obstacles and to bring this aid. We have arranged for a conference in Moscow between the United States, British and Russian authorities to settle the whole plan. No barrier must stand in the way. But why is Hitler striking at Russia, and inflicting and suffering himself or, rather, making his soldiers suffer, this frightful slaughter? It is with the declared object of turning his whole force upon the British Islands, and if he could succeed in beating the life and the strength out of us, which is not so easy, then is the moment when he will settle his account, and it is already a long one, with the people of the United States and generally with the Western Hemisphere. One by one, there is the process; there is the simple, dismal plan which has served Hitler so well. It needs but one final successful application to make him the master of the world. I am devoutly thankful that some eyes at least are fully opened to it while time remains. I rejoiced to find that the President saw in their true light and proportion the extreme dangers by which the American people as well as the British people are now beset. It was indeed by the mercy of God that he began eight years ago that revival of the strength of the American Navy without which the New World today would have to take its orders from the European dictators, but with which the United States still retains the power to marshal her gigantic strength, and in saving herself to render an incomparable service to mankind.

We had a church parade on the Sunday in our Atlantic bay. The President came on to the quarter-deck of the *Prince of Wales*, where there were mingled together many hundreds of American and British sailors and marines. The sun shone bright and warm while we all sang the old hymns which are our common inheritance and which we learned as children in our homes. We sang the hymn founded on the psalm which John Hampden's soldiers sang when they bore his body to the grave, and in which the brief, precarious span of human life is contrasted with the immutability of Him to Whom a thousand ages are but as yesterday, and as a watch in the night. We sang the sailors' hymn 'For those in peril' – and there are very many – 'on the sea'. We sang 'Onward Christian Soldiers'. And indeed I felt that this was no vain presumption, but that we had the right to feel that we were serving a cause for the sake of which a trumpet has sounded from on high.

When I looked upon that densely-packed congregation of fighting men of the same language, of the same faith, of the same fundamental laws and the same ideals, and now to a large extent of the same interests, and certainly in different degrees facing the same dangers, it swept across me that here was the only hope, but also the sure hope, of saving the world from measureless degradation.

And so we came back across the ocean waves, uplifted in spirit, fortified in resolve. Some American destroyers which were carrying mails to the United States marines in Iceland happened to be going the same way, too, so we made a goodly company at sea together.

And when we were right out in mid-passage one afternoon a noble sight broke on the view. We overtook one of the convoys which carry the munitions and supplies of the New World to sustain the champions of freedom in the Old. The whole broad horizon seemed filled with ships; seventy or eighty ships of all kinds and sizes, arrayed in fourteen lines, each of which could have been drawn with a ruler, hardly a wisp of smoke, not a straggler, but all bristling with cannons and other

144

precautions on which I will not dwell, and all surrounded by their British escorting vessels, while overhead the far-ranging Catalina air-boats soared – vigilant, protecting eagles in the sky. Then I felt that – hard and terrible and long-drawn-out as this struggle may be – we shall not be denied the strength to do our duty to the end.

'THE RESOLUTION OF THE PEOPLE IS UNCONQUERABLE'

In November 1941, Mr Churchill made a tour of some of the bombed cities of North-Eastern England and delivered the following brief speeches:

AT THE GUILDHALL, HULL, NOVEMBER 7, 1941

I wanted very much to see this city which has suffered by the malice of our assailants. I can see that it has had many of its fine buildings shattered and gutted. But I also see that it has not had the heart of its people cast down.

The resolution of the British people is unconquerable. Neither sudden nor violent shocks, nor long, cold, tiring, provoking strains and lulls can or will alter our course. No country made more strenuous efforts to avoid being drawn into this war, but I dare say we shall be found ready and anxious to prosecute it when some of those who provoked it are talking vehemently about peace. It has been rather like that in old times.

I am often asked to say how we are going to win this war. I remember being asked that last time very frequently, and not being able to give a very precise or conclusive answer. We kept on doing our best; we kept on improving. We profited by our mistakes and our experiences. We turned misfortune to good account. We were told we should run short of this or that, until the only thing we ever ran short of was Huns. We

145

did our duty. We did not ask to see too far ahead, but strode forth upon our path, guided by such lights as led us, and then one day we saw those who had forced the struggle upon the world cast down their arms in the open field and immediately proceed to beg for sympathy, mercy and considerable financial support.

Now we have to do it all over again. Sometimes I wonder why. Having chained this fiend, this monstrous power of Prussian militarism, we saw it suddenly resuscitated in the new and more hideous guise of Nazi tyranny. We have to face once more the long struggle, the cruel sacrifices, and not be daunted or deterred by feelings of vexation. With quite a little forethought, a little care and decision, and with rather a greater measure of slow persistency, we need never have had to face this thing in our lifetime or in that of our children.

However, we are all resolved to go forward. We were equally resolved when a year and three months ago we found ourselves absolutely alone, the only champion of freedom in the whole world that remained in arms. We found ourselves with hardly any weapons left. We had rescued our Army, indeed, from Dunkirk, but it had come back stripped of all its accoutrements. Every country in the world outside this island and the Empire to which we are indissolubly attached had given us up, had made up their minds that our life was ended and our tale was told. But by unflinchingly despising the manifestations of power and the threats by which we were on all sides confronted, we have come through that dark and perilous passage, now once again masters of our own destiny.

Nor are we any longer alone. As I told the House of Commons, our own steadfast conduct and the crimes of the enemy have brought other great nations to our side. One of them is struggling with Herculean vigour and with results which are profoundly significant. The other, our kith and kin across the Atlantic Ocean, is straining every nerve to equip us with all we need to carry on the struggle regardless of cost to them or of risk to their sailors and ships. They are driving forward with supplies across the ocean and aiding us to strike down and strangle the foe who molests the passage of those supplies.

Therefore we find ourselves today in a goodly company, and we are moving forward and we shall move forward steadily, however long the road may be.

I have never given any assurances of a speedy or easy or cheap victory. On the contrary, as you know, I have never promised anything but the hardest conditions, great disappointments and many mistakes. But I am sure that at the end all will be well for us in our island home, all will be better for the world, and there will be that crown of honour to those who have endured and never failed which history will accord to them for having set an example to the whole human race.

AT THE TOWN HALL, SHEFFIELD, NOVEMBER 8, 1941

This great city so intimately interwoven with our war effort has undergone this storm of fire and steel and come through with many scars, but with the conviction that however hard may be the trial, and whatever the future may bring, Sheffield will not be unequal to it.

This foul war, forced on us by human wickedness, has now gone on for more than two years. None of us can say at what moment the bugles will sound the 'Cease Fire', but of this we may be sure that, however long and stern it may be, the British Nation and the British Commonwealth of Nations will come through united, undaunted, stainless, unflinching.

When we look back over the time that has passed since world peace was broken by the brutal assault upon Poland, we see the ups and downs through which we have gone. Many disappointments have occurred, very often many mistakes, but still when we look back to fifteen months ago and remember that then we were alone and almost unarmed, and we now see our armed forces developing their strength with modern weapons; when we look across the wide stretches of European land and see that great warrior Stalin at the head of his valiant Russians; when we look westward across the ocean and see the Americans sending their war vessels out to rid the seas of pirate vermin, in order that they may carry to the fighting front line here, without regard to the opposition they may encounter, the weapons, munitions and food we require, it is a message of inspiration, because we are sure that before we get to the end of the road we shall be all together.

I urge you to continue your labours. The work of everyone is of vital importance. This is a struggle for life, a struggle in which every man and woman, old and young, can play a hero's part. The chance of glory and honour comes now here, now there, to each and everyone. However hard the task may be I know you will all be ready for that high moment. God bless you all.

In a speech to workers at a Sheffield munition works the same day, Mr Churchill said:

I give you my compliments and congratulate you on the way you are getting on with the war effort. The work you are doing plays a vital part in the war. Everyone who keeps his time is doing his best to rid the world of this curse of war and Hitlerism. I am proud to come among you because I am told you have lost only 4½ hours' time during air raids, although since January there have been 120 alerts. This is the way to stand up to it as the artillery men do with their guns, as the sailors stand on watch, as the airmen do in cutting the enemy down from the high air. You are doing your bit in the same way. Their work cannot begin until yours is finished. We have only to hold together to go safely through the dark valley, and then we will see if we can make something lasting of our victory.

WAR WITH JAPAN

Japan declared war on Great Britain and the United States on December 7, 1941. While the Emperor's emissaries were still carrying on discussions with the heads of the US State Department in Washington, Japanese planes suddenly bombed the great US naval base at Pearl Harbour and put a large part of the American fleet out of action. At the same time other

Japanese forces invaded Thailand (Siam), made landings in Malaya and the Philippines and seized the Shanghai International Settlement.

The following day Britain and the United States declared war on Japan.

As soon as I heard, last night, that Japan had attacked the United States, I felt it necessary that Parliament should be immediately summoned. It is indispensable to our system of government that Parliament should play its full part in all the important acts of State and at all the crucial moments of the war; and I am glad to see that so many Members have been able to be in their places, despite the shortness of the notice. With the full approval of the nation, and of the Empire, I pledged the word of Great Britain, about a month ago, that should the United States be involved in war with Japan, a British declaration of war would follow within the hour. I therefore spoke to President Roosevelt on the Atlantic telephone last night, with a view to arranging the timing of our respective declarations. The President told me that he would this morning send a message to Congress, which, of course, as is well known, can alone make a declaration of war on behalf of the United States, and I then assured him that we would follow immediately.

However, it soon appeared that British territory in Malaya had also been the object of Japanese attack, and later on it was announced from Tokyo that the Japanese High Command – a curious form; not the Imperial Japanese Government – had declared that a state of war existed with Great Britain and the United States. That being so, there was no need to wait for the declaration by Congress. American time is very nearly six hours behind ours. The Cabinet, therefore, which met at 12.30 today, authorised an immediate declaration of war upon Japan. Instructions were sent to His Majesty's Ambassador at Tokyo,

149

and a communication was dispatched to the Japanese Chargé
d'Affaires at 1 o'clock today to this effect:

Foreign Office, December 8

Sir,

*On the evening of December 7 His Majesty's Government
in the United Kingdom learned that Japanese forces, without
previous warning, either in the form of a declaration of war
or of an ultimatum with a conditional declaration of war, had
attempted a landing on the coast of Malaya and bombed
Singapore and Hong Kong.*

*In view of these wanton acts of unprovoked aggression,
committed in flagrant violation of international law, and particularly of Article 1 of the Third Hague Convention, relative
to the opening of hostilities, to which both Japan and the
United Kingdom are parties, His Majesty's Ambassador at
Tokyo has been instructed to inform the Imperial Japanese
Government, in the name of His Majesty's Government in
the United Kingdom, that a state of war exists between the
two countries.*

I have the honour to be, with high consideration,

Sir,

Your obedient servant,
Winston S. Churchill

Meanwhile, hostilities had already begun. The Japanese began
a landing in British territory in Northern Malaya at about
6 o'clock – 1 a.m. local time – yesterday, and they were immediately engaged by our Forces, which were in readiness. The
Home Office measures against Japanese nationals were set in
motion at 10.45 last night. The House will see, therefore, that
no time has been lost, and that we are actually ahead of our
engagements.

The Royal Netherlands Government at once marked their
solidarity with Great Britain and the United States at 3 o'clock
in the morning.

The Netherlands Minister informed the Foreign Office that
his Government were telling the Japanese Government that,

in view of the hostile acts perpetrated by Japanese forces against two Powers with whom the Netherlands maintained particularly close relations, they considered that, as a consequence, a state of war now existed between the Kingdom of the Netherlands and Japan.

I do not yet know what part Siam, or Thailand, will be called upon to play in this fresh war, but a report has reached us that the Japanese have landed troops in Singora, which is in Siamese territory, on the frontier of Malaya, not far from the landing they made on the British side of the frontier.

Meanwhile, just before Japan had gone to war, I had sent the Siamese Prime Minister the following message. It was sent off on Sunday, early in the morning:

'*There is a possibility of imminent Japanese invasion of your country. If you are attacked, defend yourself. The preservation of the full independence and sovereignty of Thailand is a British interest, and we shall regard an attack on you as an attack on ourselves.*'

It is worth while looking for a moment at the manner in which the Japanese have begun their assault upon the English-speaking world. Every circumstance of calculated and characteristic Japanese treachery was employed against the United States. The Japanese envoys, Nomura and Kurusu, were ordered to prolong their mission in the United States, in order to keep the conversations going while a surprise attack was being prepared, to be made before a declaration of war could be delivered. The President's appeal to the Emperor, which I have no doubt many Members will have read – it has been published largely in the papers here – reminding him of their ancient friendship and of the importance of preserving the peace of the Pacific, has received only this base and brutal reply. No one can doubt that every effort to bring about a peaceful solution had been made by the Government of the United States, and that immense patience and composure has been shown in the face of the growing Japanese menace.

Now that the issue is joined in the most direct manner, it only remains for the two great democracies to face their task with whatever strength God may give them. We must hold

151

ourselves very fortunate, and I think we may rate our affairs not wholly ill-guided, that we were not attacked alone by Japan in our period of weakness after Dunkirk, or at any time in 1940, before the United States had fully realised the dangers which threatened the whole world and had made much advance in its military preparation. So precarious and narrow was the margin upon which we then lived that we did not dare to express the sympathy which we have all along felt for the heroic people of China. We were even forced for a short time, in the summer of 1940, to agree to closing the Burma Road. But later on, at the beginning of this year, as soon as we could regather our strength, we reversed that policy, and the House will remember that both I and the Foreign Secretary have felt able to make increasing outspoken declarations of friendship of the Chinese people and their great leader, General Chiang-Kai-Shek.

We have always been friends. Last night I cabled to the Generalissimo assuring him that henceforward we would face the common foe together. Although the imperative demands of the war in Europe and in Africa have strained our resources, vast and growing though they are, the House and the Empire will notice that some of the finest ships in the Royal Navy have reached their stations in the Far East at a very convenient moment. Every preparation in our power has been made, and I do not doubt that we shall give a good account of ourselves. The closest accord has been established with the powerful American forces, both naval and air, and also with the strong, efficient forces belonging to the Royal Netherlands Government in the Netherlands East Indies. We shall all do our best. When we think of the insane ambition and insatiable appetite which have caused this vast and melancholy extension of the war, we can only feel that Hitler's madness has infected the Japanese mind, and that the root of the evil and its branch must be extirpated together.

It is of the highest importance that there should be no underrating of the gravity of the new dangers we have to meet, either here or in the United States. The enemy has attacked with an audacity which may spring from recklessness, but which may also spring from a conviction of strength. The ordeal to which the English-speaking world and our heroic Russian allies are being exposed will certainly be hard, especially at the outset, and will probably be long, yet when we look around us over the sombre panorama of the world, we have no reason to doubt the justice of our cause or that our strength and will-power will be sufficient to sustain it. We have at least four-fifths of the population of the globe upon our side.

We are responsible for their safety and for their future. In the past we have had a light which flickered, in the present we have a light which flames, and in the future there will be a light which shines over all the land and sea.

Mr Churchill repeated this speech on the radio the same evening, and added this appeal to munition workers.

It is particularly necessary that all munitions workers and those engaged in war industries should make a further effort proportionate to the magnitude of our perils and the magnitude of our cause. Particularly does this apply to tanks and, above all, to aircraft. Aircraft will be more than ever necessary now that the war has spread over so many wide spaces of the earth. I appeal to all those in the factories to do their utmost to make sure that we make an extra contribution to the general resources of the great alliance of free peoples that has been hammered and forged into strength amidst the fire of war.

THE WHITE HOUSE CHRISTMAS TREE

A SPEECH BROADCAST TO THE WORLD FROM THE WHITE HOUSE, WASHINGTON, AT THE TWENTIETH ANNUAL OBSERVATION OF THE LIGHTING OF THE COMMUNITY CHRISTMAS TREE, DECEMBER 24, 1941

I spend this anniversary and festival far from my country, far from my family, yet I cannot truthfully say that I feel far from home. Whether it be the ties of blood on my mother's side, or the friendships I have developed here over many years of active life, or the commanding sentiment of comradeship in the common cause of great peoples who speak the same language, who kneel at the same altars and, to a very large extent, pursue the same ideals, I cannot feel myself a stranger here in the centre and at the summit of the United States. I feel a sense of unity and fraternal association which, added to the kindliness of your welcome, convinces me that I have a right to sit at your fireside and share your Christmas joys.

This is a strange Christmas Eve. Almost the whole world is locked in deadly struggle, and, with the most terrible weapons which science can devise, the nations advance upon each other. Ill would it be for us this Christmastide if we were not sure that no greed for the land or wealth of any other people, no vulgar ambition, no morbid lust for material gain at the expense of others, had led us to the field. Here, in the midst of war, raging and roaring over all the lands and seas, creeping nearer to our hearts and homes, here, amid all the tumult, we have tonight the peace of the spirit in each cottage home and in every generous heart. Therefore we may cast aside for this night at least the cares and dangers which beset us, and make for the children an evening of happiness in a world of storm. Here, then, for one night only, each home throughout the English-speaking world should be a brightly-lighted island of happiness and peace.

Let the children have their night of fun and laughter. Let the gifts of Father Christmas delight their play. Let us grown-ups share to the full in their unstinted pleasures before we turn again to the stern task and the formidable years that lie before us, resolved that, by our sacrifice and daring, these same children shall not be robbed of their inheritance or denied their right to live in a free and decent world.

And so, in God's mercy, a happy Christmas to you all.

'PREPARATION – LIBERATION – ASSAULT'

A SPEECH TO THE CANADIAN SENATE AND HOUSE OF
COMMONS AT OTTAWA, BROADCAST TO THE WORLD,
DECEMBER 30, 1941

It is with feelings of pride and encouragement that I find
myself here in the House of Commons of Canada, invited to
address the Parliament of the senior Dominion of the Crown.
I am very glad to see again my old friend Mr Mackenzie
King, for fifteen years out of twenty your Prime Minister,
and I thank him for the too complimentary terms in which
he has referred to myself. I bring you the assurance of good
will and affection from everyone in the Motherland. We are
most grateful for all you have done in the common cause, and
we know that you are resolved to do whatever more is possible as the need arises and as opportunity serves. Canada
occupies a unique position in the British Empire because of
its unbreakable ties with Britain and its ever-growing friendship and intimate association with the United States. Canada
is a potent magnet, drawing together those in the new world
and in the old whose fortunes are now united in a deadly
struggle for life and honour against the common foe. The contribution of Canada to the Imperial war effort in troops, in
ships, in aircraft, in food and in finance has been magnificent.

The Canadian Army now stationed in England has chafed
not to find itself in contact with the enemy. But I am here to
tell you that it has stood and still stands in the key position to
strike at the invader should he land upon our shores. In a few
months, when the invasion season returns, the Canadian Army
may be engaged in one of the most frightful battles the world
has ever seen, but on the other hand their presence may help to
deter the enemy from attempting to fight such a battle on

155

British soil. Although the long routine of training and preparation is undoubtedly trying to men who left prosperous farms and businesses, or other responsible civil work, inspired by an eager and ardent desire to fight the enemy, although this is trying to high-mettled temperaments, the value of the service rendered is unquestionable, and I am sure that the peculiar kind of self-sacrifice involved will be cheerfully or at least patiently endured.

The Canadian Government have imposed no limitation on the use of the Canadian Army, whether on the continent of Europe or elsewhere, and I think it is extremely unlikely that this war will end without the Canadian Army coming to close quarters with the Germans, as their fathers did at Ypres, on the Somme, or on the Vimy Ridge. Already at Hong Kong, that beautiful colony which the industry and mercantile enterprise of Britain has raised from a desert isle and made the greatest port of shipping in the whole world – Hong Kong, that colony wrested from us for a time until we reach the peace table, by the overwhelming power of the Home Forces of Japan, to which it lay in proximity – at Hong Kong, Canadian soldiers of the Royal Rifles of Canada and the Winnipeg Grenadiers, under a brave officer whose loss we mourn, have played a valuable part in gaining precious days, and have crowned with military honour the reputation of their native land.

Another major contribution made by Canada to the Imperial war effort is the wonderful and gigantic Empire Training scheme for pilots for the Royal and Imperial Air Forces. This has now been as you know well in full career for nearly two years in conditions free from all interference by the enemy. The daring youth of Canada, Australia, New Zealand and South Africa, with many thousands from the homeland, are perfecting their training under the best conditions, and we are being assisted on a large scale by the United States, many of whose training facilities have been placed at our disposal. This scheme will provide us in 1942 and 1943 with the highest class of trained pilots, observers and air gunners in the numbers necessary to man the enormous flow of aircraft which the factories of Britain, of the Empire and of the United States are and will be producing.

I could also speak on the naval production of corvettes and above all of merchant ships which is proceeding on a scale almost equal to the building of the United Kingdom, all of which Canada has set on foot. I could speak of many other activities, of tanks, of the special forms of modern high-velocity cannon and of the great supplies of raw materials and many other elements essential to our war effort on which your labours are ceaselessly and tirelessly engaged. But I must not let my address to you become a catalogue, so I turn to less technical fields of thought.

We did not make this war, we did not seek it. We did all we could to avoid it. We did too much to avoid it. We went so far at times in trying to avoid it as to be almost destroyed by it when it broke upon us. But that dangerous corner has been turned, and with every month and every year that passes we shall confront the evil-doers with weapons as plentiful, as sharp and as destructive as those with which they have sought to establish their hateful domination.

I should like to point out to you we have not at any time asked for any mitigation in the fury or malice of the enemy. The peoples of the British Empire may love peace. They do not seek the lands or wealth of any country, but they are a tough and hardy lot. We have not journeyed all this way across the centuries, across the oceans, across the mountains, across the prairies, because we are made of sugar candy.

Look at the Londoners, the Cockneys; look at what they have stood up to. Grim and gay with their cry 'We can take it', and their war-time mood of 'What is good enough for anybody is good enough for us'. We have not asked that the rules of the game should be modified. We shall never descend to the German and Japanese level, but if anybody likes to play rough we can play rough too. Hitler and his Nazi gang have sown the wind; let them reap the whirlwind. Neither the length of the struggle nor any form of severity which it may assume shall make us weary or shall make us quit.

I have been all this week with the President of the United

States, that great man whom destiny has marked for this climax of human fortune. We have been concerting the united pacts and resolves of more than thirty States and nations to fight on in unity together and in fidelity one to another, without any thought except the total and final extirpation of the Hitler tyranny, the Japanese frenzy, and the Mussolini flop.

There shall be no halting, or half measures, there shall be no compromise or parley. These gangs of bandits have sought to darken the light of the world; have sought to stand between the common people of all the lands and their march forward into their inheritance. They shall themselves be cast into the pit of death and shame, and only when the earth has been cleansed and purged of their crimes and their villainy shall we turn from the task which they have forced upon us, a task which we were reluctant to undertake, but which we shall now most faithfully and punctiliously discharge. According to my sense of proportion, this is no time to speak of the hopes of the future, or the broader world which lies beyond our struggles and our victory. We have to win that world for our children. We have to win it by our sacrifices. We have not won it yet. The crisis is upon us. The power of the enemy is immense. If we were in any way to underrate the strength, the resources of the ruthless savagery of that enemy, we should jeopardise, not only our lives, for they will be offered freely, but the cause of human freedom and progress to which we have vowed ourselves and all we have. We cannot for a moment afford to relax. On the contrary we must drive ourselves forward with unrelenting zeal. In this strange, terrible world war there is a place for everyone, man and woman, old and young, hale and halt; service in a thousand forms is open. There is no room now for the dilettante, the weakling, for the shirker, or the sluggard. The mine, the factory, the dockyard, the salt sea waves, the fields to till, the home, the hospital, the chair of the scientist, the pulpit of the preacher – from the highest to the humblest tasks, all are of equal honour; all have their part to play. The enemies ranged against us, coalesced and combined against us, have asked for total war. Let us make sure they get it.

That grand old minstrel, Harry Lauder – Sir Harry Lauder.
I should say, and no honour was better deserved – had a song
in the last war which began, 'If we all look back on the history
of the past, we can just tell where we are.' Let us then look
back. We plunged into this war all unprepared because we
had pledged our word to stand by the side of Poland, which
Hitler had feloniously invaded, and in spite of a gallant
resistance had soon struck down. There followed those astonishing seven months which were called on this side of the
Atlantic the 'phoney' war. Suddenly the explosion of pent-up
German strength and preparation burst upon Norway, Denmark, Holland and Belgium. All these absolutely blameless
neutrals, to most of whom Germany up to the last moment
was giving every kind of guarantee and assurance, were overrun and trampled down. The hideous massacre of Rotterdam,
where 30,000 people perished, showed the ferocious barbarism
in which the German Air Force revels when, as in Warsaw
and later Belgrade, it is able to bomb practically undefended
cities.

On the top of all this came the great French catastrophe. The
French Army collapsed, and the French nation was dashed into
utter and, as it has so far proved, irretrievable confusion. The
French Government had at their own suggestion solemnly
bound themselves with us not to make a separate peace. It
was their duty and it was also their interest to go to North
Africa, where they would have been at the head of the French
Empire. In Africa, with our aid, they would have had overwhelming sea power. They would have had the recognition of
the United States, and the use of all the gold they had lodged
beyond the seas. If they had done this Italy might have been
driven out of the war before the end of 1940, and France
would have held her place as a nation in the counsels of the
Allies and at the conference table of the victors. But their
generals misled them. When I warned them that Britain would
fight on alone whatever they did, their generals told their
Prime Minister and his divided Cabinet, 'In three weeks
England will have her neck wrung like a chicken.' Some
chicken; some neck.

159

What a contrast has been the behaviour of the valiant, stout-hearted Dutch, who still stand forth as a strong living partner in the struggle! Their venerated Queen and their Government are in England, their Princess and her children have found asylum and protection here in your midst. But the Dutch nation are defending their Empire with dogged courage and tenacity by land and sea and in the air. Their submarines are inflicting a heavy daily toll upon the Japanese robbers who have come across the seas to steal the wealth of the East Indies, and to ravage and exploit its fertility and its civilisation. The British Empire and the United States are going to the aid of the Dutch. We are going to fight out this new war against Japan together. We have suffered together and we shall conquer together.

But the men of Bordeaux, the men of Vichy, they would do nothing like this. They lay prostrate at the foot of the conqueror. They fawned upon him. What have they got out of it? The fragment of France which was left to them is just as powerless, just as hungry as, and even more miserable, because more divided, than the occupied regions themselves. Hitler plays from day to day a cat-and-mouse game with these tormented men. One day he will charge them a little less for holding their countrymen down. Another day he will let out a few thousand broken prisoners of war from the 1,500,000 or 1,750,000 he has collected. Or again he will shoot a hundred French hostages to give them a taste of the lash. On these blows and favours the Vichy Government have been content to live from day to day. But even this will not go on indefinitely. At any moment it may suit Hitler's plans to brush them away. Their only guarantee is Hitler's good faith, which, as everyone knows, biteth like the adder and stingeth like the asp.

But some Frenchmen there were who would not bow their knees and who under General de Gaulle have continued the fight on the side of the Allies. They have been condemned to death by the men of Vichy, but their names will be held and are being held in increasing respect by nine Frenchmen out of every ten throughout the once happy, smiling land of

France. But now strong forces are at hand. The tide has turned against the Hun. Britain, which the men of Bordeaux thought and then hoped would soon be finished, Britain with her Empire around her carried the weight of the war alone for a whole long year through the darkest part of the valley. She is growing stronger every day. You can see it here in Canada. Anyone who has the slightest knowledge of our affairs is aware that very soon we shall be superior in every form of equipment to those who have taken us at the disadvantage of being half armed.

The Russian armies, under their warrior leader, Josef Stalin, are waging furious war with increasing success along the thousand-mile front of their invaded country. General Auckinleck, at the head of a British, South African, New Zealand and Indian army, is striking down and mopping up the German and Italian forces which had attempted the invasion of Egypt. Not only are they being mopped up in the desert, but great numbers of them have been drowned on the way there by the British submarines and the RAF in which Australian squadrons played their part.

As I speak this afternoon an important battle is being fought around Jedabia. We must not attempt to prophesy its result, but I have good confidence. All this fighting in Libya proves that when our men have equal weapons in their hands and proper support from the air they are more than a match for the Nazi hordes. In Libya, as in Russia, events of great importance and of most hopeful import have taken place. But greatest of all, the mighty Republic of the United States has entered the conflict, and entered it in a manner which shows that for her there can be no withdrawal except by death or victory.

Mr Churchill then spoke in French as follows:

Et partout dans la France occupée et inoccupée (car leur sort est égal), ces honnêtes gens, ce grand peuple, la nation française, se redresse. L'espoir se rallume dans les coeurs d'une race guerrière, même désarmée, berceau de la liberté révolutionnaire et terrible aux vainqueurs esclaves. Et partout, on voit le point du jour, et la lumiere grandit, rougeâtre, mais claire. Nous ne perdons jamais la confiance que la France jouera le rôle des hommes libres et qu'elle reprenda par des voies dures sa place dans la grande compagnie des nations libératrices et victorieuses.

Ici, au Canada, où la langue française est honorée et parlée, nous nous tenons prêts et armés pour aider et pour saluer cette résurrection nationale.

(*Translation*)

And everywhere in France, occupied and unoccupied, for their fate is identical, these honest folk, this great people, the French nation, are rising again. Hope is springing up again in the hearts of a warrior race, even though disarmed, cradle of revolutionary liberty and terrible to slavish conquerors. And everywhere dawn is breaking and light spreading, reddish yet, but clear. We shall never lose confidence that France will play the role of free men again and, by hard paths, will once again attain her place in the great company of freedom-bringing and victorious nations. Here in Canada, where the French language is honoured and spoken, we are armed and ready to help and to hail this national resurrection.

Mr Churchill then continued in English:

Now that the whole of the North American continent is becoming one gigantic arsenal, and armed camp; now that the immense reserve power of Russia is gradually becoming apparent; now that long-suffering, unconquerable China sees help approaching; now that the outraged and subjugated nations can see daylight ahead, it is permissible to take a broad forward view of the war.

We may observe three main periods or phases of the struggle that lies before us. First there is a period of consolidation, of combination, and of final preparation. In this period, which will certainly be marked by much heavy fighting, we shall still be gathering our strength, resisting the assaults of the enemy, and acquiring the necessary overwhelming air superiority and shipping tonnage to give our armies the power to traverse, in whatever numbers may be necessary, the seas and oceans which, except in the case of Russia, separate us from our foes. It is only when the vast shipbuilding programme on which the United States has already made so much progress, and which you are powerfully aiding, comes into full blood, that we shall be able to bring the whole force of our manhood and of our modern scientific equipment to bear upon the enemy. How long this period will take depends upon the vehemence of the effort put into production in all our war industries and shipyards.

The second phase which will then open may be called the phase of liberation. During this phase we must look to the recovery of the territories which have been lost or which may yet be lost, and also we must look to the revolt of the conquered peoples from the moment that the rescuing and liberating armies and air forces appear in strength within their bounds. For this purpose it is imperative that no nation or region overrun, that no Government or State which has been conquered, should relax its moral and physical efforts and preparation for the day of deliverance. The invaders, be they German or Japanese, must everywhere be regarded as infected persons to be shunned and isolated as far as possible. Where active resistance is impossible, passive resistance must be maintained. The invaders and tyrants must be made to feel that their fleeting triumphs will have a terrible reckoning, and that they are hunted men and that their cause is doomed. Particular punishment will be reserved for the quislings and traitors who make themselves the tools of the enemy. They will be handed over to the judgement of their fellow countrymen.

There is a third phase which must also be contemplated, namely, the assault upon the citadels and the homelands of the guilty Powers both in Europe and in Asia. Thus I endeavour in a few words to cast some forward light upon the dark, inscrutable mysteries of the future. But in this forecasting the course along which we should seek to advance, we must never forget that the power of the enemy, and the action of the enemy may at every stage affect our fortunes. Moreover, you will notice that I have not attempted to assign any time-limits to the various phases. These time-limits depend upon our exertions, upon our achievements, and on the hazardous and uncertain course of the war.

Nevertheless I feel it is right at this moment to make it clear that, while an ever-increasing bombing offensive against Germany will remain one of the principal methods by which we hope to bring the war to an end, it is by no means the only method which our growing strength now enables us to take into account. Evidently the most strenuous exertions must be made by all. As to the form which those exertions take, that is for each partner in the grand alliance to judge for himself in consultation with others and in harmony with the general scheme. Let us then address ourselves to our task, not in any way underrating its tremendous difficulties and perils, but in good heart and sober confidence, resolved that, whatever the cost, whatever the suffering, we shall stand by one another, true and faithful comrades, and do our duty, God helping us, to the end.

'THROUGH THE STORM'

A BROADCAST SURVEY OF THE WAR SITUATION, FEBRUARY 15, 1942

Nearly six months have passed since at the end of August I made a broadcast directly to my fellow-countrymen; it is therefore worth while looking back over this half-year of struggle for life, for that is what it has been, and what it is, to see what has happened to our fortunes and to our prospects.

At that time in August I had the pleasure of meeting the President of the United States and drawing up with him the declaration of British and American policy which has become known to the world as the Atlantic Charter. We also settled a number of other things about the war, some of which have had an important influence upon its course. In those days we met on the terms of a hard-pressed combatant seeking assistance from a great friend who was, however, only a benevolent neutral.

In those days the Germans seemed to be tearing the Russian armies to pieces and striding on with growing momentum to Leningrad, to Moscow, to Rostov, and even farther into the heart of Russia. It was thought a very daring assertion when the President declared that the Russian armies would hold out till the winter. You may say that the military men of all countries – friend, foe and neutral alike – were very doubtful whether this would come true. As for us, our British resources were stretched to the utmost. We had already been for more than a whole year absolutely alone in the struggle with Hitler and Mussolini. We had to be ready to meet a German invasion of our own island; we had to defend Egypt, the Nile Valley and the Suez Canal. Above all we had to bring in across the Atlantic in the teeth of the German and Italian U-boats and aircraft the food, raw materials and finished munitions without which we could not live, without which we could not wage war. We have to do all this still.

It seemed our duty in those August days to do everything in our power to help the Russian people to meet the prodigious onslaught which had been launched against them. It is little enough we have done for Russia, considering all she has done to beat Hitler and for the common cause. In these circumstances, we British had no means whatever of providing effectively against a new war with Japan. Such was the outlook when I talked with President Roosevelt in the middle of August on board the good ship *Prince of Wales*, now, alas, sunk beneath the waves. It is true that our position in August 1941 seemed vastly better than it had been a year earlier in 1940, when France had just been beaten into the awful prostration in which she now lies, when we were almost entirely unarmed in our own island, and when it looked as if Egypt and all the Middle East would be conquered by the Italians who still held Abyssinia and had newly driven us out of British Somaliland. Compared with those days of 1940, when all the world except ourselves thought we were down and out for ever, the situation the President and I surveyed in August

1941 was an enormous improvement. Still, when you looked at it bluntly and squarely — with the United States neutral and fiercely divided, with the Russian armies falling back with grievous losses, with the German military power triumphant and unscathed, with the Japanese menace assuming an uglier shape each day — it certainly seemed a very bleak and anxious scene.

How do matters stand now? Taking it all in all, are our chances of survival better or are they worse than in August 1941? Are we up or down? What has happened to the principles of freedom and decent civilisation for which we are fighting? Are they making headway, or are they in greater peril? Let us take the rough with the smooth, let us put the good and bad side by side, and let us try to see exactly where we are. The first and greatest of events is that the United States is now unitedly and whole-heartedly in the war with us. The other day I crossed the Atlantic again to see President Roosevelt. This time we met not only as friends, but as comrades standing side by side and shoulder to shoulder in a battle for dear life and dearer honour in the common cause and against a common foe. When I survey and compute the power of the United States and its vast resources and feel that they are now in it with us, with the British Commonwealth of Nations all together, however long it lasts, till death or victory, I cannot believe there is any other fact in the whole world which can compare with that. That is what I have dreamed of, aimed at and worked for, and now it has come to pass.

But there is another fact, in some ways more immediately effective. The Russian armies have not been defeated, they have not been torn to pieces. The Russian people have not been conquered or destroyed. Leningrad and Moscow have not been taken. The Russian armies are in the field. They are not holding the line of the Urals or the line of the Volga. They are advancing victoriously, driving the foul invader from that native soil they have guarded so bravely and love so well. More than that: for the first time they have broken the Hitler legend. Instead of the easy victories and abundant

166

booty which he and his hordes had gathered in the west, he has found in Russia so far only disaster, failure, the shame of unspeakable crimes, the slaughter or loss of vast numbers of German soldiers, and the icy wind that blows across the Russian snow.

Here, then, are two tremendous fundamental facts which will in the end dominate the world situation and make victory possible in a form never possible before. But there is another heavy and terrible side to the account, and this must be set in the balance against these inestimable gains. Japan has plunged into the war, and is ravaging the beautiful, fertile, prosperous and densely populated lands of the Far East. It would never have been in the power of Great Britain while fighting Germany and Italy – the nations long hardened and prepared for war – while fighting in the North Sea, in the Mediterranean and in the Atlantic – it would never have been in our power to defend the Pacific and the Far East single-handed against the onslaught of Japan. We have only just been able to keep our heads above water at home; only by a narrow margin have we brought in the food and the supplies; only by so little have we held our own in the Nile Valley and the Middle East. The Mediterranean is closed, and all our transports have to go around the Cape of Good Hope, each ship making only three voyages in the year. Not a ship, not an aeroplane, not a tank, not an anti-tank gun or an anti-aircraft gun has stood idle. Everything we have has been deployed either against the enemy or awaiting his attack. We are struggling hard in the Libyan Desert, where perhaps another serious battle will soon be fought. We have to provide for the safety and order of liberated Abyssinia, of conquered Eritrea, of Palestine, of liberated Syria, and redeemed Iraq, and of our new ally, Persia. A ceaseless stream of ships, men and materials has flowed from this country for a year and a half, in order to build up and sustain our armies in the Middle East, which guard those vast regions on either side of the Nile Valley. We had to do our best to give substantial aid to Russia. We gave it her in her darkest hour, and we must not fail in our undertaking now. How then in this posture, gripped and held and battered as we were, could we have provided for the safety of the Far East against such an avalanche of fire and steel as has been hurled upon us by Japan? Always, my friends, this thought overhung our minds.

There was, however, one hope and one hope only – namely that if Japan entered the war with her allies, Germany and Italy, the United States would come in on our side, thus far more than repairing the balance. For this reason, I have been most careful, all these many months, not to give any provocation to Japan, and to put up with the Japanese encroachments, dangerous though they were, so that if possible, whatever happened, we should not find ourselves forced to face this new enemy alone. I could not be sure that we should succeed in this policy, but it has come to pass. Japan has struck her felon blow, and a new, far greater champion has drawn the sword of implacable vengeance against her and on our side.

I shall frankly state to you that I did not believe it was in the interests of Japan to burst into war both upon the British Empire and the United States. I thought it would be a very irrational act. Indeed, when you remember that they did not attack us after Dunkirk when we were so much weaker, when our hopes of United States help were of the most slender character, and when we were alone, I could hardly believe that they would commit what seemed to be a mad act. Tonight the Japanese are triumphant. They shout their exultation around the world. We suffer. We are taken aback. We are hard pressed. But I am sure even in this dark hour that 'criminal madness' will be the verdict which history will pronounce upon the authors of Japanese aggression, after the events of 1942 and 1943 have been inscribed upon its sombre pages.

The immediate deterrent which the United States exercised upon Japan – apart of course from the measureless resources of the American Union – was the dominant American battle fleet in the Pacific, which, with the naval forces we could spare, confronted Japanese aggression with the shield of superior sea-power. But, my friends, by an act of sudden violent surprise, long-calculated, balanced and prepared, and delivered under the crafty cloak of negotiation, the shield of sea-power which protected the fair lands and islands of the Pacific Ocean was for the time being, and only for the time being, dashed to the ground. Into the gap thus opened rushed the invading armies of Japan. We were exposed to the assault of a warrior race of nearly 80,000,000, with a large outfit of modern weapons, whose war lords had been planning and scheming for this day, and looking forward to it perhaps for twenty years – while all the time our good people on both sides of the Atlantic were prating about perpetual peace, and cutting down each other's navies in order to set a good example. The overthrow, for a while, of British and United States sea-power in the Pacific was like the breaking of some mighty dam; the long-gathered pent-up waters rushed down the peaceful valley, carrying ruin and devastation forward on their foam, and spreading their inundations far and wide.

No one must underrate any more the gravity and efficiency of the Japanese war machine. Whether in the air or upon the sea, or man to man on land, they have already proved themselves to be formidable, deadly and, I am sorry to say, barbarous antagonists. This proves a hundred times over that there never was the slightest chance, even though we had been much better prepared in many ways than we were, of our standing up to them alone while we had Nazi Germany at our throat and Fascist Italy at our belly. It proves something else. And this should be a comfort and a reassurance. We can now measure the wonderful strength of the Chinese people who under Generalissimo Chiang Kai-Shek have single-handed fought this hideous Japanese aggressor for four and a half years and left him baffled and dismayed. This they have done, although they were a people whose whole philosophy for many ages was opposed to war and warlike arts, and who in their agony were caught ill-armed, ill-supplied with munitions, and hopelessly outmatched in the air. We must not underrate the power and malice of our latest foe, but neither must we undervalue the gigantic, overwhelming forces which now stand in the line with us in this world-struggle for freedom, and which, once they have developed their full

169

natural inherent power, whatever has happened in the meanwhile, will be found fully capable of squaring all accounts and setting all things right for a good long time to come.

You know I have never prophesied to you or promised smooth and easy things, and now all I have to offer is hard adverse war for many months ahead. I must warn you, as I warned the House of Commons before they gave me their generous vote of confidence a fortnight ago, that many misfortunes, severe torturing losses, remorseless and gnawing anxieties lie before us. To our British folk these may seem even harder to bear when they are at a great distance than when the savage Hun was shattering our cities and we all felt in the midst of the battle ourselves. But the same qualities which brought us through the awful jeopardy of the summer of 1940 and its long autumn and winter bombardment from the air, will bring us through this other new ordeal, though it may be more costly and will certainly be longer. One fault, one crime, and one crime only, can rob the United Nations and the British people, upon whose constancy this grand alliance came into being, of the victory upon which their lives and honour depend. A weakening in our purpose and therefore in our unity – that is the mortal crime. Whoever is guilty of that crime, or of bringing it about in others, to him let it be said that it were better for him that a millstone were hanged about his neck and he were cast into the sea.

Last autumn, when Russia was in her most dire peril, when vast numbers of her soldiers had been killed or taken prisoner, when one-third of her whole munitions capacity lay, as it still lies, in Nazi German hands, when Kiev fell, and the foreign ambassadors were ordered out of Moscow, the Russian people did not fall to bickering among themselves. They just stood together and worked and fought all the harder. They did not lose trust in their leaders; they did not try to break up their Government. Hitler had hoped to find quislings and fifth columnists in the wide regions he overran, and among the unhappy masses who fell into his power. He looked for them. He searched for them. But he found none.

The system upon which the Soviet Government is founded

is very different from ours or from that of the United States. However that may be, the fact remains that Russia received blows which her friends feared and her foes believed were mortal, and through preserving national unity and persevering undaunted, Russia has had the marvellous come-back for which we thank God now. In the English-speaking world we rejoice in free institutions. We have free parliaments and a free Press. This is the way of life we have been used to. This is the way of life we are fighting to defend. But it is the duty of all who take part in those free institutions to make sure, as the House of Commons and the House of Lords have done, and will I doubt not do, that the National Executive Government in time of war have a solid foundation on which to stand and on which to act; that the misfortunes and mistakes of war are not exploited against them; that while they are kept up to the mark by helpful and judicious criticism or advice, they are not deprived of the persisting power to run through a period of bad times and many cruel vexations and come out on the other side and get to the top of the hill.

Tonight I speak to you at home; I speak to you in Australia and New Zealand, for whose safety we will strain every nerve; to our loyal friends in India and Burma; to our gallant allies, the Dutch and Chinese; and to our kith and kin in the United States. I speak to you all under the shadow of heavy and far-reaching military defeat. It is a British and Imperial defeat. Singapore has fallen. All the Malay Peninsula has been over-run. Other dangers gather about us out there, and none of the dangers which we have hitherto successfully withstood at home and in the East are in any way diminished. This, there-fore, is one of those moments when the British race and nation can show their quality and their genius. This is one of those moments when it can draw from the heart of misfortune the vital impulses of victory. Here is the moment to display that calm and poise combined with grim determination which not so long ago brought us out of the very jaws of death. Here is another occasion to show – as so often in our long story – that we can meet reverses with dignity and with renewed accessions of strength. We must remember that we are no longer alone.

We are in the midst of a great company. Three-quarters of the human race are now moving with us. The whole future of mankind may depend upon our action and upon our conduct. So far we have not failed. We shall not fail now. Let us move forward steadfastly together into the storm and through the storm.

PRIME MINISTER FOR TWO YEARS

A WORLD BROADCAST, MAY 10, 1942

I have now served for two years exactly to a day as the King's First Minister. Therefore I thought it would be a good thing if I had a talk to you on the broadcast, to look back a little on what we have come through, to consider how we stand now, and to peer cautiously, but at the same time resolutely, into the future.

The tremendous period through which we have passed has certainly been full of anxieties and exertions; it has been marked by many misfortunes and disappointments. This time two years ago the Germans were beating down Holland and Belgium by unprovoked brutal, merciless invasion, and very soon there came upon us the total defeat of France and the fatal surrender at Bordeaux. Mussolini, the Italian miscalculator, thought he saw his chance of a cheap and easy triumph, and rich plunder for no fighting. He struck at the back of a dying France, and what he believed was a doomed Britain. We were left alone – our quarter of a million Dunkirk troops saved, only disarmed; ourselves, as yet – unarmed – to face the might of victorious Germany, to face also the carefully saved-up strength of an Italy which then still ranked as a first-class Power.

Here at home in this island, invasion was near; the Mediterranean was closed to us; the long route around the Cape, where General Smuts stands on guard, alone was open; our small, ill-equipped forces in Egypt and the Sudan seemed to await destruction. All the world, even our best friends, thought that our end had come. Accordingly, we prepared ourselves to conquer or to perish. We were united in that solemn, majestic hour; we were all equally resolved at least to go down fighting. We cast calculation to the winds; no wavering voice was heard; we hurled defiance at our foes; we faced our duty, and, by the mercy of God, we were preserved.

It fell to me in those days to express the sentiments and resolves of the British nation in that supreme crisis of its life. That was to me an honour far beyond any dreams or ambitions I had ever nursed, and it is one that cannot be taken away. For a whole year after the fall of France we stood alone, keeping the flag of freedom flying, and the hopes of the world alive. We conquered the Italian Empire, we destroyed or captured almost all Mussolini's African army; we liberated Abyssinia; we have so far successfully protected Palestine, Syria, Persia and Iraq from German designs. We have suffered grievous reverses in going to the aid of the heroic Greeks; we bore unflinching many a heavy blow abroad, and still more in our cities here at home; and all this time, cheered and helped by President Roosevelt and the United States, we stood alone, neither faltering nor flagging.

Where are we now? Can anyone doubt that if we are worthy of it, as we shall be, we have in our hand our own future. As in the last war, so in this, we are moving through many reverses and many defeats to complete and final victory. We have only to endure and to persevere, to conquer. Now we are no longer unarmed; we are well armed. Now we are not alone; we have mighty allies, bound irrevocably by solemn faith and common interests to stand with us in the ranks of the United Nations. There can only be one end. When it will come, or how it will come, I cannot tell. But, when we survey the overwhelming resources which are at our disposal, once they are fully marshalled and developed – as they can be, as they will be – we may stride forward into the unknown with growing confidence.

During the time that we were alone, we were steadily growing stronger. He would have been a bold man, however, who in those days would have put down in black and white exactly how we were going to win. But, as has happened before in our island history, by remaining steadfast and unyielding – stubborn, if you will – against a Continental tyrant, we reached the moment when that tyrant made a fatal blunder. Dictators, as well as democracies and parliamentary Governments, make mistakes sometimes. Indeed, when the whole story is told, I believe it will be found that the Dictators, for all their preparations and prolonged scheming, have made greater mistakes than the democracies they have assailed. Even Hitler makes mistakes sometimes. In June last, without the slightest provocation, and in breach of a pact of non-aggression, he invaded the lands of the Russian people. At that time he had the strongest army in the world, trained in war, flushed with incredible unbroken success and equipped with limitless munitions and the most modern weapons. He had also secured for himself the advantages of surprise and treachery. Thus he drove the youth and manhood of the German nation forward into Russia.

The Russians, under their warrior chief, Stalin, sustained losses which no other country or Government has ever borne in so short a time and lived. But they, like us, were resolved never to give in. They poured out their own blood upon their native soil. They kept their faces to the foe. From the very first day to the end of the year, and on till tonight, they fought with unflinching valour. And, from the very first day when they were attacked, when no one could tell how things would go, we made a brotherhood with them, and a solemn compact to destroy Nazidom and all its works. Then Hitler made his second grand blunder. He forgot about the winter. There is a winter, you know, in Russia. For a good many months the temperature is apt to fall very low. There is snow, there is frost, and all that. Hitler forgot about this Russian winter. He must have been very loosely educated. We all heard about it at school; but he forgot it. I have never made such a bad mistake as that. So winter came, and fell upon his ill-clad armies, and with the winter came the valiant Russian counter-attacks. No one can say with certainty how many millions of Germans have already perished in Russia and its snows. Certainly more have perished than were killed in the whole four and a quarter years of the last war. This is probably an understatement. So besotted is this man in his lust for blood and conquest, so blasting is the power he wields over the lives of Germans, that he even blurted out the other day that his armies would be better clothed and his locomotives better prepared for their second winter in Russia than they were for the first.

There was an admission about the length of the war that struck a chill into German hearts as cold as the icy winds of Russia. What will be the sufferings of the German manhood in this new bloodbath? What is there in front of Hitler now? Certain it is that the Russian armies are stronger than they were last year, that they have learnt by hard experience to fight the Germans in the field, that they are well-equipped, and that their constancy and courage are unquenched. That is what is in front of Hitler. What is he leaving behind him? He leaves behind him a Europe starving and in chains; a Europe in which his execution squads are busy in a dozen countries every day; a Europe which has learned to hate the Nazi name as no name has ever been hated in the recorded history of mankind; a Europe burning for revolt whenever the opportunity comes.

But this is not all he has left behind. We are on his tracks, and so is the great Republic of the United States. Already the Royal Air Force has set about it; the British, and presently the American, bombing offensive against Germany will be one of the principal features in this year's world war. Now is the time to use our increasingly superior air strength to strike hard and continually at the home front in Germany, from which so much evil has leaked out upon the world, and which is the foundation of the whole enormous German invasion of Russia. Now, while the German armies will be bleeding and burning up their strength against the 2,000-mile Russian line, and when the news of casualties by hundreds of thousands is streaming back to the German Reich, now is the time to bring home to the German people the wickedness of their rulers, by destroying under their very eyes the factories and seaports on which their war effort depends.

German propaganda has been constantly appealing of late to British public opinion to put a stop to these severe forms of warfare, which, according to the German view, should be the strict monopoly of the *Herrenvolk*. Herr Hitler himself has not taken at all kindly to this treatment, and he has been good enough to mingle terrible threats with his whinings. He warns us, solemnly, that if we go on smashing up the German cities, his war factories and his bases, he will retaliate against our cathedrals and historic monuments – if they are not too far inland. We have heard his threats before. Eighteen months ago, in September 1940, when he thought he had an overwhelming air force at his command, he declared that he would rub out – that was the actual expression, rub out – our towns and cities. And he certainly had a good try. Now the boot is on the other leg. Herr Hitler has even called in question the humanity of these grim developments of war. What a pity this conversion did not take place in his heart before he bombed Warsaw, or massacred 20,000 Dutch folk in defenceless Rotterdam, or wreaked his cruel vengeance upon the open city of Belgrade. In those days, he used to boast that for every ton of bombs we dropped on Germany, he would drop ten times, or even a hundred times, as many on Britain. Those were his words, and that was his belief. Indeed, for a time we had to suffer very severely from his vastly superior strength and utter ruthlessness.

But now it is the other way around. We are in a position to carry into Germany many times the tonnage of high explosives which he can send here, and this proportion will increase all the summer, all the autumn, all the winter, all the spring, all the summer, and so on, till the end! The accuracy of our bombing has nearly doubled, and, with continued practice, I expect it will improve still more. Moreover, at the same time, our methods of dealing with his raiders over here have more than repaid the immense care and science bestowed upon them, and the very large scale upon which they are applied. During the month of April we have destroyed one-tenth of all the raiding aircraft which have assailed our island; whereas, acting on a scale several times as big, the losses which we have suffered have been proportionately far smaller. We have waited long for this turning of the tables, and have taken whatever came to us meanwhile.

You will remember how the German propaganda films, seeking to terrorise neutral countries and glorying in devastating violence, were wont to show rows of great German bombers being loaded up with bombs, then flying in the air in battle array, then casting down showers of bombs upon the defenceless towns and villages below, choking them in smoke and flame. All this was represented from the beginning of the war to neutral countries as the German way of making war. All this was intended to make the world believe that resistance to the German will was impossible, and that subjugation and slavery were the safest and easiest road. Those days are gone. Though the mills of God grind slowly, yet they grind exceedingly small. And for my part, I hail it as an example of sublime and poetic justice that those who have loosed these horrors upon mankind will now in their homes and persons feel the shattering strokes of just retribution.

We have a long list of German cities in which all the vital industries of the German war machine are established. All these it will be our stern duty to deal with, as we have already dealt with Lubeck, with Rostock, and half a dozen important places. The civil population of Germany have, however, an easy way to escape from these severities. All they have to do is to leave the cities where munitions work is being carried on – abandon their work, and go out into the fields, and watch their home fires burning from a distance. In this way they may find time for meditation and repentance; there they may remember the millions of Russian women and children they have driven out to perish in the snows, and the mass executions of peasantry and prisoners-of-war which in varying scales they are inflicting upon so many of the ancient and famous peoples of Europe. There they may remember that it is the villainous Hitlerite regime which is responsible for dragging Germany through misery and slaughter to ultimate ruin, and learn that the tyrant's overthrow is the first step to world liberation.

We now wait in what is a stormy lull, but still a lull, before the hurricane bursts again full fury on the Russian front. We cannot tell when it will begin; we have not so far seen any evidences of those great concentrations of German masses which usually precede their large-scale offensives. They may have been successfully concealed or may not yet have been launched eastward. But it is now the tenth of May, and the days are passing. We send our salutations to the Russian armies, and we hope that the thousands of tanks and aeroplanes which have been carried to their aid from Britain and America will be a useful contribution to their own magnificently developed and reorganised munitions resources.

There is, however, one serious matter which I must mention to you. The Soviet Government have expressed to us the view that the Germans in the desperation of their assault may make use of poison gas against the armies and peoples of Russia. We are ourselves firmly resolved not to use this odious weapon unless it is used first by the Germans. Knowing our Hun, however, we have not neglected to make preparations on a formidable scale. I wish now to make it plain that we shall treat the unprovoked use of poison gas against our Russian ally exactly as if it were used against ourselves, and if we are satisfied that this new outrage has been committed by Hitler, we shall use our great and growing air superiority in the west to carry gas warfare on the largest possible scale far and wide against military objectives in Germany. It is thus for Hitler to choose whether he wishes to add this additional horror to aerial warfare. We have for some time past been bringing our defensive and precautionary arrangements up to date, and I now give public warning so that there may be no carelessness or neglect. Of one thing I am sure: that the British people who have entered into the full comradeship of war with our Russian ally, will not shrink from any sacrifice or trial which that comradeship may require.

Meanwhile, our deliveries of tanks, aircraft and munitions to Russia from Britain and from the United States continue upon the full scale. We have the duty of escorting the northern convoys to their destination. Our sailors and merchant seamen face the fearful storms of the Arctic Circle, the lurking U-boats and shore-based aircraft, as well as attacks by German destroyers and surface craft, with their customary steadfastness and faithful courage. So far, though not without some loss both to the supply ships and their escorts, every convoy has successfully fought its way through, and we intend to persevere and fight it out on this northern route to the utmost of our strength.

Is there anything else we can do to take the weight off Russia? We are urged from many quarters to invade the continent of Europe and so form a second front. Naturally, I shall not disclose what our intentions are, but there is one thing I will say: I welcome the militant, aggressive spirit of the British nation so strongly shared across the Atlantic Ocean. Is it not far better that in the thirty-second month of this hard war we should find this general desire to come to the closest grips with the enemy, than that there should be any signs of war-weariness? Is it not far better that demonstrations of thousands of people should gather in Trafalgar Square demanding the most vehement and audacious attacks, than that there should be the weepings and wailings and peace agitations which in other lands and other wars have often hampered the action and vigour of Governments? It is encouraging and inspiring to feel the strong heartbeats of a free nation, surging forward, stern and undaunted, in a righteous cause. We must not fail them, either in daring or in wisdom.

This week, two islands have been in our minds – one is very large, the other very small – Madagascar and Malta. We have found it necessary to take precautions to prevent Madagascar falling into enemy hands, by some dishonourable and feeble drifting or connivance by Vichy, like that which injured us so much in Indo-China. It is three months since the decision was taken, and more than two months since the expedition left these shores. Its first task was to secure the splendid harbour of Diego Suarez, in the northern part of Madagascar, which, if it had fallen into Japanese hands, might have

179

paralysed all our communications with India and the Middle East. While the troops were on the sea, I must tell you I felt a shiver every time I saw the word 'Madagascar' in the newspapers. All those articles with diagrams and measured maps, showing how very important it was for us to take Madagascar and forestall the Japanese, and to be there 'first for once', as they said, filled me with apprehension. There was no question of leakage, or breach of confidence. As they say, great minds think alike. But shrewd surmise may be as dangerous as leakage. And it was with considerable relief that I learned the difficulties of our soldiers and their losses had been exaggerated, and that the operation had been swiftly and effectively carried out.

We hold this island in trust; we hold it in trust for that gallant France, which we have known and marched with, and whose restoration to her place among the great Powers of the world is indispensable to the future of Europe. Madagascar rests under the safeguard of the United Nations. Vichy, in the grip of the Germans, has been made to bluster and protest. The France that rose at St Nazaire, and will one day rise in indescribable fury against the Nazis, understands what we have done and gives us its trust.

The smaller island is Malta, a tiny rock of history and romance. Today we welcome back to our shores General Dobbie, for nearly two years the heroic defender of Malta. The burden which he has borne so honourably and for so long entitles him to release and repose. In Lord Gort we have a new impulse. His work at Gibraltar has been of the highest order. It was not his fault that our armies did not have their chance in France. He is a grand fighter. For the moment the terrific air attack on Malta has slackened. It looks as if a lot of enemy aircraft had moved eastward. I wonder why? If so, another intense air battle for Malta, upon which the enemy have concentrated such an immense preponderance of strength, and for which they have sacrificed so many of those aircraft which they now have to count more carefully every day – another intense air battle will have been definitely won. But other perils remain, and I know of no man in the British

Empire to whom I would sooner entrust the combating and beating-down of those perils than Lord Gort.

If we look back today over the course of the war as it has so far unfolded, we can see that it seems to divide itself into four very clearly defined chapters. The first ended with the over-running by the Nazis of Western Europe, and with the fall of France. The second chapter, Britain alone, ended with Hitler's attack upon Russia. I will call the third chapter which then began, 'the Russian glory'. May it long continue! The fourth chapter opened at Pearl Harbour when the military party in Japan treacherously attacked the United States and Great Britain in the Far East. That is where we are now.

The aggression of Italy in 1940 had carried the war from Europe to Africa. The aggression of Japan has involved all Asia including unconquerable China, and in one way or another has drawn in, or will draw in, the whole of the American continent. Thus the struggle has become world-wide, and the fate of all states and nations and their future is at stake. This latest chapter – universal war – confronts us with many difficulties and immense complications. But is there any thoughtful sensible person who cannot see how vastly and decisively the awful balances have turned to the advantage of the cause of freedom? It is true that the Japanese, taking advantage of our preoccupations elsewhere, and of the fact that the United States had striven for so long to keep the peace, have seized more easily and more quickly than they expected their lands of booty and desire in the East Indian Archipelago. Henceforward they will find resistance stiffening on all their widely spread fronts. They can ill-afford losses such as those they have sustained in the naval action of the Coral Sea; so far we have no detailed accounts, but it is obvious, if only from the lies the Japanese have felt compelled to tell about the sinking of a battleship of the *Warspite* class, that a most vigorous and successful battle has been fought by the United States and Australian naval forces.

The Japanese war-lords cannot be indifferent to the losses of aircraft inflicted upon them at so many points, and particularly off the northern coast of Australia, and in their repulse at Colombo and Trincomalee. At the start the pent-up, saved-up resources of Japan were bound to prevail in the Far Eastern theatre; but the strength of the United States, expressed in units of modern war-power, actual and potential, is alone many times greater than the power of Japan. And we also shall make our contribution to the final defeat and punishment of this ambitious and greedy nation. Time will, however, be needed before the true strengths on either side of the Eastern war become manifest. I am not prone to make predictions, but I have no doubt tonight that the British and American sea-power will grip and hold the Japanese, and that overwhelming air power, covering vigorous military operations, will lay them low. This would come to pass, of course very much sooner should anything happen to Hitler in Europe.

Therefore tonight I give you a message of good cheer. You deserve it, and the facts endorse it. But be it good cheer or be it bad cheer will make no difference to us; we shall drive on to the end, and do our duty, win or die. God helping us, we can do no other.

'WE SEE THE RIDGE AHEAD'

A SPEECH FROM THE STEPS OF LEEDS TOWN HALL DURING A TOUR OF THE CITY WITH DR H. V. EVATT, THE AUSTRALIAN MINISTER FOR EXTERNAL AFFAIRS, MAY 16, 1942

In the height of the second great war, it is a great pleasure to come to Leeds and bring to the citizens a word of thanks and encouragement in all the work they are doing to promote the common cause of many nations and in many lands. That cause appeals to the hearts of all those in the human race who are not already gripped by tyranny or who have not already been seduced to its insidious voice. That cause is shared by all the millions of our cousins across the Atlantic who are preparing night and day to have their will and rights respected. It appeals to the patient millions of China, who have suffered long from cruel aggression and still fight with faithful stubbornness. It appeals to the noble manhood of Russia, now at full grips with the murderous enemy, striking blow for blow and repaying better ones for blows struck at them. It appeals to all the people of Britain, without discrimination of class or party. It appeals to all the peoples of the British Empire throughout the world, and I have here at my side Dr Evatt from Australia.

I voice on behalf of this vast gathering of men and women of Leeds our warmest message of good will and comradeship to our kith and kin in Australia, who, like ourselves, lie under the menace of imminent enemy attack, and who, like ourselves, are going to strike a heavy blow on all who spring upon us.

You have had your test in battle, but lately the enemy has not been so ready to come to this island: first, because a large portion of his air force is engaged against our Russian allies, and secondly because he knows that our arrangements for meeting him, thanks to the assistance of hundreds of thousands of active, willing minds and hands, are improving in power and efficiency every day. I have seen some of your factories this morning though not as many as I should have liked to have seen, and I know well the great contributions which Leeds is making to the whole forward and upward thrust of the war.

We have reached a period in the war when it would be premature to say that we have topped the ridge, but now we see the ridge ahead. We see that perseverance, unflinching, dogged, inexhaustible, tireless, valiant, will surely carry us and our allies, the great nations of the world, and the unfortunate nations who have been subjugated and enslaved, on to one of the most deep-founded movements of humanity which have ever taken place in our history. We see that they will come to the top ridge, and then they will have a chance not only of beating down and subduing those evil forces which have withstood us so long, which have twice let ruin and havoc loose on the world, but they will have that further and grander prospect that beyond the smoke of battle and the confusion of the fight we shall have the chance to settle our countries and the whole world together, moving forward together on the high road. That is the prospect that lies before us if we do not fail. And we shall not fail.

Here in the thirty-third month of the war none of us is weary of the struggle, none of us is calling for any favours from the enemy. If he plays rough we can play rough too. Whatever we have got to take we will take, and we will give it back in even greater measure. When we began this war we were a peaceful and unarmed people. We had striven hard for peace. We had gone into folly over our desire for peace and the enemy started all primed-up and ready to strike. But now, as the months go by and the great machine keeps turning and the labour becomes skilled and habituated to its task, we are going to be the ones who have the modern scientific tackle. It is not now going to be a fight of brave men against men armed. It is going to be a fight on our side of people who have not only the resolve and the cause, but who also have the weapons.

We shall go forward together. The road upwards is stony. There are upon our journey dark and dangerous valleys through which we have to make and fight our way. But it is sure and certain that if we persevere – and we shall persevere – we shall come through these dark and dangerous valleys into a sunlight broader and more genial and more lasting than mankind has ever known.

'KEEP RIGHT ON TO THE END'

A SPEECH IN THE USHER HALL, EDINBURGH, WHEN THE PRIME MINISTER RECEIVED THE FREEDOM OF THE CITY, OCTOBER 12, 1942

I have never before been made a Freeman of any city, and though, during the war, I have been complimented by a number of invitations which I greatly value, your Freedom is

before in its history. Cruel blows like the loss of the original 51st Division in France have been borne with fortitude and silent dignity. A new 51st Division has been born, and will sustain the reputation and avenge the fortunes of its forerunner. The air bombing was endured with courage and resource. In all the Services, air and land and sea, in the merchant ships, in all the many forms of service which this great struggle has called forth, Scotsmen have gained distinction. You may indeed repeat with assurance the poet's lines:

> *Gin dangers dare we'll thole our share,*
> *Gie's but the weapons, we've the will*
> *Beyont the main to prove again*
> *Auld Scotland counts for something still.*

Let us then for a moment cross the main and take a wider view. Our enemies have been more talkative lately. Ribbentrop, Goering and Hitler have all been making speeches which are of interest because they reveal with considerable frankness their state of mind.

There is one note which rings through all these speeches; it can be clearly heard above their customary boastings and threats – the dull, low, whining note of fear. They are all speeches of men conscious of their guilt and conscious also of the law. How different from the tone of 1940 when France was struck down, when Western Europe was subjugated, when Mussolini hastened to stab us in the back, when Britain stood all alone, the sole champion in arms for the freedom and inheritance of mankind! How different are these plaintive speeches and expostulations from what we used to hear in those days!

Evidently something has happened in these two years to make these evildoers feel that aggression, war, bloodshed, the trampling down of the weak, may not be after all the whole story. There may be another side to the account. It is a long account, and it is becoming pretty clear that the day is coming when it will have to be settled. The most striking and curious part of Hitler's speech was his complaint that no one pays sufficient attention to his victories.

'Look at all the victories I have won,' he exclaims in effect. 'Look at all the countries I have invaded and struck down. Look at the thousands of kilometres that I have advanced into the lands of other people. Look at the booty I have gathered, and all the men I have killed and captured. Contrast these exploits with the performances of the Allies. Why are they not down-hearted and dismayed? How do they dare to keep up their spirits in the face of my great successes and their many misfortunes?'

I have not quoted his actual words. I have given their meaning and their sense. That is his complaint. That is the question which puzzles him and angers him. It strikes a chill into his marrow, because in his heart he knows that with all his tremendous victories and vast conquests his fortunes have declined, his prospects have darkened to an immeasurable degree in the last two years, while at the same time Britain, the United States, Russia, and China have moved forward through tribulation and sorrow, steadily forward, steadily onward, from strength to strength. He sees with chagrin and amazement that our defeats are but stepping-stones to victory, and that his victories are only the stepping-stones to ruin.

It was apparent to me that this bad man saw quite clearly the shadow of slowly and remorselessly approaching doom, and he railed at fortune for mocking him with the glitter of fleeting success. But, after all, the explanation is not so difficult.

When peaceful nations like the British and the Americans, very careless in peacetime about their defences, carefree, unsuspecting nations, peoples who have never known defeat – improvident nations I will say, feckless nations, nations who despise the military art and thought war so wicked that it could never happen again – when nations like these are set upon by highly organised, heavily-armed conspirators, planning and calculating in secret for years on end, exalting war as the highest form of human effort, glorifying slaughter and aggression, prepared and trained to the last point science and discipline can carry them, is it not natural that the peaceful, unprepared, improvident peoples should suffer terribly and that the wicked, scheming aggressors should have their reign of savage exaltation?

Ah! But that is not the end of the story. It is only the first chapter. If the great, peaceful democracies could survive the first few years of the aggressors' attack, another chapter had to be written. It is to that chapter we shall come in due time.

It will ever be the glory of this island and its Empire that we stood alone for one whole year of mortal peril, and gained the time for the good cause to arm, to organise and slowly bring the conjoined, united, irresistible forces of outraged civilisation to bear upon the criminals. That is our greatest glory.

Fear is the motive which inspires Hitler's latest outrages. From the North Cape in Norway to the Spanish frontier near Bayonne, a distance apart from its inner indentations of nearly 2,000 miles, the German invading armies are holding down by brute force and terrorism the nations of Western Europe. Norway, Denmark, Holland, Belgium, France – all are in Hitler's grip, all are seething with the spirit of revolt and revolution. Except in Denmark, whose turn will come, the Nazi firing parties are busy. Every day innocent hostages and prominent citizens are arrested haphazard and taken out and shot in cold blood, and every day hatred of the German race and name burns fiercer in the hearts of these ancient, famous States and peoples.

The British Commando raids at different points along this enormous length of coast, although so far only the forerunner of what is to come, inspire the author of so many crimes and miseries with lively anxiety. His soldiers dwell among populations who would kill them with their hands if they got the chance, and will kill them one at a time when they do get the chance. In addition, there comes out of the sea from time to time a hand of steel which plucks the German sentries from their posts with growing efficiency, amid the joy of the whole countryside.

In his fear and spite, Hitler turns upon the prisoners-of-war who are in his camps and in his power, just as he takes innocent hostages from his prisons in Norway, Belgium, Holland, France, to shoot them in the hope of breaking the spirit of their countrymen. So in flattest breach of the new conventions which still hold across the lines of world war, he vents his cruel fear and anger upon the prisoners-of-war and casts them in chains. I have always expected that this war would become worse in severity as the guilty Nazis feel the ring of doom remorselessly closing in upon them. Here in the west we have seen many savage, bestial acts, but nothing that has happened in the west so far can compare with the wholesale massacre, not only of soldiers, but of civilians and women and children, which has characterised Hitler's invasion of Russia. In Russia and in his reigns of terror in Poland and Yugoslavia, tens of thousands have been murdered in cold blood by the German Army and by the special police battalions and brigades which accompany it everywhere and take a leading part in the frightful butchery perpetrated behind the front. For every one execution Hitler has ordered in the West he has carried out two hundred – it may be many more – in Eastern and Central Europe. On the first day after he entered Kiev he shot upwards of 54,000 persons.

I say to show weakness of any kind to such a man is only to encourage him to further atrocities. And you may be assured that no weakness will be shown.

There is another reason, apart from his perverted instincts, why Hitler has begun large-scale maltreatment of British prisoners of war: he wishes to throw a new topic into the arena of world discussion and so divert men's eyes from the evident failure so far – I always say so far – of his second vast campaign against Russia.

The heroic defence of Stalingrad – the fact that the splendid Russian armies are everywhere intact, unbeaten, and unbroken, nay, counter-attacking with amazing energy along the whole front from Leningrad to the Caucasus Mountains, the fearful losses suffered by the German troops, the near approach of another Russian winter – all these grim facts, which cannot be concealed, cast their freezing shadow upon the German people already wincing under the increasing impact of British bombing. The German people turn with a stony gaze upon the leader who has brought all this upon them, and dumbly, for they dare not speak aloud, they put the terrible question – 'Why did you go there? Why did you invade Russia?'

Already Field-Marshal Goering has made haste to point out that this decision was Hitler's alone, that Hitler alone conducts the war, and that the generals of the German Army are only assistants who carry out his orders. Already Himmler, the police butcher, has been decorated, honoured and promoted in token not only of the importance of his work in shooting and hanging thousands of Russian prisoners-of-war and in torturing Poles, Czechoslovaks, Yugoslavs and Greeks, but of the increasing need for his devilish arts to be employed in the homeland of Germany itself. Evidently in such a plight it would be natural for Hitler to raise a stir in some other quarter, and what could be more attractive to such a being than to mis-handle captives who are powerless in his hands? There are other matters which should cause Hitler and his guilty but somewhat ridiculous confederate, Mussolini, to ask themselves uncomfortable questions.

The U-boat warfare still remains the greatest problem of the United Nations, but there is no reason whatever why it should not be solved by the prodigious measures of offence, of defence, and of replacement on which Britain, Canada and, above all, the United States, are now engaged. The months of August and September have been, I will not say the best, but the least bad months since January. These months have seen the new building of merchant ships which substantially outweigh the losses.

They have seen the greatest tonnage of British bombs dropped upon Germany. They have covered the most numerous safe arrivals of United States troops in the British Isles. They have marked a definite growth of Allied air superiority over Germany, Italy and Japan.

In these same months, far away in the Pacific, the Australians, with our American allies, have made a good advance in New Guinea. It is not my habit to encourage light or vain expectations, but these are solid and remarkable facts.

Surveying both sides of the account – the good and the bad, with equal composure and coolness – we must see that we have reached a stern and sombre moment in the war, one which calls in a high degree for firmness of spirit and constancy of soul.

The excitement and the emotion of those great days when we stood alone and unaided against what seemed overwhelming odds and, single-handed, saved the future of the world, are not present now. We are surrounded by a concourse of Governments and nations, all of us bound together in solemn unbreakable alliance, bound together by ties not only of honour but of self-preservation. We are able to plan our slow but sure march onward. Deadly dangers still beset us. Weariness, complacency, or discord, squabbles over petty matters, would mar our prospects.

We must all drive ourselves to the utmost limit of our strength. We must preserve and refine our sense of proportion. We must strive to combine the virtues of wisdom and of daring. We must move forward together, united and inexorable.

Thus, with God's blessing, the hopes which are now justified, which we are now entitled to feel, will not fail or wither. The light is broadening on the track, and the light is brighter too. Among the qualities for which Scotland is renowned, steadfastness holds perhaps the highest place.

Be steadfast, then, that is the message which I bring to you, that is my invocation to the Scottish people, here in this ancient capital city, one of whose burgesses I now have the honour to be. Let me use the words of your famous minstrel – he is here today – words which have given comfort and renewed strength to many a burdened heart:

> 'Keep right on to the end of the road,
> Keep right on to the end.'

CHAINED PRISONERS

Following a raid by a British force on Sark, in the Channel Islands, the Germans announced that they would put into chains prisoners taken in the Dieppe raid, alleging that Germans taken prisoner on Sark were ill-treated. Britain denied the German allegations and announced that as a reprisal 1,376 German prisoners would be chained. The Prime Minister made two statements – one in Secret Session – to the House of Commons about this situation.

A STATEMENT TO THE HOUSE OF COMMONS, OCTOBER 13, 1942

His Majesty's Government have never countenanced any general order for the tying-up of prisoners on the field of battle. Such a process, however, may be necessary from time to time under stress of circumstances, and may indeed be in the best interests of the safety of the prisoners themselves. The Geneva Convention upon the treatment of prisoners-of-war does not attempt to regulate what happens in the actual fighting. It is confined solely to the treatment of prisoners who have been securely captured and are in the responsible charge of the hostile Government. Both His Majesty's Government and the German Government are bound by this Convention. The German Government, by throwing into chains 1,376 British prisoners-of-war for whose proper treatment they are responsible, have violated Article 2 of the aforesaid Convention. They are thus attempting to use prisoners-of-war as if they were hostages upon whom reprisals can be taken for occurrences on the field of battle with which the said prisoners can have had nothing to do. The action of the German Government affronts the sanctity of the Geneva Convention, which His Majesty's Government have always been anxious to observe punctiliously.

His Majesty's Government have therefore approached the protecting Power and invited that Power to lay before the German Government our solemn protest against this breach of the Geneva Convention and to urge them to desist from it, in which case the counter-measures of a similar character which His Majesty's Government felt themselves forced to take in order to protect their prisoners-of-war in enemy hands will immediately be withdrawn.

Until we learn from the protecting Power the result of this protest, I have no further statement to make upon the subject, and I should strongly deprecate any discussion which might be prejudicial to the action of the protecting Power and consequently to the interests of the prisoners-of-war of both belligerent countries.

A STATEMENT AT A SECRET SESSION OF THE HOUSE OF COMMONS, DECEMBER 10, 1942

I have an announcement to make about the unshackling of prisoners. Last week the Germans officially informed the International Red Cross that they intended to unshackle all prisoners for the Christmas week. We had previously suggested to the Protecting Power that they should ask both countries to unshackle and we had told them that we would immediately comply with such a request. The Protecting Power has now made the request and instructions have been given by us to unshackle the German prisoners in our hands on December 12. I do not know what the response of the Germans to the Protecting Power will be, but in view of their statement about unshackling for Christmas there certainly seems a good chance that they will relieve our officers and men from the indignities they so wrongly inflicted upon them. At any rate that is what we are going to do.

I should like to make it clear that we have never had any object but to get our men unchained and it remains to be seen whether we shall achieve that object or not. There has never been in our minds any thought of reprisals in the sense of inflicting cruelty for cruelty's sake. On the other hand it does not do to give way to a bully like Hitler. I am aware that many good people have criticised the action we took but it may be that that action and the timing of its cessation will produce the result we aimed at, namely, the relief of our men. If so, it will be a matter for general satisfaction.

In order that the Swiss action may have the best chance of success, the House will realise the importance of discretion in public discussion during the next few days.

VICTORY AS A SPUR

A WORLD BROADCAST, NOVEMBER 29, 1942

Two Sundays ago all the bells rang to celebrate the victory of our Desert Army at Alamein. Here was a martial episode in British history which deserved a special recognition. But the bells also carried with their clashing joyous peals our thanksgiving that, in spite of all our errors and shortcomings, we have been brought nearer to the frontiers of deliverance. We have not reached those frontiers yet, but we are becoming ever more entitled to be sure that the awful perils which might well have blotted out our life and all that we love and cherish will be surmounted, and that we shall be preserved for further service in the vanguard of mankind.

We have to look back along the path we have trodden these last three years of toil and strife, to value properly all that we have escaped and all that we have achieved. No mood of boastfulness, of vainglory, or over-confidence must cloud our minds; but I think we have a right which history will endorse to feel that we had the honour to play a part in saving the freedom and the future of the world. That wonderful association of States and races spread all over the globe called the British Empire – or British Commonwealth if you will; I do not quarrel about it – and above all, our small island, stood in the gap alone in the deadly hour. Here we stood, firm though all was drifting; throughout the British Empire no one faltered. All around was very dark. Here we kept the light burning which now spreads broadly over the vast array of the United Nations: that is why it was right to ring out the bells, and to lift our heads for a moment in gratitude and in relief, before we turn again to the grim and probably long ordeals which lie before us and to the exacting tasks upon which we are engaged.

Since we rang the bells for Alamein, the good cause has prospered. The Eighth Army has advanced nearly four hundred miles, driving before them in rout and ruin the powerful forces, or the remnants of the powerful forces, which Rommel boasted and Hitler and Mussolini believed would conquer Egypt. Another serious battle may be impending at the entrance to Tripolitania. I make it a rule not to prophesy about battles before they are fought. Everyone must try to realise the immense distances over which the North African war ranges, and the enormous labours and self-denial of the troops who press forward relentlessly, twenty, thirty, forty and sometimes fifty miles in a single day. I will say no more than that we may have the greatest confidence in Generals Alexander and Montgomery, and in our soldiers and airmen who have at last begun to come into their own.

At the other side of Africa, a thousand miles or more to the westward, the tremendous joint undertaking of the United States and Britain which was fraught with so many hazards has also been crowned with astonishing success. To transport these large armies of several hundred thousand men, with all their intricate elaborate modern apparatus, secretly across the seas and oceans, and to strike to the hour, and almost to the minute, simultaneously at a dozen points, in spite of all the U-boats and all the chances of weather, was a feat of organisation which will long be studied with respect. It was rendered possible only by one sovereign fact – namely the perfect comradeship and understanding prevailing between the British and American staffs and troops. This majestic enterprise is under the direction and responsibility of the President of the United States, and our First British Army is serving under the orders of the American Commander-in-Chief, General Eisenhower, in whose military skill and burning energy we put our faith, and whose orders to attack we shall punctually and unflinchingly obey. Behind all lies the power of the Royal Navy, to which is joined a powerful American fleet; the whole under the command of Admiral Cunningham, and all subordinated to the Allied Commander-in-Chief.

It was not only that the U-boats were evaded and brushed aside by the powerfully escorted British and American convoys; they were definitely beaten in the ten days' conflict that followed the landings, both inside and outside the Mediterranean. Here was no more secrecy. We had many scores of ships continuously exposed; large numbers of U-boats were concentrated from all quarters; our destroyers and corvettes and our aircraft took up the challenge and wore them down and beat them off. For every transport or supply ship we have lost, a U-boat has been sunk or severely damaged; for every ton of Anglo-American shipping lost so far in this expedition, we have gained perhaps two tons in the shipping acquired or recovered in the French harbours of North and West Africa. Thus, in this respect, as Napoleon recommended, war has been made to support war.

General Alexander timed his battle at Alamein to suit exactly this great stroke from the West, in order that his victory should encourage friendly countries to preserve their strict neutrality, and also to rally the French forces in North-West Africa to a full sense of their duty and of their opportunity. Now at this moment, the First British Army is striking hard at the last remaining footholds of the Germans and Italians in Tunisia. American, British and French troops are pressing forward side by side, vying with each other in a general rivalry and brotherhood. In this there lies the hope and the portent of the future.

I have been speaking about Africa, about the 2,000 miles of coastline fronting the underside of subjugated Europe. From all this we intend, and I will go so far as to say we expect, to expel the enemy before long. But Africa is no halting-place: it is not a seat but a springboard. We shall use Africa only to come to closer grips. Anyone can see the importance to us of reopening the Mediterranean to military traffic and saving the long voyage around the Cape. Perhaps by this short cut and the economy of shipping resulting from it, we may strike as heavy a blow at the U-boats as has happened in the whole war; but there is another advantage to be gained by the mastery of the North Africa shore: we open the air battle upon a new front. In order to shorten the struggle, it is our duty to engage the enemy in the air continuously on the largest scale and at the highest intensity. To bring relief to the tortured world, there must be the maximum possible air fighting. Already, the German Air Force is a wasting asset; their new construction is not keeping pace with their losses; their front line is weakening both in numbers and, on the whole, in quality. The British, American and Russian Air Forces, already together far larger, are growing steadily and rapidly; the British and United States expansion in 1943 will be, to put it mildly, well worth watching: all we need is more frequent opportunities of contact. The new air front, from which the Americans and also the Royal Air Force are deploying along the Mediterranean shore, ought to give us these extra opportunities abundantly in 1943. Thirdly, our operations in French North Africa should enable us to bring the weight of the war home to the Italian Fascist State, in a manner not hitherto dreamed of by its guilty leaders, or still less by the unfortunate Italian people Mussolini has led, exploited and disgraced. Already the centres of war industry in Northern Italy are being subjected to harder treatment than any of our cities experienced in the winter of 1940. But if the enemy should in due course be blasted from the Tunisian tip, which is our aim, the whole of the south of Italy – all the naval bases, all the munition establishments and other military objectives wherever situated – will be brought under prolonged, scientific, and shattering air attack.

It is for the Italian people, forty millions of them, to say whether they want this terrible thing to happen to their country or not. One man, and one man alone, has brought them to this pass. There was no need for them to go to war:

no one was going to attack them. We tried our best to induce them to remain neutral, to enjoy peace and prosperity and exceptional profits in a world of storm. But Mussolini could not resist the temptation of stabbing prostrate France, and what he thought was helpless Britain, in the back. Mad dreams of imperial glory, the lust of conquest and of booty, the arrogance of long-unbridled tyranny, led him to his fatal, shameful act. In vain I warned him: he would not hearken. On deaf ears and a stony heart fell the wise, far-seeing appeals of the American President. The hyena in his nature broke all bounds of decency and even commonsense. Today his Empire is gone. We have over a hundred Italian generals and nearly three hundred thousand of his soldiers in our hands as prisoners-of-war. Agony grips the fair land of Italy. This is only the beginning, and what have the Italians to show for it? A brief promenade by German permission along the Riviera; a flying visit to Corsica; a bloody struggle with the heroic patriots of Yugoslavia; a deed of undying shame in Greece; the ruins of Genoa, Turin, Milan; and this is only a foretaste. One man and the regime he has created have brought these measureless calamities upon the hard-working, gifted, and once happy Italian people, with whom, until the days of Mussolini, the English-speaking world had so many sympathies and never a quarrel. How long must this endure?

We may certainly be glad about what has lately happened in Africa, and we may look forward with sober confidence to the moment when we can say: one continent relieved. But these successes in Africa, swift and decisive as they have been, must not divert our attention from the prodigious blows which Russia is striking on the eastern front. All the world wonders at the giant strength which Russia has been able to conserve and to apply. The invincible defence of Stalingrad is matched by the commanding military leadership of Stalin. When I was leaving the Kremlin in the middle of August, I said to Premier Stalin: 'When we have decisively defeated Rommel in Egypt, I will send you a telegram.' And he replied: 'When we make our counter-offensive here' (and he drew the arrow on the map), 'I will send you one.' Both messages have duly arrived, and both have been thankfully received.

As I speak, the immense battle, which has already yielded results of the first magnitude, is moving forward to its climax; and this, it must be remembered is only part of the Russian front, stretching from the White Sea to the Black Sea, along which, at many points, the Russian armies are attacking. The jaws of another Russian winter are closing on Hitler's armies – a hundred and eighty German divisions, many of them reduced to little more than brigades by the slaughters and privations they have suffered, together with a host of miserable Italians, Rumanians, and Hungarians, dragged from their homes by a maniac's fantasy: all these as they reel back from the fire and steel of the avenging Soviet armies must prepare themselves with weakened forces and with added pangs for a second dose of what they got last year. They have, of course, the consolation of knowing that they have been commanded and led, not by the German General Staff, but by Corporal Hitler himself.

I must conduct you back to the West – to France, where another vivid scene of this strange melancholy drama has been unfolded. It was foreseen when we were planning the descent upon North Africa that this would bring about immediate reactions in France. I never had the slightest doubt myself that Hitler would break the armistice, overrun all France, and try to capture the French fleet at Toulon; such developments were to be welcomed by the United Nations, because they entailed the extinction for all practical purposes of the sorry farce and fraud of the Vichy Government. This was a necessary prelude to that reunion of France without which French resurrection is impossible. We have taken a long step towards that unity. The artificial division between occupied and unoccupied territory has been swept away. In France all Frenchmen are equally under the German yoke, and will learn to hate it with equal intensity. Abroad all Frenchmen will fire at the common foe. We may be sure that after what has happened, the ideals and the spirit of what we have called Fighting France, will exercise a dominating influence upon the whole

French nation. I agree with General de Gaulle that the last scales of deception have now fallen from the eyes of the French people; indeed, it was time.

'A clever conqueror,' wrote Hitler in *Mein Kampf*, 'will always, if possible, impose his demands on the conquered by instalments. For a people that makes a voluntary surrender saps its own character, and with such a people you can calculate that none of those oppressions in detail will supply quite enough reason for it to resort once more to arms.' How carefully, how punctiliously he lives up to his own devilish doctrines! The perfidy by which the French fleet was ensnared is the latest and most complete example. That fleet, brought by folly and by worse than folly to its melancholy end, redeemed its honour by an act of self-immolation, and from the flame and smoke of the explosions at Toulon, France will rise again.

The ceaseless flow of good news from every theatre of war, which has filled the whole month of November, confronts the British people with a new test. They have proved that they can stand defeat; they have proved that they can bear with fortitude and confidence long periods of unsatisfactory and unexplained inaction. I see no reason at all why we should not show ourselves equally resolute and active in the face of victory. I promise nothing. I predict nothing. I cannot even guarantee that more successes are on the way. I commend to all the immortal lines of Kipling:

> If you can dream – and not make dreams your master;
>   If you can think – and not make thoughts your aim;
> If you can meet with Triumph and Disaster
>   And treat those two imposters just the same –

there is my text for this Sunday's sermon, though I have no licence to preach one. Do not let us be led away by any fairseeming appearances of fortune; let us rather put our trust in those deep, slow-moving tides that have borne us thus far already, and will surely bear us forward, if we know how to use them, until we reach the harbour where we would be.

I know of nothing that has happened yet which justifies the

hope that the war will not be long, or that bitter and bloody years do not lie ahead. Certainly the most painful experiences would lie before us if we allowed ourselves to relax our exertions, to weaken the discipline, unity and order of our array, if we fell to quarrelling about what we should do with our victory before that victory had been won. We must not build on hope or fears, but only on the continued faithful discharge of our duty, wherein alone will be found safety and peace of mind. Remember that Hitler with his armies and his secret police holds nearly all Europe in his grip. Remember that he has millions of slaves to toil for him, a vast mass of munitions, many mighty arsenals, many fertile fields. Remember that Goering has brazenly declared that whoever starves in Europe, it will not be the Germans. Remember that these villains know their lives are at stake. Remember how small a portion of the German Army we British have yet been able to engage and to destroy. Remember that the U-boat warfare is not diminishing but growing, and that it may well be worse before it is better. Then, facing the facts, the ugly facts as well as the encouraging facts, undaunted, then we shall learn to use victory as a spur to further efforts, and make good fortune the means of gaining more.

This much only I will say about the future, and I say it with an acute consciousness of the fallibility of my own judgement. It may well be that the war in Europe will come to an end before the war in Asia. The Atlantic may be calm, while in the Pacific the hurricane rises to its full pitch. If events should take such a course, we should at once bring all our forces to the other side of the world, to the aid of the United States, to the aid of China, and above all to the aid of our kith and kin in Australia and New Zealand, in their valiant struggle against the aggressions of Japan. While we were thus engaged in the Far East, we should be sitting with the United States and with our ally Russia and those of the United Nations concerned, shaping the international instruments and national settlements which must be devised if the free life of Europe is ever to rise again, and if the fearful quarrels which have rent European civilisation are to be prevented from once more disturbing the progress of the world. It seems to me that should the war end thus, in two successive stages, there will be a far higher sense of comradeship around the council table than existed among the victors at Versailles. Then the danger had passed away. The common bond between the Allies had snapped. There was no sense of corporate responsibility such as exists when victorious nations who are masters of one vast scene are, most of them, still waging war side by side in another. I should hope, therefore, that we shall be able to make better solutions – more far-reaching, more lasting solutions – of the problems of Europe at the end of this war than was possible a quarter of a century ago. It is not much use pursuing these speculations farther at this time. For no one can possibly know what the state of Europe or of the world will be, when the Nazi and Fascist tyrannies have been finally broken. The dawn of 1943 will soon loom red before us, and we must brace ourselves to cope with the trials and problems of what must be a stern and terrible year. We do so with the assurance of ever-growing strength, and we do so as a nation with a strong will, a bold heart and a good conscience.

THE DESERT ARMY

A SPEECH TO THE MEN OF THE EIGHTH ARMY AT TRIPOLI, FEBRUARY 3, 1943

General Montgomery and men of the Joint Headquarters of the Eighth Army.

The last time I saw this army was in the closing days of August on those sandy and rocky bluffs near Alamein and the Ruweisat Ridge, when it was apparent from all the signs that Rommel was about to make his final thrust on Alexandria and Cairo. Then all was to be won or lost. Now I come to you a long way from Alamein, and I find this army and its famous commander with a record of victory behind it which has undoubtedly played a decisive part in altering the whole character of the war.

The fierce and well-fought battle of Alamein, the blasting through of the enemy's seaward flank, and the thunderbolt of the armoured attack, irretrievably broke the army which Rommel had boasted would conquer Egypt, and upon which the German and Italian peoples had set their hopes. Thereafter and ever since, in these remorseless three months, you have chased this hostile army and driven it from pillar to post over a distance of more than 1,400 miles – in fact, as far as from London to Moscow. You have altered the face of the war in a most remarkable way.

What it has meant in the skill and organisation of movement and manoeuvres, what it has meant in the tireless endurance and self-denial of the troops and in the fearless leadership displayed in action, can be appreciated only by those who were actually on the post. But I must tell you that the fame of the Desert Army has spread throughout the world.

After the surrender of Tobruk, there was a dark period when many people, not knowing us, not knowing the British and the nations of the British Empire, were ready to take a disparaging view. But now everywhere your work is spoken of with respect and admiration. When I was with the Chief of the Imperial General Staff at Casablanca and with the President of the United States, the arrival of the Desert Army in Tripoli was a new factor which influenced the course of our discussions and opened up hopeful vistas for the future. You are entitled to know these things, and to dwell upon them with that satisfaction which men in all modesty feel when a great work has been finally done. You have rendered a high service to your country and the common cause.

It must have been a tremendous experience driving forward day after day over this desert which it has taken me this morning more than six hours to fly at 200 miles an hour. You were pursuing a broken enemy, dragging on behind you this ever-lengthening line of communications, carrying the whole art of desert warfare to perfection. In the words of the old hymn, you have 'nightly pitched your moving tents a day's march nearer home'. Yes, not only in the march of the army but in the progress of the war you have brought home nearer. I am here to thank you on behalf of His Majesty's Government of the British Isles and of all our friends the world over.

Hard struggles lie ahead. Rommel, the fugitive of Egypt, Cyrenaica, and Tripolitania, in a non-stop race of 1,400 miles, is now trying to present himself as the deliverer of Tunisia. Along the eastern coast of Tunisia are large numbers of German and Italian troops, not yet equipped to their previous standard, but growing stronger. On the other side, another great operation, planned in conjunction with your advance, has carried the First British Army, our American comrades, and the French armies to within 30 or 40 miles of Bizerta and Tunis. Therefrom a military situation arises which everyone can understand.

The days of your victories are by no means at an end, and with forces which march from different quarters we may hope to achieve the final destruction or expulsion from the shores of Africa of every armed German or Italian. You must have felt relief when, after those many a hundred miles of desert, you came once more into a green land with trees and grass, and I do not think you will lose that advantage. As you go forward on further missions that will fall to your lot, you will fight in countries which will present undoubtedly serious tactical difficulties, but which none the less will not have that grim character of desert war which you have known how to endure and how to overcome.

Let me then assure you, soldiers and airmen, that your fellow countrymen regard your joint work with admiration and gratitude, and that after the war when a man is asked what he did it will be quite sufficient for him to say, 'I marched and fought with the Desert Army.' And when history is written and all the facts are known your feats will gleam and glow and will be a source of song and story long after we who are gathered here have passed away.

GOOD CONFIDENCE

Throughout March and April the British Eighth Army (in the east) and the Combined British and American forces (in the west) closed in relentlessly on the Axis armies in North Africa. On April 2, General Rommel's Afrika Korps and General Von Arnim's force in Tunisia joined up to make their last stand in Northern Tunisia and five days later the Eighth Army, which had fought all the way from El Alamein, made contact with the second US Army Corps advancing from Gafsa. At the same time Allied sea- and air-power smashed continuously at German communications and supply lines across the Mediterranean. Rommel was recalled in April and Von Arnim took supreme command on the Axis side. His authority was brief. On May 6, 1943, the Allies launched their last great offensive in Tunisia and in six days finally crushed the enemy. A huge number of prisoners, including Von Arnim himself, were taken and the war in North Africa ended on May 12 in complete and overwhelming victory.

The closing stages of this great campaign, one of the most memorable in military history, are told in the following Parliamentary statements by Mr Churchill.

A STATEMENT TO THE HOUSE OF COMMONS, MARCH 24, 1943

It is my duty to let the House and the country know that this great battle now proceeding in Tunisia has by no means reached its climax and that very much hard fighting now lies before the British and United States forces. The latest information from the Mareth front – later, that is, than that published in this morning's newspapers – shows that the Germans by counter-attacks, have regained the greater part of the bridgehead which had been stormed, and that their main line of defence in that quarter is largely restored. I take occasion to make that statement, as I do not wish hopes for an easy decision to be encouraged. On the other hand, I have good confidence in the final result.

FAVOURABLE TURN

A STATEMENT TO THE HOUSE OF COMMONS,
MARCH 30, 1943

Since I informed the House last week of the check sustained on the Mareth front, the situation has turned very much in our favour. General Montgomery's decision to throw his weight on to the turning movement instead of persisting in the frontal attack has been crowned with success. Another severe defeat has been inflicted by the Desert Army upon the Axis forces they have so long pursued. According to my latest information, we occupied El Hamma last night, and our vanguards passed through Gabes this morning. The decisive breakthrough of General Freyberg's turning force was aided to an extraordinary degree by novel forms of intense air attack, in which many hundreds of British aircraft were simultaneously employed.

The enemy losses in men and material have of course been very serious to him, and the Panzer divisions in particular are remarkably mauled and enfeebled. It is, however, too soon to say what proportion of the Italian 20th and 21st Army Corps has been left behind. The operations are being prosecuted with the utmost energy.

It must be remembered that this new exploit of the Desert Army must be viewed in its relation to the general scheme of action on the whole Tunisian front. The very fine unceasing advance of the United States forces, and the increasing activities in the French sector and on the front of the British First Army, all play their part in the combinations of General

Eisenhower, the supreme commander, and his deputy, General Alexander.

I should not close, however, without uttering a warning against any underrating of the task which lies before the whole group of Allied armies and air forces in Tunisia. The country is very difficult and abounds in defensive positions, but we have every reason to be satisfied with the progress already made by our superior forces and superior equipment under their skilful resolute commanders.

Replying to a Member who asked whether General Montgomery's army included both French and New Zealand troops, the Prime Minister added to his March 30 statement:

Yes, sir. New Zealand troops have actually passed through Gabes this morning. That I am entitled to say, as they are actually in contact with the enemy.

MONTGOMERY'S SURPRISE ATTACK

A STATEMENT TO THE HOUSE OF COMMONS, APRIL 7, 1943

I have received reports from the High Command in Tunisia that a new victory has been gained by the Desert Army. At half-past four yesterday morning, in the darkness of a moonless night, General Montgomery ordered his main forces to the assault of the Akarit position north of Gabes. The advance of the British and Indian infantry divisions was preceded and covered by a barrage of about 500 guns, which is practically the Alamein scale. The enemy appeared to be taken by surprise by this attack out of pitch darkness. His fortified positions were overwhelmed, and by noon all the dominant keypoints were in our hands. A hole had been blasted in the centre of the enemy's twelve mile defensive line, through which our armoured and mobile forces were immediately ordered to advance. The enemy now fought with savage vigour to restore the situation, but all his counter-attacks were repulsed. The advance of the British armour continued, and by nightfall the open country had been reached. Over 6,000 prisoners have been taken so far. Rommel's army is now retreating northward, and is being hotly pursued. This successful battle and frontal attack should enable the Desert Army to join hands with the United States forces who have been pressing the enemy unceasingly from the west. The whole of the operations of the group of armies on the Tunisian front are being concerted by General Alexander under the supreme command of the Allied commander-in-chief, General Eisenhower.

VICTORY MESSAGES

AT THE END OF THE CAMPAIGN IN NORTH AFRICA MR WINSTON CHURCHILL SENT THE FOLLOWING MESSAGES TO THE ALLIED COMMANDERS ON MAY 11, 1943

TO GENERAL EISENHOWER
(Commander-in-Chief of the Allied Forces in North Africa)

Let me add my heartfelt congratulations to those which have been sent to you by His Majesty and the War Cabinet on the brilliant result of the North African campaign by the army under your supreme direction. The comradeship and conduct with which you have sustained troops engaged in the fierce and prolonged battle in Tunisia and the perfect understanding and harmony preserved amidst the shock of war between British and United States forces and with our French allies have proved solid foundation of victory. The simultaneous advance of British and United States armies side by side into Tunis and Bizerta is an augury full of hope for the future of the world.

Long may they march together, striking down the tyrants and oppressors of mankind.

TO GENERAL ALEXANDER
(Deputy Commander-in-Chief of the Allied Forces in North Africa)

It has fallen to you to conduct a series of battles which have ended in the destruction of the German and Italian power in Africa. All the way from Alamein to Tunis, in the ceaseless fighting and marching of the last six months, you and your brilliant lieutenant, Montgomery, have added a glorious chapter to the annals of the British Commonwealth and Empire. Your combinations in the final great battle will be judged by history as a model of the military art. But more than this, you have known how to inspire your soldiers with confidence and ardour which overcame all obstacles and outlasted all fatigue and hardship. They and their trusty United States and French allied soldiers and airmen together can now be told of the admiration and the gratitude with which the entire British nation and the Empire regard them and their famous deeds. The generous rivalry in arms of the First and Eighth British Armies has achieved victory, with full honour for each and for all.

TO AIR-CHIEF-MARSHAL TEDDER
(Air-Commander-in-Chief, Mediterranean)

It is certain the victories in Tunisia would never have been gained without the splendid exertions of the Allied air force under your skilful and comprehending direction. Will you tell Spaatz, Coningham, Doolittle and Broadhurst how much their work is admired. The united, efficient, and individual devotion to duty which enables so amazing a number of sorties to be made each day is beyond all praise.

TO GENERAL GIRAUD
(Commander-in-Chief French Forces in North Africa)

It cheers all our hearts to see a line of French divisions advancing triumphantly against the common foe, and leading German prisoners by the thousand to the rear. Accept my most hearty congratulations on the fighting spirit of the French army under your command, and the tenacity in defence and aggression in assault which it has displayed in spite of being at a disadvantage in equipment. Every good wish.

A TALK TO THE AMERICAN PRESS

DURING HIS VISIT TO WASHINGTON, MR CHURCHILL ATTENDED PRESIDENT ROOSEVELT'S PRESS CONFERENCE AND ANSWERED MANY QUESTIONS ON THE PROGRESS OF THE WAR FROM 150 AMERICAN NEWSPAPER REPRESENTATIVES, MAY 25, 1943

The Allies' future plans are to wage this war to the unconditional surrender of all who have molested us – that applies to Asia as well as to Europe.

The situation is very much more satisfactory than when I was last here. It was in this house that I got the news of the fall of Tobruk. I don't think any Englishman in the United States has ever been so unhappy as I was that day; certainly no Englishman since General Burgoyne surrendered at Saratoga.

Since the attack on Alamein and the descent on North Africa we have had a great measure of success and a decisive victory.

A year ago Russia was subjected to such a heavy attack that it seemed she might lose the Caucasus; but she, too, recovered and gained another series of successes.

Hitler has been struck two tremendous, shattering blows – Stalingrad and Tunisia. In eleven months the Allies have gained some examples of highly successful war-making, and have indisputably turned the balance.

I quote the words of your great general, Nathan Bedford

Forrest, the eminently successful Confederate leader. Asked the secret of his victories, Forrest said, 'I git thar fustest with the mostest men.' The Allies can see a changed situation. Instead of, as hitherto, getting somewhere very late with very little, we are arriving first with most.

There is danger in wishful thinking that victory will come by internal collapse of the Axis. Victory depends on force of arms, I stand pat on a knock-out, but any windfalls in the way of internal collapses will be gratefully accepted.

Italy is a softer proposition than Germany, and the Allies might be aided by a change of heart or a weakening of morale.

No one wishes to take the native soil of Italy from the Italians, who will have their place in Europe after the war. The trouble is that they allow themselves to be held in bondage by intriguers, with the result that they are now in a terrible plight. I think they would be well advised to throw themselves upon the justice of those whom they have so grossly attacked. We shall not stain our name for posterity by any cruel, inhuman acts. It is a matter for the Italians to settle among themselves. All we can do is to apply the physical stimuli which we have at our disposal to bring about a change of mind in these recalcitrant persons. Of this you may be sure: we shall continue to operate on the Italian donkey at both ends, with a carrot and with a stick.

* * *

I am only too anxious to increase the war effort in the Far East. It will be prosecuted with the utmost vigour. We have talked about that, and reached some sound and good decisions. Both the Asiatic and European wars will now be waged with equal force – they will be concurrent, not consecutive. The forces we have at our disposal now make this possible.

It is a matter of the application of our munitions of war, which is a question of shipping. Our principle is that all soldiers and all ships must be engaged all the time on the widest front possible. We are the big animal now, shaking the life out of the smaller animal, and he must be given no rest, no chance to recover.

*   *   *

It is matter of poetic justice that the Allies have attained air superiority, the weapon with which the enemy chose to attempt to subjugate the world. The greater Allied superiority in manufactures will, so far as the air war is concerned, be decisive.

Two thousand tons of bombs were dropped on Dortmund, with, I believe, a highly satisfactory impression.

The recent heavy air blows against the Axis will be continued without cessation, but not to the exclusion of other methods.

To draw the conclusion from my speech before Congress that the United Nations are concentrating on bombing alone as a means of beating Germany would be distorting it. The ultimate results of the incessant Allied aerial offensive against the Axis have yet to be seen. There is nothing like a twenty-four-hour service.

*   *   *

The shipping situation is improving, thanks to the prodigious American production. The surplus over sinkings is substantial, and the killings of U-boats are more than at any previous time.

New inventions and combat efforts have greatly added to the destruction of U-boats, particularly last month. Wonderful things have been thought of, and these discoveries are being freely exchanged between the American and British Navies. Supplies are crossing the ocean on an increasing scale.

*   *   *

HITLER

I know of no reason to suppose that Hitler is not in full control of his faculties and the resources of his country.

I think he probably repents that he brought appetite unbridled and ambition unmeasured to his dealings with other nations.

I have very little doubt that if Hitler could have the past back he would play his hand a little differently. He probably regrets having turned down repeated efforts to avoid war, efforts which almost brought the British Government into disrepute. I should think he now repents that he did not curb his passions before he brought the world to misery.

*   *   *

Referring to the possibility of an early meeting between General Giraud, High Commissioner for French North Africa, and General de Gaulle, leader of the Fighting French, Mr Churchill said:

It will be very satisfactory when this back-chat comes to an end and Frenchmen get together and look to the future and the duty they owe to France rather than to sectional interests.

*   *   *

Replying to a question regarding the prospects of Russia fighting Japan, Mr Churchill said:

The matter has not been overlooked, but I am not giving directions to the Russians. Russia must know that the Japs have watched her with a purely opportunist eye.

I do not feel I should ask the Government to ask any more from Russia. The Russians have held the weight of 190 German divisions and twenty-eight divisions of satellite Axis nations. They have done what no one else could do – torn part of the guts out of the German war machine. They have been grand allies in the heroic fashion.

Russia is in a better position than a year ago. I have the utmost confidence in Russia's ability to hold out this year and hurl back any attack.

'BEFORE THE AUTUMN LEAVES FALL'

A SPEECH AT THE GUILDHALL ON RECEIVING THE
FREEDOM OF THE CITY OF LONDON, JUNE 30, 1943

I am deeply grateful for the kindness with which I am treated, not only here today on this, to me, outstanding occasion, but in the whole discharge of my responsibilities.

The strain of protracted war is hard and severe upon the men at the executive summit of great countries, however lightly care may seem to sit upon them. They have need of all the help and comfort their fellow countrymen can give them. I feel myself buoyed up by your good will here today, and indeed I have felt uplifted through all these years by the consideration with which the British people have treated me, even when serious mistakes have been made. Always they have given a generous measure of trust and friendship, and I have never felt hustled or barracked or racketed in any of the decisions it is my duty to take in conjunction with my colleagues or in regard to matters it is my task to submit to Parliament.

There is no doubt that this consideration shown to their leader by the British people, although far above his deserts, is a very real and practical help in the conduct of the war. It gives me confidence to act and to dare, that is a draught of life amid many toils and burdens. Of all the wars that we have ever waged in the long continuity of our history, there has never been one which more truly united the entire British nation and British race throughout the world than this present fearful struggle for the freedom and progress of mankind.

We entered it of our own free will, without being ourselves directly assaulted. We entered it upon the conviction of purpose which was clearly comprehended by all classes and parties and by the whole mass of the people, and we have persevered together through good and evil fortune without the slightest

215

weakening of our will-power or division of our strength. We entered it ill-prepared and almost unarmed. We entered it without counting the cost, and upon a single spontaneous impulse at the call of honour.

We strove long, too long, for peace, and suffered thereby; but from the moment when we gave our guarantee that we would not stand by idly and see Poland trampled down by Nazi violence, we have never looked back, never flagged, never doubted, never flinched. We were sure of our duty, and we have discharged it and will discharge it, without swerving or slackening, to the end.

We seek no profit, we covet no territory or aggrandisement. We expect no reward and we will accept no compromise. It is on that footing that we wish to be judged, first in our own consciences and afterwards by posterity.

It is even more remarkable that the unity which has existed and endured in this small, densely-populated island should have extended with equal alacrity and steadfastness to all parts of our world-wide Commonwealth and Empire. Some people like the word Commonwealth; others, and I am one of them, are not at all ashamed of the word Empire. But why should we not have both?

Therefore I think the expression British Commonwealth and Empire may well be found the most convenient means of describing this unique association of races and religions, which was built up partly by conquest, largely by consent, but mainly unconsciously and without design, within the all-embracing golden circle of the Crown.

Wars come with great suddenness, and many of the deep, slow courses which lead to the explosion are often hidden from or only dimly comprehended by the masses of the people, even in the region most directly affected. Time, distance, the decorum of diplomacy, and the legitimate desire to preserve peace – all impose their restraints upon public discussion and upon prior arrangements.

Alone in history, the British people, taught by the lessons they had learned in the past, have found the means to attach to the Motherland vast self-governing Dominions upon whom

216

there rests no obligation, other than that of sentiment and tradition, to plunge into war at the side of the Motherland.

None of these Dominions, except Southern Ireland, which does not under its present dispensation fully accept Dominion status, has ever failed to respond, with all the vigour of democratic institutions, to the trumpet-call of a supreme crisis to the overpowering influences and impulses that make Canada, that make Australia – and we have here in Dr Evatt a distinguished Australian – that make New Zealand and South Africa send their manhood across the ocean to fight and die.

In each one of these countries, with their long and varied history behind them, this extraordinary spectacle is an outstanding example of the triumph of mind over matter, of the human heart over fear and short-sighted self-interest.

In the vast sub-continent of India, which we trust will presently find full satisfaction within the British Commonwealth of Nations, the martial races and many others have thronged to the Imperial standards. More than 2,000,000 have joined the armed forces, and have distinguished themselves in many cases during the fiercest conflicts with Germans, Italians and Japanese.

All the great countries engaged in this war count their armies by millions, but the Indian Army has a peculiar characteristic not found in the armies of Britain or the United States or Russia or France or in the armies of our foes, in that it is entirely composed of volunteers. No one has been conscripted or compelled. The same thing is broadly true throughout our great Colonial Empire.

Many scores of thousands of troops have been drawn from the immense tropical spaces, or from lonely islands nursed by the waves of every sea. Many volunteers there were for whom we could not find arms. Many there are for whom even now we cannot find opportunities. But I say that the universal ardour of our Colonial Empire to join in this awful conflict, and to continue in that high temper through all its ups and downs, is the first answer that I would make to those ignorant and envious voices who call into question the greatness of the work we are doing throughout the world, and which we shall still continue to do.

The time came when this loosely and variously knit world-spread association, where so much was left unwritten and undefined, was confronted with the most searching test of all. The mother country, the home of the kingship, this famous island, seemed to enter the very jaws of death and destruction.

Three years ago, all over the world, friend and foe alike – everyone who had not the eye of faith – might well have deemed our speedy ruin was at hand. Against the triumphant might of Hitler, with the greedy Italians at his tail, we stood alone with resources so slender that one shudders to enumerate them even now.

Then, surely, was the moment for the Empire to break up, for each of its widely-dispersed communities to seek safety on the winning side, for those who thought themselves oppressed to throw off their yoke and make better terms betimes with the all-conquering Nazi and Fascist power. Then was the time. But what happened?

It was proved that the bonds which unite us, though supple as elastic, are stronger than the tensest steel. Then it was proved that they were the bonds of the spirit and not of the flesh, and thus could rise superior alike to the most tempting allurements of surrender and the harshest threats of doom. In that dark, terrific, but also glorious hour we received from all parts of His Majesty's Dominions, from the greatest and from the smallest, from the strongest and from the weakest, from the most modern to the most simple, the assurance that we would all go down or come through together. You will forgive me if on this occasion, to me so memorable, here in the heart of mighty London I rejoice in the soundness of our institutions and proclaim my faith in our destiny.

But now I must speak of the great Republic of the United States whose power arouses no fear and whose pre-eminence excites no jealousy in British bosoms. Upon the fraternal association and ultimate alignment of policy of the United States and the British Commonwealth and Empire depends, more than on any other factor, the immediate future of the world. If they walk, or if need be march, together in harmony and in accordance with the moral and political conceptions to which the English-speaking people have given birth, and which are frequently referred to in the Atlantic Charter, all will be well. If they fall apart and wander astray from the commanding beacon-light of their destiny, there is no end or measure to the miseries and confusion which await modern civilisation.

This is not rhetorical extravagance, no genial sentiment for a festive occasion. It is the hard, cold, vindictive truth. Yet there are many light and wayward spirits in both our countries who show themselves by word and action unmindful of this fundamental fact. It is a fact in no way derogatory to other mighty nations now fighting by our side, or to any nation, great or small, making its way through the perils of the present age.

We seek no narrow or selfish combination. We trespass not at all upon the lawful interests and characteristics of any allied or friendly State. We nourish the warmest feelings of fellowship towards the valiant Russian people, with whom we have made a twenty years' treaty of friendship and mutual aid. We foresee an expanding future for the long-enduring Republic of China. We look forward to a revival of the unity and the true greatness of France. We offer loyal and faithful comradeship to all. Nevertheless, the tremendous and awe-inspiring fact stares the British and American democracies between the eyes that acting together we can help all nations safely into harbour, and that if we are divided all will toss and drift for a long time on dark and stormy seas.

You have given me this casket, which contains my title as a Freeman of the City of London. I have not always been wrong about the future of events, and if you will permit me, I shall inscribe some of these words within it as my testament, because I should like to be held accountable for them in years which I shall not see.

It is fitting in a singular manner to speak upon this theme of the fraternal association of Britain and the United States here amid the proud monuments and prouder ruins of the City of London, because nothing ever made a warmer feeling between the British and American peoples than the unflinching resistance of London to the formidable, prolonged assault of the enemy. The phrase 'London can take it', and the proof of it that was given, stirred every generous heart in the United States, and their illustrious chief, watching the whole scene of the world with eyes of experience and conviction, sustained by the Congress of the United States, came to our aid with the famous Lend-Lease Act in a manner most serviceable to the great causes which were at stake.

There is no doubt that the sympathy of the United States for the cause of freedom, and their detestation of the Nazi creed and all the menace that it bears to American institutions, drew the United States so near the edge of the conflict that the foul Japanese saw his chance to make his bid for Asiatic domination by striking his traitor blow at Pearl Harbour. Since then we and the Americans have waged war in common, sharing all alike, taking the rough with the smooth, keeping no accounts of blood or treasure – I do not say as if we were one people, but certainly as though we were one army, one navy, and one air force. And so we shall continue like brothers, certainly until the unconditional surrender of all our foes has been achieved, and I trust thereafter until all due measures have been taken so as to secure over a long period of years our safety from future ill-usage.

Should Hitler's Germany and Mussolini's Italy collapse under the flail of Soviet Russia, and the not inconsiderable exertions of the British and American armies in the Mediterranean and elsewhere, should the war industries of Germany be blasted out of existence by the British and American air-power, should this prime and capital victory be achieved before Japan has been laid low – I stand here to tell you today, as I told the Congress of the United States in your name, that every man, every ship, and every aeroplane in the King's service that can be moved to the Pacific will be sent and will be there maintained in action by the peoples of the British Commonwealth and Empire in priority over all other interests for as many flaming years as are needed to make the Japanese in their turn submit or bite the dust.

I will turn for a moment on this occasion from the tide of world events to our domestic affairs. And here it may justly be said that our slowly-wrought British institutions have proved themselves even better adapted to this crisis than to any we have known in the past. His Majesty has at his disposal a National Government composed of the leading men of all parties, officially authorised by their parties to serve the State and only the State at the present juncture.

On the home front, I submit with diffidence, but with confidence underlying it, that in the four most important spheres of finance, of labour, of agriculture, and food – and several others which I could add – an efficient, vigorous, and successful administration has been provided, and that this will bear comparison not only with what happened in the last war – which we also won and from whose lessons we have profited much – but also is not outclassed by what is happening in any other country or under any other system of government, democratic or totalitarian.

Further I declare that our vast influential newspaper Press has known how to combine independence and liveliness with discretion and patriotism. I rejoice that both Houses of Parliament have preserved and asserted, even in our most perilous and bitter periods, their full authority and freedom. And as a very old House of Commons man I may add that, if I am here today to receive as Prime Minister the honours which you pay me, it is because, and only because, of the resolute, overwhelming, unwearying support which I have received from the oldest, the most famous and the most vital of all existing Parliamentary assemblies.

Finally, of all our institutions there is none which has served us better in the hour of need than our ancient Monarchy. We rely on this, for all that we have is centred upon and at the present time is embodied by the King and Queen, most dearly beloved and honoured by all their country. We all welcome back home our gracious and gallant King from his visit to his victorious army in Africa, and, may I say, none rejoices at his return with more fervour than his Ministers who took the responsibility of advising him not to restrain his royal pleasure in respect of a journey of this peculiar character.

The general progress of the war is satisfactory. In May two great battles were won by the Allies. Everyone has heard about the victory in Tunisia, with 350,000 Germans and Italians made captive or slain, and immense quantities of war material and shipping captured or destroyed. We have rejoiced soberly but all the more profoundly at this signal military episode, which ranks with the magnificent Russian victory at Stalingrad, and takes its place in British eyes and in British annals among our most famous victories of former times.

But there was another victory. A not less notable battle was fought in May in the Atlantic against the U-boats. For obvious reasons much less has been said about that. In May the German Admiralty made extreme exertions to prevent the movement to Great Britain of the enormous convoys of food and war materials which are continually received by us from the United States, and which we must bring in safety and punctually if our war-making capacity is to be maintained. Long lines of U-boats were spread to intercept these convoys, and packs of fifteen or twenty U-boats were then concentrated upon the attempt. To meet this, British and American and Canadian forces of the sea and air hurled their strength upon the U-boats. The fighting took place mainly around the convoys, but also over wide expanses of the ocean. It ended in the total defeat of the U-boat attack.

More than thirty U-boats were certainly destroyed in the month of May, many of them foundering with their crews into the dark depths of the sea. Staggered by these deadly losses, the U-boats have recoiled to lick their wounds and mourn their dead. Our Atlantic convoys came safely through, and now, as the result of the May victory and the massacre of U-boats, we have had in June the best month from every point of view we have ever known in the whole forty-six months of the war. The prodigious ship-building exertions of the United States, and the considerable contribution of Britain and also of Canada, have produced an output of new ships which is somewhere between seven and ten times as great as our losses from enemy action in the month of June. Since the middle of May scarcely a single merchant ship has been sunk in the whole of the North Atlantic, and in June also, although the convoys are not being seriously attacked at the present time, the U-boat losses, which should certainly not be exaggerated, have been most solid and encouraging. I give these facts purposely in a form which conveys the truth without giving precise or detailed information to circles wider than those with which we are ourselves amply concerned.

There are two conclusions to be drawn from them. The first is that we must not assume that this great improvement will be maintained or that bad patches do not lie ahead. The second is that, encouraged by the growing success of our methods, we must redouble our own efforts and ingenuity. The disasters which have overtaken the U-boat campaign in May and also in June have their bearing upon another phase of our offensive war. These two months have seen the heaviest discharge of bombs upon munitions and war-time industrial centres of Germany. Nothing like the shattering effects of this upon the cities of the Ruhr and elsewhere has ever been achieved so far.

Three years ago Hitler boasted that he would 'rub out' – that was the term – the cities of Britain, and certainly in the nine months before he abandoned his attack we suffered very heavy damage to our buildings and grievous hindrance to our life and work, and more than 40,000 of our people were killed and more than 120,000 wounded. But now those who sowed the wind are reaping the whirlwind. In the first half of this year, which ends today, the Royal Air Force alone has cast upon Germany alone thirty-five times the tonnage of bombs which in the same six months of this year has been discharged upon this island. Not only has the weight of our offensive bombing grown and its accuracy multiplied, but our measures of defence, tactical and scientific, have improved beyond all compare. In one single night, nay, mainly in one single hour, we cast upon Düsseldorf, to take an example, 2,000 tons of terrible explosive and incendiary bombs for a loss of thirty-eight aircraft, while in the first half of this same year the enemy has discharged upon us no more than 1,500 tons of bombs at a cost to him of 245 aircraft.

In addition to this, the United States air fleet in this country, already so powerful and growing with extraordinary rapidity, has by its precision daylight bombing inflicted grave injuries upon the most sensitive nerve and key centres of the enemy's war production, and American crews and pilots are continually performing feats of arms of the highest skill with dauntless audacity and devotion. All these facts and tendencies, which, it must be admitted, however prosaically viewed, are by no means wholly unfavourable in their general character, must stimulate our joint exertions in the most intense degree and on an ever-larger scale.

I have never indulged in shallow or fugitive optimism, but I have thought it right to make these statements because I am sure they will not lead to the slightest complacency or to any relaxation of that superb yet awful force which is now being brought into action. These forces will be remorselessly applied to the guilty nation and its wicked leaders, who imagined their superiority of air-power would enable them to terrorise and subjugate first all Europe and afterwards the world. They will be applied, and never was there such a case of the biter bitten.

During the summer our main attack is upon that mainspring of German war industry the Ruhr; but as the nights become longer and as the United States Air Force becomes more numerous our strong arm will lengthen both by night and by day, and there is no industrial or military target in Germany that will not receive as we deem necessary the utmost application of exterminating force. The war industry of Germany has already to some extent been dispersed in the numerous smaller towns. When the cities are disposed of we shall follow it there. Presently the weight of the Russian air attack, now mainly absorbed by their long active fighting front, will contribute an additional quota to the total blitz.

This is, I can quite well believe, a sombre prospect for the German people, and one which Dr Goebbels is certainly justified in painting in the darkest hues. But when we remind ourselves of the frightful tyrannies and cruelties with which the German armies, their gauleiters and subordinate tormentors, are now afflicting almost all Europe; when we read every week of the mass executions of Poles, Norwegians, Dutchmen, Czechoslovaks, Frenchmen, Yugoslavs, and Greeks; when we see these ancient and honoured countries of whose deeds and traditions Europe is the heir, writhing under this merciless alien yoke, and when we see their patriots striking back, with every week a fiercer and more furious desperation, we may feel sure that we bear the sword of justice, and we resolve to use that sword with the utmost severity to the full and to the end.

It is at this point that the heavy defeats recently sustained by the U-boats play their part in the general attack upon German morale. Apart from his mysterious promises of revenge, the one hope which Dr Goebbels holds out to the German people is that though they suffer the extreme tribulation of air bombing, the U-boat on the ocean is inflicting equal or even more deadly injuries upon the British and American power to wage war. When that hope dies, as die it well may, it would appear to the most dispassionate observer that a somewhat bleak and raw outlook is beginning to open itself before Hitler's accomplices and dupes. We must allow these corrective processes to take their course.

Meanwhile this is certainly no time for us to indulge in sanguine predictions. Rather should we remind ourselves of St Paul's Epistle to the Corinthians – 'Wherefore let him that thinketh he standeth take heed lest he fall.' I therefore say no more than that our affairs are in considerably better posture than they were some time ago, and that we intend to remain steadfast and unwearying in doing our duty and doing our best whatever may betide.

I have still to speak of the war in the Mediterranean, about which there is so much talk at the present time. Mussolini's Italian Fascists, who are, after all, only a small privileged portion of the real Italian nation, seem to be already suffering from that war of nerves of which they and their German masters made so much use in former times. So far they have only been subjected to preliminary and discursive bombardment, but they are already speculating feverishly where the blow will fall, against how many of the shores or islands from the Gulf of Lions to the Levant, from the Riviera to the Dodecanese, it may be directed, when the blow will fall, and what will be its weight at each point. It is no part of our business to relieve their anxieties or their uncertainties.

They may remember how they themselves struck at the Turks in Tripoli in bygone years, at Abyssinia in recent times, still later at Albania, and how they fell upon Greece and set out to conquer Egypt. And they may look back regretfully to the days when they used to disturb a peaceful world, and when it rested with their pinchbeck Caesar to settle which weaker community should be struck down first.

I can do nothing to help them to resolve their fears, which, communicated to their allies, may perhaps have led to the remarkably long delay in the opening of the promised German offensive against Russia. But I have some words of caution to say to our own people. First of all, all great military operations are dominated by risks and turns of fortune. I know of no certainty in war. This is particulary true of amphibious war. Therefore any mood of over-confidence should be austerely repressed.

There is another point which should be comprehended. All large amphibious operations, especially if they require the co-operation of two or more countries, require long months of organisation with refinements and complexities hitherto unknown in war. Bold impulses, impatient desires, and sudden flashes of military instinct cannot hasten the course of events.

I cannot go farther today than to say that it is very probable there will be heavy fighting in the Mediterranean and elsewhere before the leaves of autumn fall.

For the rest, we must leave the unhappy Italians and their German tempters and taskmasters to anxieties which will aggravate from week to week and from month to month.

This, however, I will add before I sit down. We, the United Nations, demand from the Nazi, Fascist, and Japanese tyrannies unconditional surrender. By this we mean that their will-power to resist must be completely broken, and that they must yield themselves absolutely to our justice and mercy. It also means that we must take all those far-sighted measures which are necessary to prevent the world from being again convulsed, wrecked and blackened by their calculated plots and ferocious aggressions. It does not mean, and it never can mean, that we are to stain our victorious arms by inhumanity or by mere lust of vengeance, or that we do not plan a world in which all branches of the human family may look forward to what the American Constitution finely calls 'life, liberty, and the pursuit of happiness'.

Mr Churchill later made this short speech in the Mansion House at the luncheon which followed the Guildhall ceremony:

This is indeed a joyous occasion for me, and one which gives me the most lively pleasure – to be received by the ancient City of London, which I have visited so often on political business in varying atmospheres during the last forty or fifty years. To be received with such entire cordiality and treated with so much honour is an immense satisfaction to me. It refreshes me, and will make me do my very best to give good service in the difficult times that lie ahead.

We must not think that the difficult times are over. Death and damnation are no longer at the nation's throat. Survival and victory are well within our grasp, but long may be the road and hard and painful the processes by which we shall arrive at a satisfactory conclusion. But we shall come, bringing other countries with us, out of the frightful welter into which we have been plunged and by which civilisation has been threatened.

I should like to tell you how kind I think it is of you to have asked so many of my friends and colleagues and fellow-workers and chiefs of staff, with whom I am in very close association, and who do the work, and run the war, and bring the victories about. No one can tell whether the struggle will be long or short, and nobody, however bold a prophet he may be, however luxuriant in imagination, can pretend to lift up the veil which lies before the period into which we are moving. All I can say is this – that Britain holds together and retains her old traditions and greatness. However events may go, we shall not only be able to stand firmly ourselves, but to be a guide and help to others who move forward on their path.

I thank the Lord Mayor for his hospitality and for the great honour that has been done to me. This event will always rank in my mind with the very highest days of rejoicing that I have passed in my journey through the world.

THE CALL FOR A THREE-POWER TALK

A WORLD BROADCAST, AUGUST 31, 1943

At the beginning of July, I began to feel the need for a new meeting with the President of the United States and also for another conference of our joint Staffs. We were all delighted when, by a happy inspiration, President Roosevelt suggested that Quebec should be the scene, and when the Governor-General and the Government of Canada offered us their princely hospitalities. Certainly no more fitting and splendid setting could have been chosen for a meeting of those who guide the war policy of the two great Western democracies at this cardinal moment in the Second World War than we have here in the Plains of Abraham, the Château Frontenac, and the ramparts of the Citadel of Quebec, from the midst of which I speak to you now.

Here at the gateway of Canada, in mightly lands which have never known the totalitarian tyrannies of Hitler and Mussolini, the spirit of freedom has found a safe and abiding home. Here that spirit is no wandering phantom. It is enshrined in Parliamentary institutions based on universal suffrage and evolved through the centuries by the English-speaking peoples. It is inspired by the Magna Carta and the Declaration of Independence. It is guarded by resolute and vigilant millions, never so strong or so well armed as today.

Quebec was the very place for the two great Powers of sea and of the air to resolve and shape plans to bring their large and growing armies into closer contact and fiercer grips with the common foe. Here above all, in the capital and heart of French Canada, was it right to think of the French people in their agony, to set on foot new measures for their deliverance, and to send them a message across the ocean that we have not forgotten them, nor all the services that France has rendered to culture and civilisation, to the march of the human intellect and to the rights of men. For forty years or more I have believed in the greatness and virtue of France, often in dark and baffling days I have not wavered, and since the Anglo-French Agreement of 1904 I have always served and worked actively with the French in the defence of good causes.

It was therefore to me a deep satisfaction that words of hope, of comfort and recognition should be spoken, not only to those Frenchmen who, outside Hitler's clutches, march in arms with us, but also to the broad masses of the French nation who await the day when they can free and cleanse their land from the torment and shame of German subjugation. We may be sure that all will come right. We may be sure that France will rise again free, united, and independent, to stand on guard with others over the generous tolerances and brightening opportunities of the human society we mean to rescue and rebuild.

I have also had the advantage of conferring with the Prime Minister of Canada, Mr Mackenzie King, that experienced statesman who led the Dominion instantly and unitedly into the war, and of sitting on several occasions with his Cabinet, and the British and Canadian Staffs have been over the whole ground of the war together. The contribution which Canada has made to the combined effort of the British Commonwealth and Empire in these tremendous times has deeply touched the heart of the Mother Country and of all the other members of our widespread family of States and races.

From the darkest days the Canadian Army, growing stronger year by year, has played an indispensable part in guarding our British homeland from invasion. Now it is fighting with distinction in wider and ever-widening fields. The Empire Air Training Organisation, which has been a wonderful success, has found its seat in Canada, and has welcomed the flower of the manhood of Great Britain, of Australia and New Zealand to her spacious flying-fields and to comradeship with her own gallant sons.

Canada has become in the course of this war an important seafaring nation, building many scores of warships and merchant ships, some of them thousands of miles from salt water, and sending them forth manned by hardy Canadian seamen to guard the Atlantic convoys and our vital life-line across the ocean. The munition industries of Canada have played a most important part in our war economy. Last, but not least, Canada has relieved Great Britain of what would otherwise have been a debt for those munitions of no less than $2,000,000,000.

All this, of course, was dictated by no law. It came from no treaty or formal obligation. It sprang in perfect freedom from sentiment and tradition and a generous resolve to serve the future of mankind. I am glad to pay my tribute on behalf of the people of Great Britain to the great Dominion, and to pay it from Canadian soil. I only wish indeed that my other duties, which are exacting, allowed me to travel still farther afield and tell Australians, New Zealanders, and South Africans to their faces how we feel towards them for all they have done, and are resolved to do.

I mentioned just now the agreement Britain made with France almost forty years ago, and how we have stood by it, and will stand by it, with unswerving faithfulness. But there is another great nation with whom we have made a solemn treaty. We have made a twenty-year treaty of good will and mutual aid with Soviet Russia. You may be sure that we British are resolved to do our utmost to make that good with all our strength and national steadiness.

It would not have been suitable for Russia to be represented at this Anglo-American conference, which, apart from dealing with the immediate operations of our intermingled and interwoven armed forces in the Mediterranean and elsewhere, was largely, if not mainly, concerned with heating and inflaming the war against Japan, with whom the Soviet Government have a five years' treaty of non-aggression.

It would have been an embarrassing invitation for us to send. But nothing is nearer to the wishes of President Roosevelt and myself than to have a threefold meeting with Marshal Stalin. If that has not yet taken place, it is certainly not because we have not tried our best, or have not been willing to lay aside every impediment and undertake further immense journeys for that purpose. It is because Marshal Stalin, in direct command of the victorious Russian armies, cannot at the present time leave the battle-fronts upon which he is conducting operations of vital consequence – not only to Russia, which is the object of ferocious German attack, but also to the common cause of all the United Nations.

To judge by the latest news from the Russian battle-fronts Marshal Stalin is certainly not wasting his time. The entire British Empire sends him our salutes on this brilliant summer campaign, and on the victories of Orel, Kharkov, and Taganrog, by which so much Russian soil has been redeemed and so many hundreds of thousands of its invaders wiped out.

The President and I will persevere in our efforts to meet Marshal Stalin, and in the meantime it seems most necessary and urgent that a conference of the British, United States, and Russian Foreign Ministers, or their responsible representatives, should be held at some convenient place, in order not merely to explore the various important questions connected with the future arrangements for world security, but to carry their discussions to a point where the heads of States and Governments may be able to intervene.

We shall also be very glad to associate Russian representatives with us in the political decisions which arise out of the victories the Anglo-American forces have gained in the Mediterranian. In fact, there is no step which we may take, or which may be forced upon us by the unforeseeable course of this war, about which we should not wish to consult with our Russian friends and allies in the fullest confidence and candour. It would be a very great advantage to us all and indeed to the whole free world, if a unity of thought and decision upon practical measures for the longer future, as well as upon

231

strategic problems, could be reached between the two great opponents of the Hitlerite tyranny.

We have heard a lot of talk in the last two years about establishing what is called a Second Front in Northern France against Germany. Anyone can see how desirable that immense operation of war would be. It is quite natural that the Russians, bearing the main weight of the German armies on their front, should urge us ceaselessly to undertake this task and should in no way conceal their complaints and even reproaches that we have not done it before.

I do not blame them at all for what they say. They fight so well, and they have inflicted such enormous injury upon the military strength of Germany, that nothing they could say in honest criticism of our strategy, or the part we have so far been able to take in the war, would be taken amiss by us, or weaken our admiration for their own martial prowess and achievement.

We once had a fine front in France, but it was torn to pieces by the concentrated might of Hitler; and it is easier to have a front pulled down than it is to build it up again. I look forward to the day when British and American liberating armies will cross the Channel in full force and come to close quarters with the German invaders of France. You would certainly not wish me to tell you when that is likely to happen, or whether it be soon or late; but whenever the great blow is struck, you may be sure that it will be because we are satisfied that there is a good chance of continuing success, and that our soldiers' lives will be expended in accordance with sound military plans and not squandered for political considerations of any kind.

I submit to the judgement of the United Nations, and of history, that British and American strategy, as directed by our combined Chiefs of Staff, and as approved and to some extent inspired by the President and myself, has been the best that was open to us in a practical sense. It has been bold and daring, and has brought into play against the enemy the maximum effective forces that could have been deployed up to the present by Great Britain and the United States, having regard to the limitations of ocean transport, to the peculiar conditions of amphibious warfare, and to the character and training of the armies we possess, which have largely been called into being since the beginning of the war.

Personally, I always think of the Third Front as well as the Second Front. I have always thought that the Western democracies should be like a boxer who fights with two hands and not one. I believe that the great flanking movement into North Africa, made under the authority of President Roosevelt and of His Majesty's Government, for whom I am a principal agent, will be regarded in the after time as quite a good thing to do in all the circumstances.

Certainly it has reaped rich and substantial results. Africa is cleared. All German and Italian armies in Africa have been annihilated, and at least half a million prisoners are in our hands. In a brilliant campaign of thirty-eight days Sicily, which was defended by over 400,000 Axis troops, has been conquered.

Mussolini has been overthrown. The war impulse of Italy has been destroyed, and that unhappy country is paying a terrible penalty for allowing itself to be misled by false and criminal guides. How much easier it is to join bad companions than to shake them off! A large number of German troops have lately been drawn away from France in order to hold down the Italian people, in order to make Italy a battleground, and to keep the war as distant and as long as possible from German soil. By far the greater part of the German Air Force has been drawn off from the Russian front, and indeed is being engaged and worn down with ever-growing intensity, by night and day, by British and American and Canadian airmen.

More than all this, we have established a strategic initiative and potential – both from the Atlantic and from the Mediterranean – of which the enemy can neither measure the weight nor foresee the hour of application. But in the Mediterranean and in our air assaults on Germany the war has prospered. An immense diminution of Hitler's war-making capacity has been achieved by the air bombardment, and of course that bombardment will steadily increase in volume and in accuracy as each successive month passes by.

I readily admit that much of all this would have been impossible in this form or at this time, but for the valiant and magnificent exertions and triumphs of the Russian Army, who have defended their native soil against a vile and unprovoked attack with incomparable vigour, skill, and devotion, and at a terrible price in Russian blood.

No Government ever formed among men has been capable of surviving injuries so grave and cruel as those inflicted by Hitler upon Russia. But under the leadership of Marshal Stalin, and thanks also to the stand made by the British peoples when they were all alone, and to abundant British and American ammunition and supplies of all kinds, Russia has not only survived and recovered from these frightful injuries, but has inflicted, as no other force in the world could have inflicted, mortal damage on the German army machine.

Most important and significant events are taking place in the Balkans as a result of the Russian victories, and also, I believe, of the Anglo-American campaign against Italy. Thrice in the last thirty years the Bulgarian people, who owed their liberation and existence to Russia, have been betrayed against their interest, and to a large extent against their wishes, and driven by evil rulers into disaster. The fate of Boris may serve other miscreants with the reminder that the wages of sin is death.

This is also the time to remember the glorious resistance to the invaders of their native lands of the people of Yugoslavia and of Greece, and of those whom Mr Gladstone once called 'the heroic Highlanders of Montenegro'. The whole of the Balkans is aflame, and the impending collapse of Italy as a war factor will not only remove from the scene the most numerous of their assailants, but will also bring help nearer to those unconquerable races. I look forward with confidence to the day when Yugoslavia and Greece will once again be free – free to live their own lives and decide their own destiny. I take this opportunity to send a message of encouragement to these people and their Governments, and to the Kings of Greece and Yugoslavia, who have never faltered for one moment in their duty, and whom we hope to see restored to their thrones by the free choice of their liberated peoples.

234

Let us then all go forward together, making the best of ourselves and the best of each other; resolved to apply the maximum forces at our command without regard to any other single thought than the attack and destruction of those monstrous and evil dominations which have so nearly cost each and all of us our national lives and mankind its future.

Of course, as I told you, a large part of the Quebec discussions was devoted to the vehement prosecution of the war against Japan. The main forces of the United States and the manhood of Australia and New Zealand are engaged in a successful grapple with the Japanese in the Pacific. The principal responsibility of Great Britain against Japan at present lies on the Indian front and in the Indian Ocean. The creation of a Combined Anglo-American Command over all the forces – land, sea, and air – of both countries in that theatre, similar to what has proved so successful in North-West Africa, has now been brought into effect.

A supreme commander of the South-East Asia front has been chosen, and his name has been acclaimed by British, American, and Chinese opinion. He will act in constant association with Generalissimo Chiang Kai-Shek. It is true that Lord Louis Mountbatten is only forty-three. It is not often under modern conditions and in established military professions that a man gets so great a chance so early. But if an officer having devoted his life to the military art does not know about war at forty-three, he is not likely to learn much more about it later on. As Chief of Combined Operations, Lord Louis has shown rare powers of organisation and resourcefulness. He is what – pendants notwithstanding – I will venture to call 'a complete triphibian', that is to say, a creature equally at home in three elements – earth, air, and water – and also well accustomed to fire. We all wish the new Command and its commander full success in their novel, varied, and certainly most difficult task.

I have been asked several times since I crossed the Atlantic whether I think the Germans will give in this year or whether they will hold out through another – which will certainly be worse for them. There are those who take an over-sanguine

235

view. Certainly we see all Europe rising under Hitler's tyranny. What is now happening in Denmark is only another example. Certainly we see the Germans hated as no race has ever been hated in human history, or with such good reason. We see them sprawled over a dozen once free and happy countries, with their talons making festering wounds, the scars of which will never be effaced. Nazi tyranny and Prussian militarism, those two loathsome dominations, may well foresee and dread their approaching doom.

We cannot measure the full force of the blows which the Russian armies are striking and are going to strike. We cannot measure, though we know it is enormous, the havoc wrought in Germany by our bombing; nor the effects upon a population who have lived so long by making wars in the lands of others, and now, for the first time for more than a century, are having blasting and desolating war brought to their hearths and homes. We cannot yet measure what further results may attend the Anglo-American campaign in the Mediterranean, nor what depression the marked failure, for the time being, of the U-boat warfare on which German hopes were set, or the consequences of the shattering blows which are being struck, may engender in the German mind.

We pass here into the sphere of mass psychology, never more potent than in this modern age. Yet I consider that there are dangers in allowing our minds to dwell unduly upon the favourable circumstances which surround us, and which are so vividly and effectively brought to our notice every day by Press and broadcast.

For myself, I regard all such speculation as to when the war will end as at this moment vain and unprofitable. We did not undertake this task because we had carefully counted the cost, or because we had carefully measured the duration. We took it on because duty and honour called us to it, and we are content to drive on until we have finished the job. If Almighty God in His mercy should lighten or shorten our labours and the torment of mankind, all His servants will be thankful. But the United Nations feel conscious both as States, and as hundreds of millions of individuals, of being called to a high duty,

236

which they will unflinchingly and tirelessly discharge with whatever strength is granted to them, however long the ordeal may last.

See how those who stray from the true path are deceived and punished. Look at this wretched Mussolini and his son-in-law and accomplice Ciano, on whom the curse of Garibaldi has veritably fallen. I have heard that Ciano, explaining one day why Mussolini had plunged his dagger into the back of falling France and dreamed himself almost among the Caesars, said that such a chance would not occur again in 5,000 years. Certainly in June, 1940, the odds and omens seemed very favourable to Fascist ambition and greed.

It is not given to the cleverest and the most calculating of mortals to know with certainty what is their interest. Yet it is given to quite a lot of simple folk to know every day what is their duty. That is the path along which the British Commonwealth and Empire, the great Republic of the United States, the vast Union of Soviet Socialist Republics, the indomitable and innumerable people of China – all the United Nations – that is the path along which we shall march till our work is done and we may rest from our labours, and the whole world may turn with hope, with science, with good sense, and dear-bought experience, from war to lasting peace.

THE WOMEN OF BRITAIN

Throughout the war the hard work and heroism of the women of Britain in the Fighting Services, in Civil Defence and in all sections of industry was an inspiring example to the world. The Prime Minister paid tribute to them in the following speech delivered at a meeting of 6,000 women at the Royal Albert Hall, London.

SEPTEMBER 29, 1943

This impressive and representative gathering marks a definite recognition of the part which women are playing in our struggle for right and freedom. I remember in 1939, at Manchester, making an appeal for a million women to come forward into the war effort in all its forms. That was thought to be a very extravagant proposal at the time, but it is not a third of what has since been required and of what has been forthcoming.

We are engaged in total war. We are engaged in a struggle for life. Although you cannot say that the peril is as imminent as it was in 1940, during that year when we were all alone, nevertheless, if this war were so handled that the unity of national effort were diminished, that its pace and vigour were slackened, that we fell apart, that apathy overtook us, and if this were typical throughout the forces of the United Nations, then indeed another set of dangers, not perhaps so catastrophic in their aspect, but none the less deadly in their character, would march upon us. The war would languish, our soldiers would find themselves short of munitions and services just at the time when they would need them most, just at the time when their action was growing to an ever larger scale.

And the enemy – what is their hope? Their hope is that we shall get wearied, that the democracies will faint and falter on the long road, and that now, in the fifth year of the war, there will be doubts, despondencies and slackness; and then they hope that out of this they will be able, consolidated in their central fortress of Europe or in their remote home islands of Japan, to extract from our weariness and from any divisions which might appear among us the means of making terms to enable them to repair their losses, to regather their forces, and to open upon the world in, it may be, a decade, another war, even more terrible than that through which we are passing. Therefore, the ideas of total war, of fighting for life, must be continually in your mind.

The war effort of our forty-six millions living in Great Britain and Northern Ireland is at the present time justly admired by our allies. Upon the whole, there is no community engaged in this war which is more smoothly, effectively, and exhaustively organised for war; there is no community which presents so many different sides and varieties of war effort.

238

We have to guard the seas; we have to bring in our food and materials; we have to guard our homes against the ever-present threat of oversea attacks, we have to be ready to meet intensive and novel forms of air attack at any time; we have to grow a far greater proportion of our own food than we ever did before; we have to carry on all our vast production of munitions; we have to build warships and merchant ships in large numbers; we have to maintain the life of our civilian population, and take care of the sick, the old and the broken. All this has to be done by this community, and I say that it is a spectacle of marvellous organisation which our country presents at the present time.

This war effort could not have been achieved if the women had not marched forward in millions and undertaken all kinds of tasks and work for which any other generation but our own – unless you go back to the Stone Age – would have considered them unfitted; work in the fields, heavy work in the foundries and in the shops, very refined work on radio and precision instruments, work in the hospitals, responsible clerical work of all kinds, work throughout the munitions factories, work in the mixed batteries – I take a special interest in those – most remarkable societies where there are more women than men, and where the weapons are handled with the utmost skill and proficiency. These mixed batteries have saved scores of thousands of strong men from static employment, and set them free for the field armies and the mobile batteries. Nothing has been grudged, and the bounds of women's activities have been definitely, vastly, and permanently enlarged.

It may seem strange that a great advance in the position of women in the world in industry, in controls of all kinds, should be made in time of war and not in time of peace. One would have thought that in the days of peace the progress of women to an ever larger share in the life and work and guidance of the community would have grown, and that, under the violences of war, it would be cast back. The reverse is true. War is the teacher, a hard, stern, efficient teacher. War has taught us to make these vast strides forward towards a far more complete equalisation of the parts to be played by men and women in society.

I said that now that the conditions in this island present an incomparable example, among the United Nations, of unified, concerted war effort. I cannot expect, after four years of war, that there is much slack to take up; but my friend Mr Bevin, the Minister of Labour, has the greatest possible difficulty in providing for even the approved demands which are made upon him by all the Departments of the State. We are fully extended now, and what we have to do is to hold it, to maintain this effort, through the fifth year of war, or the sixth if need be; for we will never stop until we have achieved our purpose.

In the forthcoming year you will see larger armies fighting, you will see more powerful air forces striking at the hearts of the enemy's country; but the actual demands made upon the British population cannot be greatly increased. The augmentation of munitions will follow from the smoother running of the great processes which are already at work, rather than from any multiplications of the human beings engaged in production. We are, as I say, full out, and to hold that and to maintain that is a tremendous task, and one that will require the utmost firmness of character in all His Majesty's subjects, and extreme care, diligence and vigilance on the part of those who are entrusted with public office in any form. All will be needed in order that we may keep up the tremendous pace at which we are moving, for whatever time is necessary in order to secure the complete, the absolute victory of the good cause.

It is a good cause. No one has any doubt about that. All over the world men and women, under every sky and climate, of every race, creed and colour, all have the feeling that in the casting-down of this monstrous Nazi engine of tyranny, cruelty, greed and aggression – in the casting of it down shattered in pieces, something will affect in a decisive manner its future destinies, and which will even in our own time be marked by very sensible improvement in the conditions under which the great masses of the people live.

240

Freedom will be erected on unshakable foundations, and at her side will be Right and Justice; and I am sure of this, that when the victory is gained we shall show a poise and temper as admirable as that which we displayed in the days of our mortal danger, that we shall not be led astray by false guides either into apathy and weakness or into brutality, but that the name of our dear country, our island home, will, by our conduct, by our clairvoyance, by our self-restraint, by our inflexible tenacity of purpose, long stand in honour amongst the nations of the world.

In all this the women of Britain have borne, are bearing, and will continue to bear, a part which excites admiration among our allies, and will be found to have definitely altered those social and sex balances which years of convention had established.

I have no fear of the future. Let us go forward into its mysteries, let us tear aside the veils which hide it from our eyes, and let us move onward with confidence and courage. All the problems of the post-war world, some of which seem so baffling now, will be easier of solution once decisive victory has been gained, and once it is clear that victory won in arms has not been cast away by folly or by violence when the moment comes to lay the broad foundations of the future world order, and it is time to speak great words of peace and truth to all.

'BEATING THE LIFE OUT OF GERMANY'

Week by week, throughout 1943, the air offensive against Germany grew more powerful and the devastation inflicted on the industrial areas and communications more crippling.

On October 11, Mr Winston Churchill sent messages of congratulations on the great air attack to Lieut-General Jacob L. Devers, Commanding-General European Theatre of Operations, United States Army Air Force, and Air Chief Marshal Sir Arthur Harris, Commander-in-Chief, Bomber Command.

TO GENERAL DEVERS

I shall be obliged if you will convey to General Eaker and his command the thanks of the British War Cabinet for the magnificent achievements of the Eighth Air Force in the Battle of Germany in recent days, culminating in their remarkable successes of last week.

In broad daylight the crews of your bombers have fought their way through the strongest defence which the enemy could bring against them, and have ranged over the length and breadth of Germany, striking with deadly accuracy many of the most important hostile industrial installations and ports.

Your bombers and the fighters which support them in these fierce engagements have inflicted serious losses on the German Air Force, and, by forcing the enemy to weaken other fronts, have contributed notably to the successes of the Allied arms everywhere.

The War Cabinet extend their congratulations also to the ground crews of the Eighth Air Force, without whose technical skill and faithful labour these feats of arms would not be possible.

I am confident that with the ever-growing power of the Eighth Air Force, striking alternate blows with the Royal Air Force Bomber Command, we shall together inexorably beat the life out of industrial Germany, and thus hasten the day of final victory.

TO AIR CHIEF-MARSHAL HARRIS

The War Cabinet have asked me to convey to you their compliments on the recent successes of Bomber Command, whose deeds in the first week of October mark yet another stage in the offensive against Germany.

The War Cabinet realise that the results of this campaign are not restricted to damage which can be seen and photographed, but are reflected with equal significance in the extent to which the German Air Force has been forced from the offensive to the defensive, both operationally and in new construction, and

242

compelled to concentrate more and more of its resources on the protection of Germany against bombing attacks from the west, to the benefit of our own and Allied forces on the other European fronts.

Your command, with day-bomber formations of the Eighth Air Force fighting alongside it, is playing a foremost part in the converging attack on Germany now being conducted by the forces of the United Nations on a prodigious scale. Your officers and men will, I know, continue their efforts in spite of the intense resistance offered, until they are rewarded by the final downfall of the enemy.

These growing successes have only been achieved by the devotion, endurance, and courage for which Bomber Command is renowned. Airmen and airwomen of Britain, the Dominions, and our allies have worked wholeheartedly together to perfect the mighty offensive weapon which you wield in a battle watched by the world.

I request you to bring this message to the attention of all members of your command.

ILLNESS

In December, 1943, the people of the Allied nations were shocked to learn that Mr Churchill had been taken seriously ill following his meetings with Marshal Stalin and President Roosevelt and was suffering from pneumonia. From Egypt the Prime Minister went to Marrakesh for convalescence and issued the following message for general publication.

DECEMBER 29, 1943

Now that I am leaving the place where I have been staying for 'an unknown destination', after more than a fortnight's illness, I wish to express my deep gratitude to all who have sent me kind messages or otherwise helped me. I had planned to visit the Italian front as soon as the conferences were over,

243

but on December 11, I felt so tired out that I had to ask General Eisenhower for a few days' rest before proceeding. This was accorded me in the most generous manner.

The next day came the fever, and the day after, when the photographs showed that there was a shadow on one of my lungs, I found that everything had been foreseen by Lord Moran. Excellent nurses and the highest medical authorities in the Mediterranean arrived from all quarters as if by magic. This admirable M and B, from which I did not suffer any inconvenience, was used at the earliest moment, and after a week's fever the intruders were repulsed. I hope all our battles will be equally well conducted. I feel a good deal better than at any time since leaving England, though of course a few weeks in the sunshine are needed to restore my physical strength.

I did not feel so ill in this attack as I did last February. The M and B, which I may also call Moran and Bedford, did the work most effectively. There is no doubt that pneumonia is a very different illness from what it was before this marvellous drug was discovered. I have not at any time had to relinquish my part in the direction of affairs, and there has been not the slightest delay in giving the decisions which were required from me. I am now able to transact business fully. I have a highly efficient nucleus staff, and am in full daily correspondence with London; and though I shall be resting for a few weeks I shall not be idle, providing of course that we do not have any setbacks.

I thought that some of those who have been so kind as to inquire, or express themselves in friendly terms, about me, would like to have this personal note from me, which they will please take as conveying my sincere thanks.

'THE HOUR OF OUR GREATEST EFFORT IS APPROACHING'

A WORLD BROADCAST, MARCH 26, 1944

I hope you will not imagine that I am going to try to make you some extraordinary pronouncement tonight, and tell you exactly how all the problems of mankind in war and peace are going to be solved. I only thought you would like me to have a short talk with you about how we are getting on, and to thank you for all the kindness with which you have treated me in spite of my many shortcomings.

It is a year almost to a day since I spoke to you on the broadcast here at home. This has been a time of disappointments as well as successes. But there is no doubt that the good news has far outweighed the bad, and that the progress of the United Nations towards their goal has been solid, continual and growing quicker.

The long and terrible march which the rescuing Powers are making is being accomplished stage by stage, and we can now say, not only with hope but with reason, that we shall reach the end of our journey in good order, and that the tragedy which threatened the whole world and might have put out all its lights and left our children and descendants in darkness and bondage – perhaps for centuries – that tragedy will not come to pass.

He is a rash man who tries to prophesy when, how, and under what conditions victory will come, but come it will. That at least is sure. It is also certain that unity of aims and action and singleness of purpose among us all – Britons at home, Allies abroad – will make it come sooner.

A year ago the Eighth Army, which had marched 1,500 miles across the desert from Alamein, was in battle for the Mareth Line, and the First British Army and the American

245

army were fighting their way forward through Tunisia. We were all confident of victory, but we did not know that in less than two months the enemy would be driven with heavy slaughter from the African continent, leaving at one stroke 335,000 prisoners and dead in our hands.

Since then the successful campaign in Sicily brought about the fall of Mussolini and the heartfelt repudiation by the Italian people of the Fascist creed. Mussolini indeed escaped to eat the bread of affliction at Hitler's table, to shoot his son-in-law, and help the Germans wreak vengeance upon the Italian masses whom he had professed to love, and over whom he had ruled for more than twenty years. This fate and judgement, more terrible than death, has overtaken the vainglorious dictator who stabbed France in the back and thought his crime had gained him the empire of the Mediterranean.

The conquest of Sicily and Naples brought in their train the surrender of Sardinia and the liberation of Corsica, islands which had been expected to require for themselves a serious expedition and a hard campaign. We now hold one-third of the mainland of Italy. Our progress has not been as rapid or decisive as we had hoped. I do not doubt that we shall be victors both at the Anzio beachhead and on the main front to the southward, and that Rome will be rescued.

Meanwhile we have swept out of the struggle sixty-six Italian divisions, and we are holding in Italy, for the most part in close action, nearly twenty-five German divisions and a noteworthy part of the German air force, all of whom can burn and bleed in the land of their former ally while other even more important events which might require their presence are impending elsewhere.

We have been disappointed in the Aegean Sea and its many islands, which we have not yet succeeded in dominating, but these setbacks in the Eastern Mediterranean are offset and more than offset by the panic and frenzy which prevail in Hungary, Rumania, and Bulgaria, by the continued activities of the Greek guerillas, and, above all, by the heroic struggles of the Partisans of Yugoslavia under the leadership of Marshal Tito.

In the Near and Middle East we have certainly travelled a long way forward from those autumn days of 1940 when we stood all alone, when Mussolini was invading Egypt, when we were driven out of British Somaliland, when all Ethiopia was in Italian chains, and when we wondered whether we could defend the Suez Canal, the Nile Valley, the Sudan, and British East Africa. There is much still to be done in the Balkans and the Eastern Mediterranean, but here again I do not doubt that the task will be finished in a workmanlike manner.

We who dwell in the British Isles must celebrate with joy and thankfulness our deliverance from the mortal U-boat peril, which deliverance lighted the year which has ended. When I look back upon the fifty-five months of this hard and obstinate war, which makes ever more exacting demands upon our life-springs of energy and contrivance, I still rate highest among the dangers we have overcome the U-boat attacks upon our shipping, without which we cannot live or even receive the help which our Dominions and our grand and generous American ally have sent us.

But there are other deliverances which we should never forget. There was the mining peril, the sea-mining peril, which loomed so large in 1939, and which has been mastered by superior science and ingenuity, and by the often forgotten but almost unsurpassed devotion to duty of our minesweeper crews and the thousands of ships they work and man that we may eat and live and thus fight for the good cause. We have been delivered from the horrors of invasion at a time when we were almost unarmed.

We have endured without swerving or failing the utmost fury which Hitler could cast upon us from the air, and now the tables are turned, and those who sought to destroy their enemies by the most fearful form of warfare are themselves reeling and writhing under the prodigious blows of British and American air-power. We had ourselves a large air force in these islands this time last year. We have a larger one today.

Besides all that, our American allies have now definitely overtaken and outnumbered us in the mighty air force they have established here. The combination in true brotherhood

247

of these two air forces – either of which is nearly as large in number as, and in power is much greater than, the whole air force of Germany, aided as it will be by another Allied air force in Italy almost as large, now established there, will produce results in these coming months which I shall not attempt to measure in advance, but which will certainly be of enormous advantage to the cause of the Allies.

Not only have the British and Americans this great preponderance in numbers, which enables them to send 1,000 bombers as often as the enemy is able to send 100 against us, but also, by sharing all our secrets with one another, we have won the leadership in the marvels of radar both for attack and defence.

Surveying these famous and massive events, land, sea, and air, in the war waged by the two western allies, Britain and the United States, against Hitlerism, we are entitled – nay bound – to be encouraged, to be thankful, and to resolve to do better than we have ever done before.

It would be quite natural if our Soviet friends and allies did not appreciate the complications and difficulties which attend all sea-crossing – amphibious is the word – operations on a large scale. They are the people of the great land spaces, and when they face a threat to the sacred soil of Russia it is by land that they march out to meet and attack their foes. Our tasks are different. But the British and American peoples are filled with genuine admiration for the military triumphs of the Russian armies.

I have paid repeated tributes to their splendid deeds, and now I must tell you that the advance of their armies from Stalingrad to the Dniester river, with vanguards reaching out towards the Pruth, a distance of 900 miles, accomplished in a single year, constitutes the greatest cause of Hitler's undoing. Since I spoke to you last not only have the Hun invaders been driven from the lands they had ravaged, but the guts of the German Army have been largely torn out by Russian valour and generalship.

The peoples of all the Russias have been fortunate in finding in their supreme ordeal of agony a warrior leader, Marshal

Stalin, whose authority enabled him to combine and control the movements of armies numbered by many millions upon a front of nearly 2,000 miles, and to impart a unity and a concert to the war direction in the east which has been very good for Soviet Russia and for all her allies.

I have now dealt with the progress of the war against Hitlerite Germany. But I must also speak of the other gigantic war which is proceeding against the equally barbarous and brutal Japanese. This war is waged in vast preponderance by the fleets, air forces, and armies of the United States. We have accepted their leadership in the Pacific Ocean just as they have accepted our leadership in the Indian theatre.

We are proud of the contribution made by Australia and New Zealand against Japan. The debt which the British Empire and Commonwealth of Nations owe to the United States for the fact that their operations against the Japanese shielded Australia and New Zealand from Japanese aggression and from mortal peril during a period when the Mother Country was at full stretch in the struggle against Germany and Italy is one that will never be forgotten in any land where the Union Jack is flown.

Remarkable success has attended the work of the American Navy and of the American, Australian, and New Zealand troops. The progress in New Guinea is constant. The American victories in the Pacific, and in particular their latest conquest and liberation of the Marshall Islands, constitute superb examples of the combination of naval, air, and military force.

It is possible that the war in the Pacific may progress more rapidly than was formerly thought possible. The Japanese are showing signs of grave weakness. The attrition of their shipping, especially their oil tankers, and of their air forces, on all of which President Roosevelt dwelt with sure foresight a year ago, has become not merely evident but obvious.

The Japanese have not felt strong enough to risk their Fleet in a general engagement for the sake of their outer defence line. In this they have been prudent, considering the immense expansion of the United States naval power since the Japanese treacherous assault on Pearl Harbour. What fools the Japanese ruling caste were to bring against themselves the mighty, latent war-energies of the great Republic, all for the sake of carrying out a base and squalid ambuscade!

The British Empire and Commonwealth of Nations have pledged themselves to fight side by side with the United States against Japan no matter what it costs or how long it lasts. Actually we have suffered from the Japanese injuries even greater than those which have roused the armed wrath of the American Union. In our theatre of war, in Burma and the Bay of Bengal, we shall strive our utmost to aid the Americans in their contacts with China and to add to our own.

The more we can fight and engage the Japanese, and especially wear down their air-power, the greater the diversion we make from the Pacific theatre and the more help we give the operations of the United States.

In Burma those plans which were prepared last August at Quebec are now being put into practice. Young men are at the helm. Admiral Mountbatten has infused a spirit of energy and confidence into the heavy forces gathered to recover Burma and by that means to defend the frontiers of India and reopen the road to China. Our airborne operations enable us to attack the Japanese in rear. They for their part have also got behind our front by infiltration at various places, and fierce fighting is going on at many points.

It is too soon to proclaim results in this vast area of mountain and jungle, but in nearly every combat we are able to count three or four times more Japanese dead, and that is what matters, than we have ourselves suffered in killed, wounded, and missing.

Individual fighting superiority in the jungle has definitely passed to the British and Indian soldiers as compared with the Japanese. Farther to the north an American column of experienced jungle-fighters and a considerable Chinese army under General Stilwell, of the United States Service, are progressing with equal mastery. Later on I shall make to you or to Parliament a further report on all this hard fighting, which, mind you, is not by any means decided yet. Meanwhile we have placed a powerful battle-fleet under Admiral Somerville in

Indian waters in order to face the main part of the Japanese Fleet should it turn westward after having declined battle against the Americans.

When I spoke a year ago I drew attention to the possibility that there would be a prolonged interval between the collapse of Hitler and the downfall of Japan. I still think there will be an interval, but I do not consider it will necessarily be as long an interval as I thought a year ago. But be it long or short, we shall go through with our American brothers with our utmost strength to the very end.

I have now tried to carry you as if in a Mosquito aircraft on reconnoitring duty over the world-wide expanse of this fell and ferocious war, and I trust you have gained not only some glimpses of particular scenes, but also a feeling of the relative size and urgency of the various things that are going on. There are, as you see, quite a lot of things going on.

Still, I remember that when I spoke to you on March 21 of last year, I gave up the main part of what I said to what we were planning to do to make our island a better place for all its people after the war was over, whenever that should be.

I told you there would have to be a General Election and a new House of Commons, and that if I were still thought fit to be of any further use, I should put to the country a Four Years' Plan to cover the transition period between war and peace, and to bring the soldiers, sailors, and airmen back to a land where there would be food, work, and homes for all. I dwelt on how wrong it would be to make promises which could not be fulfilled and for one set of politicians to try to outbid another in visionary scheming and dreaming. But I mentioned five or six large fields in which practical action would have to be taken.

Let me remind you of them. A reform and advance on a great scale in the education of the people and a nation-wide uplifting of their physical health. I spoke of the encouragement of agriculture and food production and the vigorous revival of healthy village life. I dwelt upon the importance of a national compulsory insurance scheme for all classes, for all purposes, from the cradle to the grave, and of a sound scheme of demobilisation which would not delay the rebuilding of industry and would not seem unfair to the fighting men.

I also spoke about the maintenance of full employment, and about the rebuilding of our cities and the housing of the people, and I made a few tentative suggestions about economic and financial policy, and what one may well call the importance of making both ends meet. All this was to happen after war was over. No promises were to be made beforehand; but every preparation that was possible, without impeding the war effort, including legislative preparation, was to be set on foot.

Now, my friends, as your unfailing kindness encourages me to call you, I am a man who has no unsatisfied ambitions except to beat the enemy and help you in any way I think right, and therefore I hope you will not suppose, that in what I am going to say to you I am looking for votes or trying to glorify this party or that.

But I do feel I may draw your attention to the fact that several of these large measures, which a year ago I told you might be accomplished after the war was over, have already been shaped and framed and presented to Parliament and the public.

For instance, you have the greatest scheme of improved education that has ever been attempted by a responsible Government. This will soon be on the Statute book. It involves a heavy cost upon the State; but I do not think we can maintain our position in the post-war world unless we are an exceptionally well-educated people, and unless we can handle easily and with comprehension the problems and inventions of the new scientific age.

Then there is the very far-reaching policy of a National Health Service, which has already been laid before Parliament in outline and has received a considerable measure of acceptance. Before this session is out we shall lay before you our proposals for the extension of National Insurance, upon which a vast amount of patient work has been done.

So here you have, or will have very shortly, three of the important measures which I thought would be put off till after the war, already fashioned and proclaimed at a time when no one can tell when the war will end, and all this has been done without relaxing the war effort or causing any party strife to mar the national unity.

But there are several other large problems upon which Ministers and their assistants have toiled and wrought which are far advanced, and, indeed, if this process continues and the war goes on long enough, the greater part of my Four Years' Plan of a year ago may well be perfected and largely in operation before we reach the General Election and give the people a chance to say what they think about it.

Now I must say that one might have expected that His Majesty's Government would receive many compliments on the remarkable progress they have made, not only with the war, but with the preparations for social and domestic welfare at the armistice or peace. Last October I thought the time had come to ask the King to appoint Lord Woolton Minister of Reconstruction with a seat in the War Cabinet. His was a record which rightly commanded respect.

However, there is a large number of respectable and even eminent people, who are not at all burdened with responsibility, who have a lot of leisure on their hands, and who feel most sincerely that the best work they can do at this present time of hard effort and anxiety is to belabour the Government with criticism, and condemn them as unprofitable servants because they are not, in the midst of this deadly struggle, ready at any moment to produce fool-proof solutions for the whole future of the world as between nation and nation, as between victors and vanquished, as between man and man, as between Capital and Labour, as between the State and the individual, and so forth and so on.

The harshest language is used, and this National Government, which has led the nation and the Empire, and, as I hold, a large part of the world, out of mortal danger, through the dark valleys into which they had wandered largely through their own folly back to the broad uplands where the stars of peace and freedom shine, is reviled as a set of dawdlers and muddlers unable to frame a policy, or take a decision, or make a plan and act upon it.

253

I know you, around your firesides, will not forget that this Administration, formed in the hour of disaster by the leaders of the Conservative, Labour, and Liberal Parties banded together in good faith and good will, has brought the British Isles and the British Commonwealth and Empire 'out of the jaws of death, back from the mouth of hell, while all the world wondered'. I know you will not forget that.

There are two subjects of domestic policy which I mentioned last year on which we have not yet produced our course of action. The first is housing. We set before ourselves, as a prime responsibility, the provision of homes for all who need them, with priority for our service men as and when they come home from the war.

Let me first of all lay down this absolute rule. Nothing can or must be done in housing or rehousing which, by weakening or clogging the war effort, prolongs the war. Neither labour nor material can be diverted in any way which hampers the vast operations which are in progress or impending.

Subject to that, there are three ways in which the business of housing and rehousing the people should be attacked.

I do not take the view myself that we were a nation of slum-dwellers before the war. Nearly 5,000,000 new approved houses or dwellings were built in this small island between the two wars, and the British people as a whole were better housed than almost any people on the continent of Europe or, I will add, in many parts of the United States of America.

But now about a million homes have been destroyed or grieviously damaged by the fire of the enemy. This offers a magnificent opportunity for rebuilding and replanning, and, while we are at it, we had better make a clean sweep of all those areas of which our civilisation should be ashamed.

However, I have given my word that, so far as it may lie in my power, the soldiers when they return from the war and those who have been bombed out and made to double up with other families shall be restored to homes of their own at the earliest possible moment.

The first attack must evidently be made upon houses which are damaged but which can be reconditioned into proper dwellings. This must go forward during the war, and we hope to have broken the back of it during the war. It is a war measure, for our allies are here among us in vast numbers, and we must do our best for them.

The second attack on the housing problem will be made by what are called the prefabricated or emergency houses.

On this the Minister of Works, Lord Portal, is working wonders. I hope we may make up to half a million of these, and for this purpose not only plans but actual preparations are being made during the war on a nation-wide scale.

Factories are being assigned, the necessary set-up is being made ready, materials are being earmarked as far as possible, the most convenient sites will be chosen. The whole business is to be treated as a military evolution handled by the Government, with private industry harnessed to its service; and I have every hope and a firm resolve that several hundred thousand of our young men will be able to marry several hundred thousand of our young women and make their own four years' plan.

Now what about these emergency houses? I have seen the full-sized model myself, and steps are being taken to make sure that a good number of housewives have a chance of expressing their views about it. These houses will make a heavy demand upon the steel industry, and will absorb in a great measure its overflow and expansion for war purposes.

They are, in my opinion, far superior to the ordinary cottage as it exists today; not only have they excellent baths, gas or electric kitchenettes and refrigerators; but their walls carry fitted furniture – chests of drawers, hanging cupboards and tables – which today it would cost £80 to buy.

Moreover, for the rest of the furniture, standard articles will be provided and mass-produced, so that no heavy capital charge will fall upon the young couples, or others who may become tenants. Owing to the methods of mass-production which will be used, I am assured that these houses, including the £80 worth of fitted furniture, will be available at a very moderate rent. All these emergency houses will be publicly owned, and it will not rest with any individual tenants to keep them in being after they have served their purpose of tiding over the return of the fighting men and after permanent dwellings are available. As much thought has been and will be put into this plan as was put into the invasion of Africa, though I readily admit that it does not bear comparison in scale with the kind of things we are working at now. The swift production of these temporary houses is the only way in which the immediate needs of our people can be met in the four or five years that follow the war.

In addition to this and to the reconditioning of the damaged dwellings, we have the programme of permanent rebuilding which the Minister of Health has recently outlined and by which we shall have 200,000 or 300,000 permanent houses built or building by the end of the first two years after the defeat of Germany. For these, 200,000, sites are already owned by the local authorities.

Side by side with this comes the question of the employment of the building trade. We do not want a frantic splurge of building, to be followed by a sharp contraction of the trade. I have sympathy with the building trade and with the bricklayers. They are apt to be the first to be taken for the wars, and in time of peace they all know, as they work at their job, that when it is finished they may have to look for another. If we are to secure the best results, it will be necessary that our Twelve Years' Plan for the building trade, on which Mr Bevin and Lord Portal have spent so much time, shall guarantee steady employment for long periods and increased reward for increased efforts or superior skill, and this will be carried out. Then we are told by the busy wiseacres: 'How can you build houses without the land to put them on? When are you going to tell us your plans for this?'

But we have already declared, in 1941, that all land needed for public purposes shall be taken at prices based on the standards of values of March 31, 1939. This was a formidable decision of State policy which selected property in land for a special restrictive imposition. Whereas stocks and shares and many classes of real property have gone up in value during the war, and when agricultural land, on account of the new proposals and prospects open to farmers, has also risen in value, the State has the power, which it will on no account surrender, to claim all land needed *bona fide* for war industry or for public purposes, at values fixed before wartime conditions supervened.

There are certain hard cases which will be best adjusted by Parliamentary debate, but in the main, you may be sure that ample land will be forthcoming when and where it is needed for all the houses, temporary or permanent, required to house our people far better than they have ever been housed before.

Nobody need be deterred from planning for the future by the fear that they may not be able to obtain the necessary land. Legislation to enable local authorities to secure any land required for the reconstruction of our towns has been promised and will be presented to Parliament this session.

There are some comfortable people, of course, who want to put off everything until they have planned and got agreed in every feature a White Paper or a blueprint for the regeneration of the world, before, of course, asking the electors how they feel about it. The people would rather postpone building the homes for the returning troops until they had planned out every acre in the country to make sure the landscape is not spoiled. In time of war we have to face immediate needs and stern realities, and it surely is better to do that than to do nothing while preparing to do everything.

Here is my difficulty. I cannot take any step that will hinder the war – and no one except the very clever ones can tell when the war will end, or whether it will end suddenly or peter out. Therefore, there must be an emergency plan, and that is what Ministers concerned have been working at for some time past. But in spite of this and of all I have said, I cannot guarantee that everything will be perfect or that if the end of the war came suddenly, as it might do, there will not be an interval when things will be pretty rough. But it will not be a long interval, and it will be child's play compared to what we have gone through.

Nor need we be frightened about the scale of this task. It looks to me a small one – this housing – compared with some of those we have handled and are handling now. The value of the land involved is between one-twentieth and one-thirtieth of the cost of the houses to be built upon it, and our population itself is unhappily about to enter upon a period of numerical decline which can only be checked by the most robust treatment of housing and all its ancillaries.

There is one other question on which I should like to dwell tonight, but for a reason which I will mention later I only intend to utter a passing reassurance. I mean demobilisation. Now I know as much about this as most people, because I was Secretary of State for War and Air at the time of the great demobilisation after the last war, when in about six months we brought home from abroad, released from military service, and restored to their families, nearly 3,000,000 men.

Great plans had been prepared before the Armistice by the planners to bring home all the key men first, and any soldier who could get a telegram from someone at home saying that he was wanted for a key job had priority over the man who had borne the burden and heat of the war. The troops did not think this was fair, and by the time I went to the War Office a convulsion of indiscipline shook the whole of our splendid Army, which had endured unmoved all danger, slaughter, and privation. I persuaded the Cabinet to reverse this foolish and inequitable plan and substitute the simple rule 'First out first home', and the process of demobilisation went forward in a smooth and orderly fashion.

Now my friend Mr Bevin, the Minister of Labour, for whose deep sagacity and knowledge of the wage-earning masses I have high admiration, has devised a very much less crude, but equally fair and healthy scheme, in which I have the greatest confidence, in which all concerned may have the greatest confidence. Why am I not going to tell you all about it tonight, or why will Mr Bevin not tell you about it in the near future?

Here is the reason. This is no time to talk about demobilisation. The hour of our greatest effort and action is approaching. We march with valiant allies who count on us as we count on them. The flashing eyes of all our soldiers, sailors, and airmen must be fixed upon the enemy on their front. The only homeward road for all of us lies through the arch of victory. The magnificent armies of the United States are here or are pouring in. Our own troops, the best trained and best equipped we have ever had, stand at their side in equal numbers and in true comradeship. Leaders are appointed in whom we all have faith. We shall require from our own people here, from Parliament, from the Press, from all classes, the same cool, strong nerves, the same toughness of fibre, which stood us in good stead in those days when we were all alone under the blitz.

And here I must warn you that in order to deceive and baffle the enemy as well as to exercise the forces, there will be many false alarms, many feints, and many dress rehearsals. We may also ourselves be the object of new forms of attack from the enemy. Britain can take it. She has never flinched or failed. And when the signal is given, the whole circle of avenging nations will hurl themselves upon the foe and batter out the life of the cruellest tyranny which has ever sought to bar the progress of mankind.

THE LANDING IN NORMANDY

STATEMENTS TO THE HOUSE OF COMMONS ON THE LIBERATION OF ROME AND THE LANDING IN FRANCE, JUNE 6 AND 8, 1944

The House should, I think, take formal cognisance of the liberation of Rome by the Allied armies under the command of General Alexander, with General Clark of the United States Service and General Oliver Leese in command of the Fifth and Eighth Armies respectively. This is a memorable and glorious event, which rewards the intense fighting of the last five months in Italy. The original landing, made on January 22 at Anzio, has, in the end, borne good fruit. In the first place, Hitler was induced to send to the south of Rome eight or nine divisions which he may well have need of elsewhere. Secondly, these divisions were repulsed, and their teeth broken, by the successful resistance of the Anzio bridgehead forces in the important battle which took place in the middle of February. The losses on both sides were heavy – the Allies losing about 20,000 men, and the Germans about 25,000 men. Thereafter, the Anzio bridgehead was considered by the enemy to be impregnable.

Meanwhile, the great regrouping of the main army had to take place before the attacks could be renewed. These attacks were at first unsuccessful, and Cassino still blocked the advance. On May 11, General Alexander began his present operation, and after unceasing and intense fighting by the whole of the armies, broke into the enemy's lines and entered the Liri Valley. It is noteworthy that, counting from right to left, the whole of the Polish, British Empire, French, and United States forces broke the German lines in front of them by frontal attack. That has an important bearing on other matters, which I shall come to before I sit down.

At what was judged the right moment the bridgehead force, which by this time had reached a total of nearly 150,000 men, fell upon the retiring enemy's flank and threatened his retreat. The junction of the main armies with the bridgehead forces drove the enemy off his principal lines of retreat to the north, forcing a great part of his army to retire in considerable disorder with heavy losses, especially in material, through mountainous country. The Allied forces, with great rapidity, were regrouped, with special emphasis on their left flank, which soon deployed against Rome after cutting the important highway. The American and other forces of the Fifth Army broke through the enemy's last line and entered Rome, where the Allied troops have been received with joy by the population. This entry and liberation of Rome mean that we shall have the power to defend it from hostile air attack, and to deliver it from the famine with which it was threatened. However, General Alexander's prime object has never been the liberation of Rome, great as are the moral, political and psychological advantages of that episode. The Allied forces, with the Americans in the van, are driving ahead, northwards, in relentless pursuit of the enemy. The destruction of the enemy army has been, throughout, the single aim, and they are now being engaged at the same time along the whole length of the line as they attempt to escape to the north. It is hoped that the 20,000 prisoners already taken will be followed by further captures in future, and that the condition of the enemy's army, which he has crowded into Southern Italy, will be decisively affected.

It would be futile to attempt to estimate our final gains at the present time. It is our duty, however, to pay the warmest tribute of gratitude and admiration to General Alexander for the skill with which he has handled this army of so many different States and nations, and for the tenacity and fortitude with which he has sustained the long periods when success was denied. In General Clark the United States Army has found a fighting leader of the highest order, and the qualities of all Allied troops have shone in noble and unjealous rivalry. The great strength of the air forces at our disposal, as well as the preponderance in armour, has undoubtedly contributed in a notable and distinctive manner to the successes which have been achieved. We must await further development in the Italian theatre before it is possible to estimate the magnitude and quality of our gains, great and timely though they certainly are.

I have also to announce to the House that during the night and the early hours of this morning the first of the series of landings in force upon the European continent has taken place. In this case the liberating assault fell upon the coast of France. An immense armada of upwards of 4,000 ships, together with several thousand smaller craft, crossed the Channel. Massed airborne landings have been successfully effected behind the enemy lines, and landings on the beaches are proceeding at various points at the present time. The fire of the shore batteries has been largely quelled. The obstacles that were constructed in the sea have not proved so difficult as was apprehended. The Anglo-American allies are sustained by about 11,000 first-line aircraft, which can be drawn upon as may be needed for the purposes of the battle. I cannot, of course, commit myself to any particular details. Reports are coming in in rapid succession. So far the commanders who are engaged report that everything is proceeding according to plan. And what a plan! This vast operation is undoubtedly the most complicated and difficult that has ever taken place. It involves tides, wind, waves, visibility, both from the air and the sea standpoint, and the combined employment of land, air and sea forces in the highest degree of intimacy and in contact with conditions which could not and cannot be fully foreseen.

There are already hopes that actual tactical surprise has been attained, and we hope to furnish the enemy with a succession of surprises during the course of the fighting. The battle that has now begun will grow constantly in scale and in intensity for many weeks to come, and I shall not attempt to speculate upon its course. This I may say, however. Complete unity prevails throughout the Allied armies. There is a brotherhood in arms between us and our friends of the United States. There is complete confidence in the supreme commander, General Eisenhower, and his lieutenants, and also in the commander of the Expeditionary Force, General Montgomery. The ardour and spirit of the troops, as I saw myself, embarking in these last few days was splendid to witness. Nothing that equipment, science or forethought could do has been neglected, and the whole process of opening this great new front will be pursued with the utmost resolution both by the commanders and by the United States and British Governments whom they serve.

Later in the day the Prime Minister made a further statement as follows:

I have been at the centres where the latest information is received, and I can state to the House that this operation is proceeding in a thoroughly satisfactory manner. Many dangers and difficulties which at this time last night appeared extremely formidable are behind us. The passage of the sea has been made with far less loss than we apprehended. The resistance of the batteries has been greatly weakened by the bombing of the Air Force, and the superior bombardment of our ships quickly reduced their fire to dimensions which did not affect the problem. The landings of the troops on a broad front, both British and American – Allied troops, I will not give lists of all the different nationalities they represent – but the landings along the whole front have been effective, and our troops have penetrated in some cases several miles inland. Lodgements exist on the broad front.

The outstanding feature has been the landings of the airborne troops, which were on a scale far larger than anything that has been seen so far in the world. These landings took place with extremely little loss and with great accuracy. Particular anxiety attached to them, because the conditions of light prevailing in the very limited period of the dawn – just before the dawn – the conditions of visibility made all the difference. Indeed, there might have been something happening at the last minute which would have prevented airborne troops from playing their part. A very great degree of risk had to be taken in respect of the weather.

But General Eisenhower's courage is equal to all the necessary decisions that have to be taken in these extremely difficult and uncontrollable matters. The airborne troops are well established, and the landings and the follow-ups are all proceeding with much less loss – very much less – than we expected. Fighting is in progress at various points. We have captured various bridges which were of importance, and which were not blown up. There is even fighting proceeding in the town of Caen, inland. But all this, although a very valuable first step – a vital and essential first step – gives no indication of what may be the course of the battle in the next days and weeks, because the enemy will now probably endeavour to concentrate on this area, and in that event heavy fighting will soon begin and will continue without end, as we can push troops in and he can bring other troops up. It is, therefore, a most serious time that we enter upon. Thank God, we enter upon it with our great allies and all in good heart and all in good friendship.

On June 8 the Prime Minister made the following brief reference to the fighting in France:

I do not propose to make any statement about the battle today, and shall not do so unless something exceptional turns up. As a matter of fact, I think that all the points which have occurred to me are very fully met in the excellent reports furnished by our able and upright Press. But I would say this, that if this is the last time I speak to the House before the weekend I earnestly hope that when Members go to their constituencies they will not only maintain morale, so far as that is necessary, but also give strong warnings against over-optimism, against the idea that these things are going to be settled with a run, and that they will remember that although great dangers lie behind us, enormous exertions lie before us.

THE FLYING BOMB

STATEMENTS TO THE HOUSE OF COMMONS, JULY 6 AND 25, 1944

[July 6, 1944]

I consider that His Majesty's Government were right in not giving out a great deal of information about the flying bombs until we knew more about them and were able to measure their effect. The newspapers have in an admirable manner helped the Government in this, and I express my thanks to them. The time has come, however, when a fuller account is required and a wider field of discussion should be opened and in my opinion such a discussion is no longer hampered by the general interest. I would at the same time enjoin upon hon Members and the public outside to watch their step in anything they say, because a thing which might not strike one as being harmful at all might give some information to the enemy which would be of use to him and a detriment to us. Still, a very wide field of discussion will be open henceforth.

Let me say at the outset that it would be a mistake to underrate the serious character of this particular form of attack. It has never been underated in the secret circles of the Government. On the contrary up to the present time the views which we formed of the force and extent of the danger were considerably in excess of what has actually happened. The probability of such an attack has, among other things, been under continuous intense study and examination for a long time. During the early months of 1943 we received through our many and varied Intelligence sources, vague reports that the Germans were developing a new long-range weapon with which they proposed to bombard London. At first our information led us to believe that a rocket weapon would be used. Just over a year ago the Chiefs of Staff proposed to me that the Joint Parliamentary Secretary to the Minister of Supply, my hon Friend the Member for Norwood (Mr Sandys), should be charged with the duty of studying all the intelligence as it came in and reporting what truth, if any, there was in these reports and advising the Chiefs of State and the War Cabinet as to countermeasures. Long before this time my right hon Friend the Home Secretary, whose vigilance has been unceasing, had begun to strengthen the street shelters generally, and he now intensified this work so that these shelters are by no means ill adapted to withstand the blast effects of the bombs at present being used.

The House will realise that the enemy took all possible precautions to conceal his designs from us. Nevertheless, as the result of searching investigations by agents and by reconnaissance, we had, by July 1943, succeeded in locating at Peenemunde, on the Baltic, the main experimental station both for the flying bomb and the long-range rocket. In August last the full strength of Bomber Command was sent out to attack those installations. The raids were costly, on account of the great distances into Germany which had to be flown, but very great damage was done to the enemy and his affairs, and a number of key German scientists, including the head scientist, who were all dwelling together in a so-called Strength-Through-Joy establishment, were killed. This raid delayed by many months the development and bringing into action of both these weapons.

About this time we had also located at Watten, in the Pas de Calais, the first of the large structures which appeared to be connected with the firing of a long-range rocket. This site was very heavily attacked as long ago as September, and has been under continual treatment since by the heaviest weapons borne by the British and American Air Forces. We also carried out a most thorough air reconnaissance of the whole of North-West France and Belgium. This was an immense task, and not without its cost, but in the result we discovered in October last that, in addition to the large structures of the Watten type, other structures, in greater numbers, were being erected all along the French coast between Havre and Calais. I meditated at that time whether I should make a statement to the House in Secret Session on the subject, but on the whole, everything being in such a hypothetical condition, I thought that might cause needless alarm, and that we had better proceed step by step till we had greater assurances as to what we could say.

The reconnaissance which we carried out was an immense task, but it yielded very important information. Eventually we found that about 100 of these rather smaller sites all along the French coast between Havre and Calais were being erected, and we concluded that they would be the firing-points for a jet-propelled projectile much smaller than the rocket to which our thoughts had first then turned. All these hundred firing points were continuously bombed since last December, and every one of them was destroyed by the Royal Air Force, with the wholehearted assistance of the growing United States airpower. If it had not been for our bombing operations in France and Germany, the counter-preparations in which we indulged, the bombardment of London would no doubt have started perhaps six months earlier and on a very much heavier scale. Under the pressure of our counter-measures, the enemy, who felt, among other impulses, the need of having something to boast about and carrying on a war of nerves in order to steady the neutrals and satellites and assuage his own public opinion, developed a new series of prefabricated structures which could be rapidly assembled and well camouflaged, especially during periods of cloudy weather. It is from those comparatively light and very rapidly erected structures that the present attack is being made.

What is the scale of this attack? The hundred firing-sites which were destroyed, assuming that the enemy's production of the missiles was adequate, could have delivered a vastly greater discharge of HE on London per day than what we have now. I think it is only just to the British and American Air Forces to record that diminution by their untiring and relentless efforts in the scale of the attack to which we are now exposed. The new series of firing-points, like the first, have been heavily and continuously bombed for several months past. As new sites are constructed or existing ones repaired, our bombing attacks are repeated. Every effort is used to destroy the structures, and also to scatter the working parties and to deal with other matters concerned with the smooth running of this system of attack. The total weight of bombs so far dropped on flying bomb and rocket targets in France and Germany, including Peenemunde, has now reached about 50,000 tons, and the number of reconnaissance flights now totals many thousands. The scrutiny and interpretation of the tens of thousands of air photographs obtained for this purpose have alone been a stupendous task discharged by the Air Reconnaissance and Photographic Interpretation Unit of the RAF.

These efforts have been exacting to both sides, friend and foe. Quite a considerable proportion of our flying-power has been diverted for months past from other forms of offensive activity. The Germans, for their part, have sacrificed a great deal of manufacturing strength which would have increased their fighter and bomber forces working in conjunction with their hard-pressed armies on every front. It has yet to be decided who has suffered and will suffer the most in the process. There has, in fact, been in progress for a year past an unseen battle into which great resources have been poured by both sides. This invisible battle has now flashed into the open, and we shall be able, and indeed obliged, to watch its progress at fairly close quarters.

To the blood-curdling threats which German propaganda has been making in order to keep up the spirit of their people and of their satellites, there have been added the most absurd claims about the results of the first use of the secret weapon. I minimise nothing, I assure the House, but I think it right to correct those absurdities by giving some actual facts and figures, knowledge of which, although they may not be known to the enemy, will do him very little good, in my opinion and in the opinion of my advisers. Between 100 and 150 flying bombs, each weighing about one ton, are being discharged daily, and have been so discharged for the last fortnight or so from the firing-points in France. Considering the modest weight and small penetration-power of these bombs, the damage they have done by blast effect has been extensive. It cannot at all be compared with the terrific destruction by fire and high explosives with which we have been assaulting Berlin, Hamburg, Cologne, and scores of other German cities, and other war manufacturing points in Germany.

This form of attack is, no doubt, of a trying character, a worrisome character, because of its being spread out throughout the whole of the twenty-four hours, but people have just got to get used to that. Everyone must go about his duty and his business, whatever it may be – every man or woman – and then, when the long day is done, they should seek the safest shelter that they can find and forget their cares in well-earned sleep. We must neither underrate nor exaggerate. In all up to six a.m. today, about 2,750 flying bombs have been discharged from the launching-stations along the French coast. A very large proportion of these have either failed to cross the Channel or have been shot down and destroyed by various methods, including the great deployment of batteries, aircraft and balloons which have been very rapidly placed in position. Batteries move to any position in which they are required and take up their positions rapidly, but once on the site great improvements can be made in the electrical connections and so forth; and the Air Force, confronted with the somewhat novel problem of chasing a projectile, has found new methods every day.

Therefore, I say, a very large proportion of those that were discharged from the other side has been shot down and destroyed by various methods. Sometimes shooting them down means that they explode upon the ground. Therefore the places where they should be shot down are better chosen where successful hits do not necessarily mean explosions in a built-up area. I am very careful to be vague about areas. The weather, however, during the month of June has been very unfavourable to us for every purpose. In Normandy, it has robbed us in great part of the use of immense superiority. These battles in Normandy are being waged without that extraordinary and overwhelming exceptional aid of the vast air force we had collected for the purpose. When the weather improves a new great reinforcement will come into play. In Britain the bad weather has made more difficult the work and combination of the batteries and aircraft. It has also reduced the blows we strike at every favourable opportunity at the launching-stations or suspicious points on the other side of the Channel.

Nevertheless, the House will, I think, be favourably surprised to learn that the total number of flying bombs launched from the enemy's stations have killed almost exactly one person per bomb. That is a very remarkable fact, and it has kept pace roughly week by week. Actually the latest figures are 2,754 flying bombs launched and 2,752 fatal casualties sustained. They are the figures up to six o'clock this morning. Well, I am bound to say I was surprised when, some time ago, I perceived this wonderful figure. This number of dead will be somewhat increased by people who die of their injuries in hospital. Besides these there has been a substantially larger number of injured, and many minor injuries have been caused by splinters of glass. A special warning of this danger was issued by the Ministries of Home Security and Health, and in giving wide publicity to the recommendations for reducing this risk the newspapers have also rendered a most useful service.

As this battle – for such it is – may be a somewhat lengthy affair, I do not propose to withhold the number of casualties.

I will give the number because I believe the exaggerated rumours and claims that are made are more harmful than the disclosure of the facts. I will now give the casualties up to date, and thereafter they will be given in the usual form, at monthly intervals, by the Minister of Home Security. The total number of injured detained in hospital is about 8,000. This does not include minor injuries treated at first-aid posts and out-patients' departments of hospitals, and not needing detention at the hospital even for a single day. Of those detained in hospital a large proportion has, in fact, been discharged after a few days. Here let me say that the casualty and first-aid services of Greater London are working excellently. This machine has been well tested in the past, and it has been continually reviewed, kept up to date, and improved in the light of experience. It is not at all strained beyond its capacity and, naturally, we draw from other parts of the country which are not affected to strengthen the central machine.

So far as hospital accommodation is concerned, we prepared for so many more casualties in the Battle of Normandy than have actually occurred so far that we have, for the present, a considerable immediate emergency reserve in which to disperse patients. The injured are speedily transferred to hospitals in safer districts, and I am glad to say that penicillin, which up to now has had to be restricted to military uses, will be available for the treatment of all flying-bomb casualties. Here I must say a word about our American friends and allies in London, from the highest official to the ordinary soldier whom one meets, who have, in every way, made common cause with us and been forthcoming as helpers, wardens and assistants of every kind. No one can visit a bombed site where an explosion has recently taken place without seeing how very quickly they are, in large numbers, on the scene and running any risk to give a helping hand to anyone in distress. And the same is true of the great headquarters under General Eisenhower, where they are conducting this great battle, and where, apart from that, every conceivable assistance is given to our Forces and aid services. It will be another tie, I think, between our two peoples, when they see something of what we go through in

London and take a generous part in bearing our burden. A very high proportion of these casualties I have mentioned – somewhat around 10,000 – not always severe or mortal, have fallen upon London, which presents to the enemy – now I have mentioned it the phrase 'Southern England' passed out of currency – a target eighteen miles wide by, I believe, over twenty miles deep, and it is, therefore, the unique target of the world for the use of a weapon of such gross inaccuracy.

The flying bomb is a weapon literally and essentially indiscriminate in its nature, purpose and effect. The introduction by the Germans of such a weapon obviously raises some grave questions upon which I do not propose to trench today.

Slight repairs to buildings are being done as quickly as possible. As a temporary measure these are usually rough protective repairs to roofs and windows. A large force of building workers is engaged on this work. Copious reinforcements have been brought in, and are being brought in, from the provinces by the Minister of Labour, and are arriving here daily. Repairs to a very large number of houses have already been carried out, but there are areas where the blast damage is at present somewhat ahead of our growing repair forces. This will be remedied as time goes on.

As to evacuation, as I have said, everyone must remain at his post and discharge his daily duty. This House would be affronted if any suggestion were made to it that it should change its location from London. Here we began the war, and here we will see it ended. We are not, however, discouraging people who have no essential work to do from leaving London at their own expense if they feel inclined to do so by the arrangements they make. In fact they assist our affairs by taking such action at their own expense. We do not need more people in London than are required for business purposes of peace and war. For people of small means, who are not engaged in war work and wish to leave, registers have been opened and arrangements will be made for their transfer as speedily as possible to safer areas. Children are already being sent at their parents' wish out of the danger areas, which are

271

by no means exclusively confined to the Metropolis. There is, of course, the bomb highway over which the robots all pass before reaching that point of Southern England which I have ventured to particularise this morning. Children are being sent, if their parents wish, out of the danger areas, and in all cases mothers with small children, or pregnant women, will be given full facilities by the State. And we do not propose to separate the mother from the child except by her wish, for a terrible thing happened last time. Mothers were separated from children of two or three years of age, and, after a period, when they had saved up money and got time to go down and see them, the children hardly knew them. I hope now with our growing strength, reserves and facilities for removal, we shall be able to say to a mother with three or four children, 'If you wish to leave, it is perfectly possible. Arrangements will be made to take you into the country with your children. If you wish them to go by themselves and you wish to stay here with your husband, or because of your job, then arrangements can be made that way too.' We do not consider that the scale of attack under which we lie at present justifies Governmental compulsion in any case. In order to speed these arrangements, the Minister of War Transport, Lord Leathers, has arranged that the railways should provide a larger service of trains from the London stations.

All these matters and many others are reviewed daily, or almost daily, certainly whenever necessary, by the Civil Defence Committee over which the Minister of Home Security has so long presided. He has presided over it since those dark days when he took over the care of London, especially, which he knew so well, in the old original blitz. Upon this Committee sit either the heads or the representatives of every single Department concerned, and the War Cabinet is always available to confirm any decision which involves high policy. There is no delay. Matters are settled with very great speed, but a very great power is given to this Committee, and questions about what I may call the social side of the flying bomb, the social reactions, should be addressed either to the Minister of Home Security, who will answer them himself, or to the

Minister of Health, who has a great sphere of responsibility.

A good many questions can be asked, but the House, I am sure, would wish to have a check-up on them beforehand, because a perfectly innocent and proper question might have some connection which would tell the enemy more than we need tell him. After all, the Germans keep large Intelligence services, always prying about and trying to find out everything they can, and really we ought to leave them something to do. I can see lots of questions that could well be discussed here, and if there were some particular kind of question we wanted to talk over among ourselves, such procedure is always available to the House. I am not going to attempt to parade to the House the many difficult matters that have been settled. I have mentioned a good many of them. I could give a complete list, and if I have left anything out, that is a thing that can be reserved for a future day. We can with confidence leave our civil organisation to do its work under the watchful supervision of the House of Commons. We have had many periods in the war in which the Government have relied on the House of Commons to keep them in close touch with the people and the populations affected, and we have welcomed many helpful suggestions. I think we can have great confidence in our civil organisation, for it has immense experience and has handled machinery which has stood far greater strains than this.

On the operational side, a special committee has been set up to review, concert and advise upon all counter-measures, both offensive and defensive, to deal with the flying bomb. This committee consists of the Joint Parliamentary Secretary to the Ministry of Supply as chairman; Air-Marshal Hill, who is in charge of ADGB (Air Defence of Great Britain); General Pile, who has been our highly competent commander-in-chief of the Ack-Ack Command since the beginning of the war; the Deputy Chief of the Air Staff; and a representative of the deputy Allied commander, Air-Marshal Tedder. This committee has at its disposal a great number of able scientists and engineers who are studying from the technical standpoint the improvement of our counter-measures. The committee reports to me personally, to the Chiefs of Staff, and, finally, to the War Cabinet. There is an organisation for getting quick decisions from all the authorities concerned.

The House will ask: What of the future? Is this attack going to get worse, or is it going to be beat like the magnetic mine, or beat like the attempted destruction of Britain by the aeroplane, or beat as the U-boat campaign was beat? Will new developments on the other hand, of a far more formidable character, come upon us? Will the rocket bomb come? Will improved explosives come? Will greater ranges, faster speeds, and larger war-heads come upon us? I can give no guarantee that any of these evils will be entirely prevented before the time comes, as come it will, when the soil from which these attacks are launched has been finally liberated from the enemy's grip. In the meantime I can only say that when I visited various scenes of bomb explosions on Saturday, only one man of many hundreds whom I saw asked a question. The question was: 'What are you going to do about it?' I replied: 'Everything in human power, and we have never failed yet.' He seemed contented with the reply. That is the only promise I can make.

I must, however, make it perfectly plain – I do not want there to be any misunderstanding on this point – that we shall not allow the battle operations in Normandy or the attacks we are making against special targets in Germany to suffer. They come first, and we must fit our own domestic arrangements into the general scheme of war operations. There can be no question of allowing the slightest weakening of the battle in order to diminish in scale injuries which, though they may inflict grievous suffering on many people and change to some extent the normal, regular life and industry of London, will never stand between the British nation and their duty in the van of a victorious and avenging world. It may be a comfort to some to feel that they are sharing in no small degree the perils of our soldiers overseas, and that the blows which fall on them diminish those which in other forms would have smitten our fighting men and their allies. But I am sure of one thing, that London will never be conquered and will never fail, and that her renown, triumphing over every ordeal, will long shine among men.

A Member asked what facilities there would be to bring to the attention of Ministers points affecting the lives of the people, their welfare and safety, and the Prime Minister replied:

I would venture to make a suggestion on the spur of the moment. That is, that the Minister of Home Security should depute someone to whom Members could refer, and, if they did not get satisfaction in that way, they could take such other measures as are open. I feel that there will be questions, small questions, but in some cases very painful questions, and I am anxious that the House should keep in close touch with the Government in this affair, which we are all in together, as in so many others. But it seems to me that it would be a good thing if my right hon Friend deputed someone who was a member of his committee to see Members who were anxious about this matter. I did something like this myself twenty-five years ago during demobilisation after the last war, and it gave great satisfaction. At that time questions amounted to several hundreds a day. If there is any better way of doing it, I will talk it over with my right hon Friend, and he will make some statement to the House.

A Member raised the question of the opening of deep shelters, and the Prime Minister said:

I am afraid that I overlooked that in my speech. We always regarded these deep shelters as a reserve, and it has now been decided to make use of them. The Home Secretary is much to be congratulated in having these up his sleeve, and we must make use of them in the manner which is most effective to further our general plans, not merely as places where particular individuals can camp out indefinitely, but as part of the general movement and life of London.

Questioned about evacuation, the Prime Minister said:

The case of the old and infirm must be considered and will be considered. This is one of the first matters to which my right hon Friend will give his attention, but I think the children are the first consideration.

When another Member urged the need for a public Debate, the Prime Minister replied:

That might easily do something which the hon Gentleman would be the last to wish. Something might be said which might help the enemy. Every word is read and eagerly scanned in order to try to make up a case. A Debate in public very often consists of criticism, quite naturally, because those who are satisfied remain silent. I am not sure that we need unduly stress the troubles we have to face and mean to conquer, by a public Debate during which at any moment it might be necessary for the Minister to say that we ought to go into Secret Session.

It would be better to do what has been promised, that is, have a discussion without the enemy listening. I know a good deal about all this business. I have very good advisers who check, I can assure hon Members, what I say, so that I do not inadvertently let out something detrimental; but hon Members have not the same opportunity. A perfectly well-meaning speech might be resented by the troops when it got around and make them say: 'Well they have said this in the House of Commons.' We must be careful, and therefore I should not recommend a full public Debate.

A Member said he had received many letters urging reprisals, and the Prime Minister replied:

I have said deliberately that that is a subject which raises grave considerations and upon which I do not intend to embark. That, I am sure, is the best way in which to leave it. Might I appeal to the House not to pursue unduly these interrogations today? I weighed my words very carefully, and I should like them to represent what we have to put before the House and the people.

Mr Edgar Granville, MP for Eye, asked about the effect of blast on glass, whether tape should be used and whether the Prime Minister would give instructions for doors and shelters to be open. The Prime Minister replied:

Really, these are not questions for me to answer.

Mr Granville: 'They save people's lives. Apparently that does not matter to some hon Members.' The Prime Minister replied:

The hon Gentleman has no right to suggest that other hon Members do not care about saving people's lives, or that he has any monopoly of human charity – or any marked pre-eminence in human genius.

Asked to inform Members of the House what Government Departments were responsible for dealing with the various questions arising out of the flying bomb attacks, the Prime Minister made the following statement on July 25:

[July 25, 1944]

The following statement shows the Civil Departments principally concerned and the main fields of responsibility of each Department. Any necessary co-ordination of the regional activities of the Civil Departments mentioned is effected by the Regional Commissioner. Civil problems arising from flying-bomb attacks are dealt with by the Civil Defence Committee, which is a Ministerial committee, on which all Departments concerned are represented under the chairmanship of the Home Secretary and Minister of Home Security.

Home Office and Ministry of Home Security:
    Police.

National Fire Service.
Civil Defence Services (other than first aid posts and ambulances).
Fire Guards.
Demolition and clearance.
Salvage and storage of furniture.
Provision of air raid shelters.
Glass protection.
Public warning and industrial alarm system.
Casualty statistics.

Ministry of Health:
Casualty services (first aid posts, ambulances and hospitals).
Evacuation of priority classes.
Rest centres, billeting and care of the homeless.
General supervision and direction of first aid repairs by local authorities to house property.
Restoration of sewers and water services.
Equipment and management of air raid shelters.
Health and comfort of shelters.

Ministry of Food:
Emergency feeding arrangements.

Board of Education:
Air raid shelter in schools.
Education of evacuated children.

Ministry of Works:
Allocation of all labour engaged on various classes of first aid work, according to requirements.
Control of use of building materials, and allocation and distribution of first aid repair materials and necessary plant.
Assisting local authorities' first aid repair of houses with the Special Repair Service and contractors who are being brought in from outside.

278

Ministry of Labour and National Service:
Supply of all classes of labour.

Board of Trade:
Claims in respect of insurable commodities under the War Risks Insurance Act or private chattels or business equipment under the War Damage Act.

Ministry of Fuel and Power:
Restoration of gas and electricity supplies.

General Post Office:
Repairs to telecommunications.

Ministry of Aircraft Production (Emergency Services Organisation):
Repairs to war production factories.

War Damage Commission (Questions should be addressed to the Chancellor of the Exchequer):
Claims in respect of war damage to land and buildings.

Assistance Board (Questions should be addressed to the Minister of Labour):
Relief of distress schemes.

Minister of Pensions:
Claims for injuries, etc.

Minister of Information:
Press censorship.
Communications of information to the public, otherwise than as provided by the Department concerned.

Ministry of War Transport:
General transport services.

THE FRUITS OF *1944*

When I look back over the wartime years I cannot help feeling that time is an inadequate and even capricious measure of their duration. At one moment they seem so long, at another so short. Sometimes events are galloping forward at breathless speed; sometimes there are long, hard, anxious pauses which we have to bear. Anniversaries like this seem to recur with extreme rapidity when you get to one and look back at the other. It seems such a very brief span, and yet the intervening months are so packed with incident and so burdened with toil that as you retrace your steps mentally over them you cannot believe that they have not lasted for several years. It is hard to remember how long ago this war began, and one can never be quite sure whether it has lasted a flash or an age.

I had a very shrewd suspicion, my Lord Mayor, when I received your gracious invitation, that you would probably propose the health of His Majesty's Ministers and I must hold myself in readiness for the task of making some reply, and I thought that I would see whether I could get some hint out of what I had said last year, when this agreeable event and festival was also celebrated. I saw that I was then congratulating you upon the year of victory of 1943. I was congratulating the City of London on that memorable and exhilarating year of almost unbroken success, and I was recounting a long succession of places and countries which had been cleared of the enemy – all Africa, Sicily, Sardinia, Corsica, and one-third of Italy were in the hands of the British and United States armies. The mighty war which the United States was waging in the Pacific had prospered beyond all hope, and in Russia Marshal Stalin's armies were already rolling triumphantly forward to cleanse their native land of the German invader.

But the events of 1943 have been far surpassed by those of 1944. Rome and Athens, Paris and Brussels and Belgrade, all have been rescued, and by their own exertions have largely rescued themselves, from German oppression. All of Hitler's satellites have turned against him. Not only have they been struck down, but they have actually turned their arms upon his baleful coercion. Slaves, driven so far against their interests, against their honour, against, in many cases, their inclination, have had a chance to turn upon the slave-driver, and may now wreak the vengeance which is due as much from them as from any of the free countries which fought from the beginning. Both in the east and in the west the Allied vanguards stand on German soil.

The U-boat menace has for the time being – I always put that sort of remark in, because life is full of changes and hazards in these years – the U-boat menace has for the time being been practically effaced. There was one recent month in which up to the last day they did not sink a single ship. On the last day they got one – therefore the matter was hardly of a character to be specially mentioned. But that great peril which hung over us for so long and at times concentrated the whole attention of the defence organisation of this country, and of the United States has been effaced, and from the air there rains down on the guilty German land a hail of fire and explosive of ever-increasing fury. We have had our own experience, and we know how severe the ordeal may be; but I can assure you that we have not suffered one-tenth, and we shall not suffer one-tenth of what is being meted out to those who first started and developed this cruel and merciless form of attack. Such are some of the fruits – for if I tried to name them all I should indeed vex your patience – of 1944, and no one can be blamed, provided that he does not slacken his or her efforts for a moment – no one can be blamed for hoping that victory may come to the Allies and peace may come to Europe in 1945.

When I was here last year I could not tell you that I was about to start for the meeting of the three great Allies – the heads of the three Governments – at Teheran. There it was that the plans were made and the agreements and decisions taken which were executed with so much precision and with a degree of combination to which Marshal Stalin referred in his wise and weighty speech a few days ago. Now I do not mind saying that it is high time we had another triple conference, and that such a meeting might easily abridge the sufferings of mankind and set a term to the fearful process of destruction which is now ravaging the earth.

The prospects of such a meeting have been vastly improved by the results of the Presidential Election in the United States for which we waited so breathlessly on Tuesday last. I see on looking back on my past records that when I was here last year I appealed to both the British and the American public to be very careful that the electioneering did not in any way ruffle the good will that existed throughout the English-speaking world, and was so great an aid to our armies.

It is certainly remarkable that the whole of this tremendous turmoil of the United States elections should have been carried through without any stirring of the ancient moth-eaten and threadbare controversies which are to be found in the history books between Great Britain and her American kins-men and now brothers-in-arms. We were very careful our-selves to avoid even the slightest semblance of mixing ourselves up with American political affairs, and I offer my compliments to Parliament, to the Press, and to public men of all parties and of no party – perhaps especially to them – for the care and restraint which have made all potential indiscretions die upon their lips.

Now that the event is over and the results have been de-clared, there are a few things I should like to say about the American Presidential Election. Let us first of all express our gratitude to both of the great parties in America for the manner in which the interests of the Alliance and the prosecu-tion of the war have been held high above the dust of party conflict. The United States has set an example to the world of how democratic institutions can be worked with the utmost vigour and freedom without injury to the permanent interests of the State. We know that we in Britain have in the Republican Party of the United States vast numbers of friends and well-wishers, and that the upholding of Anglo-American relations is cherished by tens of millions in both the great parties over there.

I am sure that everyone will have been moved by the spirited and sportsmanlike manner in which Governor Dewey at the moment of defeat offered his congratulations to his opponent, and pledged himself and his party to work wholeheartedly for the world cause. What a model this should be to those States where political differences are often not soluble by words or votes, where the question of who is to be in and who is to be out may be a matter of life and death, or be settled by violence and intrigue, and where there may be but a short step between being the ruler and being the victim!

Here in this country, the forerunner of all the democratic and parliamentary conceptions of modern times, we in this country, who are very old at the game of party politics hard fought out, have learned how to carry through and debate great fiercely contested political issues without the severance of national life, and even in most cases without the severance of personal and private friendships. However we may regret it, it seems almost certain that we too in this old island shall have our General Election in 1945, and I am confident that it will be conducted by all concerned with a liveliness and robust vigour which will gratify the political emotions and the combative instincts of our people at home, without destroying the marvellous underlying unity and sense of brotherhood which have long subsisted in this country and have reached their highest degree amid the perils from which we have been delivered, and in the Government composed of men of all parties who will, I am sure, preserve to their latest day sentiments of warm comradeship in this great episode and tremendous time of trouble which no ordinary political differences will ever be able to disturb.

We have strictly avoided any expression of opinion about party issues in the United States, but at this moment now I feel free to express on personal grounds the very great joy which it gives me to know that my intimate wartime co-operation with

President Roosevelt will be continued in the months that lie immediately before us. These are months profoundly interwoven with the future of both our countries, and also, we trust, through the future association of our two countries, interwoven with the peace and progress of the whole world.

I have spoken of the famous capital cities that have been freed by the costly fighting of this stern but very glorious year, and we have in General Koenig, the Governor of Paris and in the Burgomaster of Brussels, living representatives to bring home to us the splendid events which have so recently taken place.

The attention of the Western Allies and, indeed, of the world has naturally been dominated by the decisive battle in Normandy in which Anglo-American armies have destroyed or pulverised the structure of German resistance in France. The brilliant exploitation of that victory enabled the Americans to sweep the enemy from France, aided by the audacious and gallant Maquis, and enabled the British to clear the Channel coast and to drive the enemy out of Belgium and out of a large part of Holland.

How many times, when a great battle has been won, have its results been thrown away by tardiness or lack of vigour in pursuit. Here we have seen under General Eisenhower's supreme direction the highest results surely and firmly seized and held at every stage.

It is nearly always right to pursue a beaten foe with all one's strength, and even to run serious risks in doing so; but, of course, there comes a time when the pursuers outstrip the utmost limits of their own supplies, and where the enemy, falling back on his own depots, is able once again to form a front. This showed itself very plainly in the serious and continuous fighting which broke out on the Moselle and in that neighbourhood, when the American advance, thrust forward with so much impetus and *élan*, came up against a hard core of regathered enemy resistance. A pause in the Allied advance was inevitable, and during the last two months the bringing-up of supplies and reinforcements and the improvements of harbours have been the main preoccupation of the Supreme Allied

284

Command, apart from the heavy fighting I have spoken of on the Moselle. But during these last eight or ten weeks two considerable struggles have been fought by armies under British command, in both of which Canadian and Polish forces were represented, and in both of which a large proportion of United States troops fought with their customary distinction.

The first of these two great operations was in Italy under General Alexander. They have surmounted the terrible barrier of the Apennines and the Gothic Line, and this has carried us into the valley of the Po. The progress of the season has, however, brought us to very bad weather – quite exceptional weather for this time of the year – and progress there is hard. The forcing of this mountain line, so strongly fortified and held by a hostile German army practically as large as our own, already constitutes a great feat of arms, and has cost us and our allies very nearly 50,000 casualties.

The second interim battle has been in the Netherlands under Field-Marshal Montgomery. It has opened the Scheldt, and will very shortly place the great port of Antwerp at the disposal of the northern flank of the Allied armies, which will presently move into Germany for the final struggle. In these two operations – in Italy and in Holland and Belgium – very heavy losses have been sustained, in the greatest proportion by the British and Canadian forces. In both we have been aided by our valiant allies. In both opportunities have been offered for the display of superb heroism, and deeds have been done which, when they are known and when they can be studied with the attention they deserve, will long figure in song and story and long light the martial annals of our race and nation.

I thought it right to point out in a precise and definite manner these two important and prolonged battles which have been fought – one in the Apennines and one around the Scheldt. They are only the prelude to further great operations which must be conducted in the months to come. I felt that it had not perhaps been realised how very great has been the efforts which we have so largely had the honour to make and that it was appropriate to place them in their proper setting in the unfolding chain of this hard and obstinate war.

Now we stand on the threshold of Germany, and it will take the full exertions of the three great Powers and every scrap of strength and sacrifice that they can give to crush down the desperate resistance which we must expect from the deadly military antagonist at last so largely beaten back to his own lair. I cannot today any more than on the other four occasions when I have been called on to respond to this toast – I cannot offer you an easy future even on the continent of Europe. Supreme efforts must be made. It is always in the last lap that races are either gained or lost. The effort must be forthcoming. This is no moment to slacken.

Hard as it may seem after five long years of war, every man and woman in this land must show what they are capable of doing, and I am sure that our soldiers at the front will not be found incapable of that extra effort which is necessary to crown all that has been attained and, above all, to bring this frightful slaughter and devastation in Europe to an end within the shortest possible period of time. I can assure you that that, at any rate, is the dominant thought of His Majesty's Government.

Although it is our duty to work hard – and we have worked hard – to produce large schemes of social improvement and advance, although it is our duty to make preparations for the change-over from war to peace, from war in Europe to war in Japan, in far distant Asia, although we are bound to work as hard as we can, nothing must be allowed to stand in the way of the prosecution of the war to its ultimate conclusion. If we were to fail in that we should not be worthy either of your confidence or of the kindness which has led you to drink our health this afternoon.

THANKSGIVING DAY

A SPEECH AT A CONCERT AT THE ROYAL ALBERT HALL,
LONDON, IN CELEBRATION OF AMERICAN THANKS-
GIVING DAY, NOVEMBER 23, 1944

We have come here tonight to add our celebration to those
which are going forward all over the world wherever Allied
troops are fighting, in bivouacs and dug-outs, on battlefields,
on the high seas, and in the highest air. Always this annual
festival has been dear to the hearts of the American people.
Always there has been that desire for thanksgiving, and never,
I think, has there been more justification, more compulsive
need than now.

It is your Day of Thanksgiving, and when we feel the truth
of the facts which are before us, that in three or four years
the peaceful, peace-loving people of the United States, with all
the variety and freedom of their life in such contrast to the
iron discipline which has governed many other communities
– when we see that in three or four years the United States
has in sober fact become the greatest military, naval, and air
Power in the world – that, I say to you in this time of war, is
itself a subject for profound thanksgiving.

We are moving forward in this struggle which spreads over
all the lands and all the oceans; we are moving forward surely,
steadily, irresistibly, and perhaps, with God's aid, swiftly,
towards victorious peace. There again is a fitting reason for
thanksgiving.

I have spoken of American thanksgiving. Tonight here,
representing vaster audiences and greater forces moving outside this hall, it is both British and American thanksgiving
that we may celebrate. And why is that? It is because under the
compulsion of mysterious and all-powerful destiny we are
together. We are joined together, shedding our blood side by

287

side, struggling for the same ideals, until the triumph of the great causes which we serve shall have been made manifest.

But there is a greater Thanksgiving Day which still shines ahead, which beckons the bold and loyal and warm-hearted, and that is when this union of action which has been forced upon us by our common hatred of tyranny, which we have maintained during these dark and fearful days, shall become a lasting union of sympathy and good-feeling and loyalty and hope between all the British and American peoples, wherever they may dwell. Then, indeed, there will be a Day of Thanksgiving, and one in which all the world will share.

TROOPS' WELFARE IN THE FAR EAST

A SPEECH TO THE HOUSE OF COMMONS, DECEMBER 20, 1944

I have been asked to make a statement which I have prepared in conjunction with the Ministers at the head of the War Office and the India Office. Many Members of the House have very properly been concerned about the welfare of our forces serving in the Far East. The Service Departments, and in particular the War Office, who have the greatest interest in this subject, have for many months made preparation in conjunction with the Government of India for the reception of the great forces which are assembled and assembling in the Far Eastern theatre, and not least among their activities has been the provision of such stores and equipment as may be necessary on a reasonable basis for the well-being and contentment of those forces. But in my view the time has now come when the influence of the Government machine as a whole, civil as well as military, must be brought to bear upon this important question. For this reason the Under-Secretary of State for the Home Department (Lord Munster) has recently made a tour of India and the Burma front for the purpose of examining the situation on the spot and reporting to the Government about the improvements which are required. His report is being published as a White Paper, and will be available in the Vote Office before the House rises this evening.

The Government and the House are indebted to him for the manner in which he has discharged this responsible task. His report calls attention to a considerable number of matters in which improvement is urgently required. At the same time, he has rightly recognised the difficulties which have had to be faced by the authorities charged with these matters, and he has presented what is I think a very fair and helpful picture of the situation. It is important in arriving at a judgement on these matters, to realise that the task of providing suitable amenities for troops serving in the East is far more intricate and harder than for troops serving under European conditions. The great spaces to be covered, the lack of ordinary European amenities of life anywhere except in large towns, and the small numbers of European women who can devote their services voluntarily to the provision of amenities, are great handicaps. The Government of India, since 1942, have had to receive a very large increase in the number of European troops in India, and their resources have been strained to the utmost to provide accommodation and to fulfil military construction programmes essential for operations. A great deal has been done to improve and expand welfare facilities for the British forces, but clearly more can be achieved if additional resources and personnel can be provided from outside India.

The Government will apply themselves energetically to this problem. The Government of India and the South-East Asia Command have already been asked for a detailed statement of the help they require to make good the deficiencies in the welfare field to which Lord Munster has drawn attention.

One of our first concerns is, naturally, the welfare of the sick and wounded. Lord Munster visited thirty-four hospitals in the course of his tour. I am glad to say that he reports from a layman's point of view that he is satisfied that the medical facilities are maintained at a high standard of efficiency, in spite of the administrative difficulties of an extended front and poor communications. He has drawn attention to certain shortages of medical personnel in India. These are the reflection of general shortages. Every effort is being made to improve the position, but the Government have to pay regard to the many other claims, both civilian and service, on the available supply of doctors and nurses. Consideration is being given urgently to his proposal that further members of the Voluntary Aid Detachment should be sent out to India, and to the other proposals he makes to improve the present position.

In some directions it will not be possible to achieve what we desire until the defeat of Germany enables greater resources to be diverted to the East. But plans have been made and directions are being given so that when these greater resources become available, they can be diverted without loss of time to the amelioration of the conditions of service of the men and women of the Service and the Merchant Navy who are called upon to continue the fight against Japan. At that stage a greater volume of air transport should become available, and this will render practicable an improvement in the facilities for the conveyance of fresh food and other comforts to the troops in the forward areas, and for the movement of men on urgent compassionate leave and to some extent on ordinary leave from the front. It will also make possible a wider use of air transport for the evacuation of casualties and the improvement of the transport of mails. A plan is being prepared under which the rapidity of mails can be progressively improved and the charges reduced. The immediate target is to carry by air all letter mail to the Far East, and it is hoped to achieve this early in 1945. The Under-Secretary of State for the Home Department has drawn attention in his report to the inadequacy of accommodation in leave centres and static camps in the Far Eastern theatres. A thorough revision of the present scales of accommodation and amenities in these centres and camps has already been ordered. Attention is being given to the adoption of modern methods of construction, the extension of fly-proofing of buildings, and the provision in greater quantities of modern appurtenances, including refrigerators, shower baths, and good furniture. These improvements will proceed as resources permit. Special attention is also being given to the provisions of a varied diet and up-to-date hygienic systems of preparing and cooking food.

Measures are being taken as a matter of urgency which will in due course improve the supplies of beer available for the forces in India. Indian production of beer has already been expanded to the fullest extent which is practicable without the import of raw materials and plant, but I hope it will be found possible to increase further both imported supplies and Indian production. Arrangements are also well advanced to produce in India cigarettes of a type more palatable to British troops. Trial brands have already been issued with a view to large-scale production when it is known which type is preferred by the men. Measures are also in hand to accelerate the provision of cinema apparatus and wireless equipment, most of which I should mention can only be obtained from the USA. The value of the work done by British women for the well-being of the troops in India has been proved. Steps are now being taken to encourage more British women, both those who are residents in India now and volunteers from home, to undertake this important and valuable contribution to the welfare of the troops. Canteen services are not the responsibility of NAAFI in this theatre, but the Government of India are taking special steps to improve and to enlarge the local organisation.

It has also been decided that special consideration will be given to service men and their families in assessing priorities for the allotment of houses and furniture after the war. The wives and families of service men engaged in the Far Eastern theatre will, of course share in this preferential treatment. In order that service men overseas may keep abreast of important developments in social policy at home, pamphlets explaining new legislation on matters of major importance will be prepared and distributed to service men and merchant seamen.

The House will have observed that in recent months a good deal more attention has been paid by the general public in this country to the efforts and achievements of our men in the Far East. The Ministry of Information and other authorities concerned recognise that this sympathetic interest must be fed by a service of reliable information as to what goes on there. Both the authorities at home and those in control of information on the spot will continue their efforts to maintain and improve the sources of such a service.

Although it is not a matter referred to in his report, Lord Munster has drawn my attention to the uncertainty which prevails in the minds of the men on the subject of the length of time for which they will be required to serve in the East. The position seems to have been made clear by the Secretary of State for War on September 26 and by me on November 17. But it will perhaps be useful if I restate the position so far as those serving in India and SEAC are concerned.

British officers and men of the British Army serving in the East are eligible for posting to the Home Establishment under the Python scheme. This was explained by the Secretary of State for War in his statement. This scheme is not applicable to British officers of the Indian Army, but does apply to British service officers and men attached to the Indian Army. The intention is to reduce the period of service in the Far East to the shortest period which is practicable, and generally speaking, priority for posting to the Home Establishment under this scheme is given to those who have served longest away from this country. It is hoped before very long to have posted home all those who have served for more than four years in India and SEAC. In fact the aim is to reduce the qualifying period for repatriation from those theatres to a few months under four years. There may be unavoidable exceptions to this in cases where individuals or specialist personnel cannot be spared for operational reasons, or where trained replacements cannot yet be provided; but this is the general policy, which will be carried out to the furthest extent that war allows.

In addition there is the twenty-eight day leave scheme which I recently announced to the House. This is designed to give a short period of leave at home to men who have been engaged in exceptionally arduous conditions but who may not come within the scope of the Python scheme for some time. The selection is made at the discretion of the commanders-in-chief concerned. But naturally, length of absence will be taken into account. Moreover, the current scheme whereby men are posted back to the United Kingdom on exceptional grounds of compassion will continue to operate. Men who receive leave under the short leave scheme will return again to service in the Far East, but as far as is practicable in present circumstances men repatriated under the Python scheme will not.

British officers and men belonging to the Indian Army are not eligible for posting to this country under the Python scheme. Home posting is impossible, because the Indian Army has no home establishment; and transfer to the British Army for this purpose would involve the loss to the Indian Army of an officer who has received special training for service with Indian troops. In lieu of the Python schemes a leave scheme has been introduced under which British officers of the Indian Army can receive sixty-one days' leave at home. There are many officers of the Indian Army with very long periods of overseas services and at present no officer with less than five years' service is considered for leave, as it is obviously equitable that those with the longest service abroad should receive leave first. The short leave scheme also applies to British officers and other ranks of the Indian Army, and they are eligible on the same basis as those of the British Army.

His Majesty's Government are giving constant attention to the needs of the men and women serving in the Far East. I have issued instructions to those concerned on the spot and to Departments here that in relation to operational needs a higher priority must be given to the requirements for welfare and amenities for the forces in the Far East than hitherto. I have also at the desire of the Secretary of State for War, appointed Lieut-General King to be my personal representative in the India and South-East Asia Commands for welfare matters. It will be General King's duty to ascertain how matters are progressing and to report to me on difficulties which may arise and on the assistance which is required from this country. He will be concerned with the welfare of all three Services and the Merchant Navy, and will have a staff suitably composed for that purpose. The rapidity with which improvements can be effected must to a large extent depend on the progress of the war in Europe, but we shall press on in the meantime with every measure for which our resources are available.

PRESIDENT ROOSEVELT

A SPEECH TO THE HOUSE OF COMMONS, APRIL 17, 1945

I beg to move:

'That an humble Address be presented to His Majesty to convey to His Majesty the deep sorrow with which this House has learned of the death of the President of the United States of America, and to pray His Majesty that in communicating his own sentiments of grief to the United States Government, he will also be generously pleased to express on the part of this House their sense of the loss which the British Commonwealth and Empire and the cause of the Allied nations have sustained, and their profound sympathy with Mrs Roosevelt and the late President's family, and with the Government and people of the United States of America.'

My friendship with the great man to whose work and fame we pay our tribute today began and ripened during this war. I had met him, but only for a few minutes, after the close of the last war, and as soon as I went to the Admiralty in September 1939, he telegraphed inviting me to correspond with him direct on naval or other matters if at any time I felt inclined. Having obtained the permission of the Prime Minister, I did so. Knowing President Roosevelt's keen interest in sea warfare, I furnished him with a stream of information about our naval affairs, and about the various actions, including especially the action of the Plate River, which lighted the first gloomy winter of the war.

When I became Prime Minister, and the war broke out in

all its hideous fury, when our own life and survival hung in the balance, I was already in a position to telegraph to the President on terms of an association which had become most intimate and, to me, most agreeable. This continued through all the ups and downs of the world struggle until Thursday last, when I received my last message from him. These messages showed no falling-off in his accustomed clear vision and vigour upon perplexing and complicated matters. I may mention that this correspondence which, of course, was greatly increased after the United States entry into the war, comprises to and fro between us, over 1,700 messages. Many of these were lengthy messages, and the majority dealt with the more difficult points which come to be discussed upon the level of heads of Governments only after official solutions have not been reached at other stages. To this correspondence there must be added our nine meetings – at Argentia, three in Washington, at Casablanca, at Teheran, two at Quebec and, last of all, at Yalta, comprising in all about 120 days of close personal contact, during a great part of which I stayed with him at the White House or at his home at Hyde Park or in his retreat in the Blue Mountains, which he called Shangri-la.

I conceived an admiration for him as a statesman, a man of affairs, and a war leader. I felt the utmost confidence in his upright, inspiring character and outlook, and a personal regard – affection I must say – for him beyond my power to express today. His love of his own country, his respect for its constitutions, his power of gauging the tides and currents of its mobile public opinion, were always evident, but added to these were the beatings of that generous heart which was always stirred to anger and to action by spectacles of aggression and oppression by the strong against the weak. It is, indeed, a loss, a bitter loss to humanity that those heart-beats are stilled for ever.

President Roosevelt's physical affliction lay heavily upon him. It was a marvel that he bore up against it through all the many years of tumult and storm. Not one man in ten millions, stricken and crippled as he was, would have attempted to plunge into a life of physical and mental exertion and of hard, ceaseless political controversy. Not one in ten millions would have tried, not one in a generation would have succeeded, not only in entering this sphere, not only in acting vehemently in it, but in becoming indisputable master of the scene. In this extraordinary effort of the spirit over the flesh, of will-power over physical infirmity, he was inspired and sustained by that noble woman his devoted wife, whose high ideals marched with his own, and to whom the deep and respectful sympathy of the House of Commons flows out today in all fullness.

There is no doubt that the President foresaw the great dangers closing in upon the pre-war world with far more prescience than most well-informed people on either side of the Atlantic, and that he urged forward with all his power such precautionary military preparations as peacetime opinion in the United States could be brought to accept. There never was a moment's doubt, as the quarrel opened, upon which side his sympathies lay. The fall of France, and what seemed to most people outside this island, the impending destruction of Great Britain, were to him an agony, although he never lost faith in us. They were an agony to him not only on account of Europe, but because of the serious perils to which the United States herself would have been exposed had we been overwhelmed or the survivors cast down under the German yoke. The bearing of the British nation at that time of stress, when we were all alone, filled him and vast numbers of his countrymen with the warmest sentiments towards our people. He and they felt the blitz of the stern winter of 1940–41, when Hitler set himself to rub out the cities of our country, as much as any of us did, and perhaps more indeed, for imagination is often more torturing than reality. There is no doubt that the bearing of the British and, above all, of the Londoners, kindled fires in American bosoms far harder to quench than the conflagrations from which we were suffering. There was also at that time, in spite of General Wavell's victories – all the more, indeed, because of the reinforcements which were sent from this country to him – the apprehension widespread in the United States that we should be invaded by Germany after the fullest preparation in the spring of 1941. It was in February that the President sent to

England the late Mr Wendell Willkie, who, although a political rival and an opposing candidate, felt as he did on many important points. Mr Willkie brought a letter from Mr Roosevelt, which the President had written in his own hand, and this letter contained the famous lines of Longfellow:

> '. . . Sail on, O ship of State!
> Sail on, O Union, strong and great!
> Humanity with all its fears,
> With all the hopes of future years,
> Is hanging breathless on thy fate!'

At about that same time he devised the extraordinary measure of assistance called Lend-Lease, which will stand forth as the most unselfish and unsordid financial act of any country in all history. The effect of this was greatly to increase British fighting power, and for all the purpose of the war effort to make us, as it were, a much more numerous community. In that autumn I met the President for the first time during the war at Argentia in Newfoundland, and together we drew up the declaration which has since been called the Atlantic Charter, and which will, I trust, long remain a guide for both our peoples and for other people in the world.

All this time in deep and dark and deadly secrecy, the Japanese were preparing their act of treachery and greed. When next we met in Washington, Japan, Germany and Italy had declared war upon the United States, and both our countries were in arms, shoulder to shoulder. Since then we have advanced over the land and over the sea through many difficulties and disappointments, but always with a broadening measure of success. I need not dwell upon the series of great operations which have taken place in the Western Hemisphere, to say nothing of that other immense war proceeding on the other side of the world. Nor need I speak of the plans which we made with our great ally, Russia, at Teheran, for these have now been carried out for all the world to see.

But at Yalta I noticed that the President was ailing. His captivating smile, his gay and charming manner, had not deserted him, but his face had a transparency, an air of purification, and often there was a faraway look in his eyes. When I took my leave of him in Alexandria harbour I must confess that I had an indefinable sense of fear that his health and his strength were on the ebb. But nothing altered his inflexible sense of duty. To the end he faced his innumerable tasks unflinching. One of the tasks of the President is to sign maybe a hundred or two State papers with his own hand every day, commissions and so forth. All this he continued to carry out with the utmost strictness. When death came suddenly upon him 'he had finished his mail'. That portion of his day's work was done. As the saying goes, he died in harness, and we may well say in battle harness, like his soldiers, sailors, and airmen, who side by side with ours are carrying on their task to the end all over the world. What an enviable death was his! He had brought his country through the worst of its perils and the heaviest of its toils. Victory had cast its sure and steady beam upon him.

In the days of peace he had broadened and stabilised the foundations of American life and union. In war he had raised the strength, might and glory of the great Republic to a height never attained by any nation in history. With her left hand she was leading the advance of the conquering Allied armies into the heart of Germany, and with her right, on the other side of the globe, she was irresistibly and swiftly breaking up the power of Japan. And all the time ships, munitions, supplies, and food of every kind were aiding on a gigantic scale her allies, great and small, in the course of the long struggle.

But all this was no more than worldly power and grandeur, had it not been that the causes of human freedom and of social justice, to which so much of his life had been given, added a lustre to this power and pomp and warlike might, a lustre which will long be discernible among men. He has left behind him a wave of resolute and able men handling the numerous interrelated parts of the vast American war machine. He has left a successor who comes forward with firm step and sure conviction to carry on the task to its appointed end. For us, it remains only to say that in Franklin Roosevelt there died the greatest American friend we have ever known, and the greatest champion of freedom who has ever brought help and comfort from the new world to the old.

UNCONDITIONAL SURRENDER

A WORLD BROADCAST, MAY 8, 1945

Yesterday morning at 2.41 a.m. at Headquarters, General Jodl, the representative of the German High Command, and Grand Admiral Doenitz, the designated head of the German State, signed the act of unconditional surrender of all German land, sea, and air forces in Europe to the Allied Expeditionary Force, and simultaneously to the Soviet High Command.

General Bedell Smith, Chief of Staff of the Allied Expeditionary Force, and General François Sevez signed the document on behalf of the supreme commander of the Allied Expeditionary Force, and General Susloparov signed on behalf of the Russian High Command.

Today this agreement will be ratified and confirmed at Berlin where Air-Chief-Marshal Tedder, deputy supreme commander of the Allied Expeditionary Force, and General de Lattre de Tassigny will sign on behalf of General Eisenhower. Marshal Zhukov will sign on behalf of the Soviet High Command. The German representatives will be Field-Marshal Keitel, Chief of the High Command, and the commanders-in-chief of the German Army, Navy, and Air Forces.

Hostilities will end officially at one minute after midnight tonight (Tuesday, May 8), but in the interests of saving lives the 'Cease fire' began yesterday to be sounded all along the front, and our dear Channel Islands are also to be freed today.

The Germans are still in places resisting the Russian troops, but should they continue to do so after midnight they will, of course, deprive themselves of the protection of the laws of war, and will be attacked from all quarters by the Allied troops. It is not surprising that on such long fronts and in the existing disorder of the enemy the orders of the German High Command should not in every case be obeyed immediately. This does not, in our opinion, with the best military advice at our disposal, constitute any reason for withholding from the nation the facts communicated to us by General Eisenhower of the unconditional surrender already signed at Rheims, nor should it prevent us from celebrating today and tomorrow (Wednesday) as Victory-in-Europe days.

Today, perhaps we shall think mostly of ourselves. Tomorrow we shall pay a particular tribute to our Russian comrades, whose prowess in the field has been one of the grand contributions to the general victory.

The German war is therefore at an end. After years of intense preparation, Germany hurled herself on Poland at the beginning of September 1939; and, in pursuance of our guarantee to Poland and in agreement with the French Republic, Great Britain, the British Empire and Commonwealth of Nations, declared war upon this foul aggression. After gallant France had been struck down we, from this island and from our united Empire, maintained the struggle singlehanded for a whole year until we were joined by the military might of Soviet Russia, and later by the overwhelming power and resources of the United States of America.

Finally almost the whole world was combined against the evil-doers, who are now prostrate before us. Our gratitude to our splendid allies goes forth from all our hearts in this island and throughout the British Empire.

We may allow ourselves a brief period of rejoicing; but let us not forget for a moment the toil and efforts that lie ahead. Japan, with all her treachery and greed, remains unsubdued. The injury she has inflicted on Great Britain, the United States and other countries, and her detestable cruelties, call for justice and retribution. We must now devote all our strength and resources to the completion of our task, both at home and abroad. Advance, Britannia. Long live the cause of freedom. God save the King.

GRATITUDE TO PARLIAMENT

After making his broadcast announcement of Germany's unconditional surrender, the Prime Minister read the same statement to the House of Commons a few minutes later, and added:

That is the message which I have been instructed to deliver to the British nation and Commonwealth. I have only two or three sentences to add. They will convey to the House my deep gratitude to this House of Commons, which has proved itself the strongest foundation for waging war that has ever been seen in the whole of our long history. We have all of us made our mistakes, but the strength of the Parliamentary institution has been shown to enable it at the same moment to preserve all the title-deeds of democracy while waging war in the most stern and protracted form. I wish to give my hearty thanks to men of all parties, to everyone in every part of the House where they sit, for the way in which the liveliness of Parliamentary institutions has been maintained under the fire of the enemy, and for the way in which we have been able to persevere – and we could have persevered much longer if need had been – till all the objectives which we set before us for the procuring of the unlimited and unconditional surrender of the enemy had been achieved. I recollect well at the end of the last war, more than a quarter of a century ago, that the House when it heard the long list of the surrender terms, the armistice terms, which had been imposed upon the Germans, did not feel inclined for debate or business, but desired to offer thanks to Almighty God, to the Great Power which seems to shape and design the fortunes of nations and the destiny, of man; and I therefore beg, Sir, with your permission to move:

'That this House do now attend at the Church of St Margaret, Westminster, to give humble and reverent thanks to Almighty God for our deliverance from the threat of German domination.'

This is the identical Motion which was moved in former times.

'THIS IS YOUR VICTORY'

During the celebrations which followed the announcement of Germany's unconditional surrender the Prime Minister made two short speeches from the balcony of the Ministry of Health building to the crowds in Whitehall.

[MAY 8, 1945]

God bless you all. This is your victory! It is the victory of the cause of freedom in every land. In all our long history we have never seen a greater day than this. Everyone, man or woman, has done their best. Everyone has tried. Neither the long years, nor the dangers, nor the fierce attacks of the enemy, have in any way weakened the independent resolve of the British nation. God bless you all.

[MAY 9, 1945]

My dear friends, I hope you have had two happy days. Happy days are what we have worked for, but happy days are not easily worked for. By discipline, by morale, by industry, by good laws, by fair institutions – by those ways we have won through to happy days for millions and millions of people.

You have been attacked by a monstrous enemy – but you never flinched or wavered.

Your soldiers were everywhere in the field, your airmen in the skies – and never let us forget our grand Navy. They dared and they did all those feats of adventure and audacity which have ever enabled brave men to wrest victory from obstinate and bestial circumstances. And you people at home have taken all you had to take – which was enough, when all is said and done. You never let the men at the front down. No one ever asked for peace because London was suffering.

London, like a great rhinoceros, a great hippopotamus, saying: 'Let them do their worst. London can take it.' London could take anything.

My heart goes out to the Cockneys. Any visitors we may happen to have here today – and many great nations are represented here, by all those who have borne arms with us in the struggle – they echo what I say when I say 'GOOD OLD LONDON!'

In every capital of the victorious world there are rejoicings tonight, but in none is there any lack of respect for the part which London has played.

I return my hearty thanks to you for never having failed in the long, monotonous days and in the long nights black as hell.

God bless you all. May you long remain as citizens of a great and splendid city. May you long remain as the heart of the British Empire.

'FORWARD TILL THE WHOLE TASK IS DONE'

A WORLD BROADCAST, MAY 13, 1945

It was five years ago on Thursday last that His Majesty the King commissioned me to form a National Government of all parties to carry on our affairs. Five years is a long time in human life, especially when there is no remission for good conduct. However, this National Government was sustained by Parliament and by the entire British nation at home and by all our fighting men abroad, and by the unswerving co-operation of the Dominions far across the oceans and of our Empire in every quarter of the globe. After various episodes had occurred it became clear last week that so far, things have worked out pretty well, and that the British Commonwealth and Empire stand more united and more effectively power-ful than at any time in its long romantic history. Certainly we are – this is what may well, I think, be admitted by any fair-minded person – in a far better state to cope with the problems and perils of the future than we were five years ago.

For a while our prime enemy, our mighty enemy, Germany, overran almost all Europe. France, who bore such a frightful strain in the last great war, was beaten to the ground and took some time to recover. The Low Countries, fighting to the best of their strength, were subjugated. Norway was overrun. Mussolini's Italy stabbed us in the back when we were, as he thought, at our last gasp. But for ourselves – our lot, I mean – the British Commonwealth and Empire, we were absolutely alone.

In July, August and September, 1940, forty or fifty squadrons of British fighter aircraft in the Battle of Britain broke the teeth of the German air fleet at odds of seven or eight to one. May I repeat again the words I used at that momentous hour: 'Never in the field of human conflict was so much owed by so many to so few.' The name of Air-Chief-Marshal Lord Dowding will always be linked with this splendid event. But conjoined with the Royal Air Force lay the Royal Navy, ever ready to tear to pieces the barges, gathering from the canals of Holland and Belgium, in which a German invading army could alone have been transported. I was never one to believe that the invasion of Britain, with the tackle that the enemy had at that time, was a very easy task to accomplish. With the autumn storms, the immediate danger of invasion in 1940 passed.

Then began the blitz, when Hitler said he would 'rub out our cities'. That's what he said, 'rub out our cities'. This blitz was borne without a word of complaint or the slightest sign of flinching, while a very large number of people – honour to them all – proved that London could 'take it', and so could our other ravaged centres. But the dawn of 1941 revealed us still in jeopardy. The hostile aircraft could fly across the approaches to our island, where forty-six millions of people had to import half their daily bread and all the materials they needed for peace or war; these hostile aircraft could fly across the approaches from Brest to Norway and back again in a single flight. They could observe all the movements of our shipping in and out of the Clyde and Mersey, and could direct upon our convoys the large and increasing numbers of U-boats with which the enemy bespattered the Atlantic – the survivors or successors of which U-boats are now being collected in British harbours.

The sense of envelopment, which might at any moment turn to strangulation, lay heavy upon us. We had only the north-western approach between Ulster and Scotland through which to bring in the means of life and to send out the forces of war. Owing to the action of Mr de Valera, so much at variance with the temper and instinct of thousands of Southern Irishmen who hastened to the battle-front to prove their ancient valour, the approaches which the Southern Irish ports and airfields, could so easily have guarded were closed by the hostile aircraft and U-boats. This was indeed a deadly moment in our life, and if it had not been for the loyalty and friendship of Northern Ireland we should have been forced to come to close quarters with Mr de Valera or perish for ever from the earth. However, with a restraint and poise to which, I say, history will find few parallels, His Majesty's Government never laid a violent hand upon them, though at times it would have been quite easy and quite natural, and we left the de Valera Government to frolic with the Germans and later with the Japanese representatives to their heart's content.

When I think of these days I think also of other episodes and personalities. I think of Lieutenant-Commander Esmonde, VC, of Lance-Corporal Kenneally, VC, and Captain Fegen, VC, and other Irish heroes that I could easily recite, and then I must confess that bitterness by Britain against the Irish race dies in my heart. I can only pray that in years which I shall not see the shame will be forgotten and the glories will endure, and that the peoples of the British Isles as of the British Commonwealth of Nations will walk together in mutual comprehension and forgiveness.

My friends, when our minds turn to the north-western approaches we will not forget the devotion of our merchant seamen, and our mine-sweepers out every night, and so rarely mentioned in the headlines. Nor will we forget the vast, inventive, adaptive, all-embracing and, in the end, all-controlling power of the Royal Navy, with its evermore potent new ally, the air. These have kept the life-line open. We were able to breathe; we were able to live; we were able to strike. Dire deeds we had to do. We had to destroy or capture the French fleet which, had it ever passed undamaged into German hands would, together with the Italian fleet, have perhaps enabled the German Navy to face us on the high seas. This we did. We had to make the dispatch to General Wavell all around the Cape, at our darkest hour, of the tanks – practically all we had in the island – and this enabled us as far back as November 1940, to defend Egypt against invasion and hurl back with the loss of a quarter of a million captives and with heavy slaughter the Italian armies at whose tail Mussolini had already planned to ride into Cairo or Alexandria.

Great anxiety was felt by President Roosevelt, and indeed by thinking men throughout the United States, about what would happen to us in the early part of 1941. The President felt to the depths of his being that the destruction of Britain would not only be an event fearful in itself, but that it would expose to mortal danger the vast and as yet largely unarmed potentialities and the future destiny of the United States. He feared greatly that we should be invaded in that spring of 1941 and no doubt he had behind him military advice as good as any that is known in the world, and he sent his recent Presidential opponent, the late Mr Wendell Willkie, to me with a letter in which he had written in his own hand the famous lines of Longfellow, which I quoted in the House of Commons the other day.

We were, however, in a fairly tough condition by the early months of 1941, and felt very much better about ourselves than in those months immediately after the collapse of France. Our Dunkirk army and field force troops in Britain, almost a million strong, were nearly all equipped or re-equipped. We had ferried over the Atlantic 1,000,000 rifles and 1,000 cannon from the United States, with all their ammunition, since the previous June. In our munition works, which were becoming very powerful, men and women, had worked at their machines till they dropped senseless from fatigue.

Nearly 1,000,000 of men, growing to 2,000,000 at the peak, although working all day had been formed into the Home Guard. They were armed at least with rifles, and armed also with the spirit 'Conquer or Die'.

Later in 1941, when we were still alone, we sacrificed unwillingly, to some extent unwittingly, our conquests of the winter in Cyrenaica and Libya in order to stand by Greece; and Greece will never forget how much we gave, albeit unavailingly, of the little we had. We did this for honour. We repressed the German-instigated rising in Iraq. We defended Palestine. With the assistance of General de Gaulle's indomitable Free French we cleared Syria and the Lebanon of Vichyites and of German aviators and intriguers. And then in June 1941, another tremendous world event occurred.

You have no doubt noticed in your reading of British history – and I hope you will take pains to read it, for it is only from the past that one can judge the future, and it is only from reading the story of the British nation, of the British Empire, that you can feel a well-grounded sense of pride to dwell in these islands – you have sometimes noticed in your reading of British history that we have had to hold out from time to time all alone, or to be the mainspring of coalitions, against a Continental tyrant or dictator, and we have had to hold out for quite a long time: against the Spanish Armada, against the might of Louis XIV, when we led Europe for nearly twenty-five years under William III and Marlborough, and a hundred and fifty years ago, when Nelson, Pitt and Wellington broke Napoleon, not without assistance from the heroic Russians of 1812. In all these world wars our island kept the head of Europe or else held out alone.

And if you hold out alone long enough, there always comes a time when the tyrant makes some ghastly mistake which alters the whole balance of the struggle. On June 22, 1941, Hitler, master as he thought himself of all Europe – nay, indeed, soon to be master of the world, so he thought – treacherously, without warning, without the slightest provocation, hurled himself on Russia and came face to face with Marshal Stalin and the numberless millions of the Russian people. And then at the end of the year Japan struck a felon blow at the United States at Pearl Harbour, and at the same time attacked us in Malaya and Singapore. Thereupon Hitler and Mussolini declared war on the Republic of the United States.

Years have passed since then. Indeed every year seems to me almost a decade. But never since the United States entered the war have I had the slightest doubt that we should be saved, and that we only had to do our duty in order to win. We have played our part in all this process by which the evil-doers have been overthrown, and I hope I do not speak in vain or boastful words, but from Alamein in October 1942, through the Anglo-American invasion of North Africa, of Sicily, of Italy, with the capture of Rome, we marched many miles and never knew defeat. And then last year, after two years' patient preparation and marvellous devices of amphibious warfare – and mark you, our scientists are not surpassed in any nation in the world, especially when their thought is applied to naval matters – last year on June 6 we seized a carefully-selected little toe of German-occupied France and poured millions in from this island, and from across the Atlantic, until the Seine, the Somme, and the Rhine all fell behind the advancing Anglo-American spearheads. France was liberated. She produced a fine army of gallant men to aid her own liberation. Germany lay open.

Now from the other side the mighty military achievements of the Russian people, always holding many more German troops on their front than we could do, rolled forward to meet us in the heart and centre of Germany. At the same time, in Italy, Field-Marshal Alexander's army of so many nations, the largest part of which was British or British Empire, struck their final blow and compelled more than a million enemy troops to surrender. This Fifteenth Army Group, as we call it, British and Americans joined together in almost equal numbers, are now deep in Austria, joining their right hand with the Russians and their left with the United States armies of General Eisenhower's command. It happened, as you may remember – but memories are short – that in the space of three days we received the news of the unlamented departures of Mussolini and Hitler, and in three days also surrenders were made to Field-Marshal Alexander and Field-Marshal Montgomery of over 2,500,000 soldiers of this terrible warlike German army.

I shall make it clear at this moment that we never failed to recognise the immense superiority of the power used by the United States in the rescue of France and the defeat of Germany. For our part, British and Canadians, we have had about one-third as many men over there as the Americans, but we have taken our full share of the fighting, as the scale of our losses shows. Our Navy has borne incomparably the heaviest burden in the Atlantic Ocean, in the narrow seas and the Arctic convoys of Russia, while the United States Navy has had to use its immense strength mainly against Japan. We made a fair division of labour, and we can each report that our work is either done or going to be done. It is right and natural that we should extol the virtues and glorious services of our own most famous commanders, Alexander and Montgomery, neither of whom was ever defeated since they began together at Alamein. Both of them have conducted in Africa, in Italy, in Normandy and in Germany, battles of the first magnitude and of decisive consequence. At the same time we know how great is our debt to the combining and unifying command and high strategic direction of General Eisenhower.

And here is the moment when I pay my personal tribute to the British Chiefs of the Staff with whom I worked in the closest intimacy throughout these heavy, stormy years. There have been very few changes in this small, powerful and capable body of men who, sinking all Service differences and judging the problems of the war as a whole, have worked together in perfect harmony with each other. In Field-Marshal Brooke, in Admiral Pound, succeeded after his death by Admiral Andrew Cunningham, and in Marshal of the Air Portal, a team was formed who deserved the highest honour in the direction of the whole British war strategy and in its relations with that of our allies.

It may well be said that our strategy was conducted so that the best combinations, the closest concert, were imparted into the operations by the combined staffs of Britain and the United States, with whom, from Teheran onwards, the war leaders of Russia were joined. And it may also be said that never have the forces of two nations fought side by side and intermingled in the lines of battle with so much unity, comradeship and brotherhood as in the great Anglo-American armies. Some people say: Well, what would you expect, if both nations speak the same language, have the same laws, have a great part of their history in common, and have very much the same outlook upon life with all its hope and glory? Isn't it just the sort of thing that would happen? And others may say: It would be an ill day for all the world and for the pair of them if they did not go on working together and marching together and sailing together and flying together, whenever something has to be done for the sake of freedom and fair play all over the world. That is the great hope of the future.

There was one final danger from which the collapse of Germany has saved us. In London and the south-eastern counties we have suffered for a year from various forms of flying bombs – perhaps you have heard about this – and rockets, and our Air Force and our Ack-Ack batteries have done wonders against them. In particular the Air Force, turned on in good time on what then seemed very slight and doubtful evidence, hampered and vastly delayed all German preparations. But it was only when our armies cleaned up the coast and overran all the points of discharge, and when the Americans captured vast stores of rockets of all kinds near Leipzig, which only the other day added to the information we had, and when all the preparations being made on the coasts of France and Holland could be examined in detail, in scientific detail, that we knew how grave had been the peril, not only from rockets and flying bombs but from multiple long-range artillery which was being prepared against London. Only just in time did the Allied armies blast the viper in his nest. Otherwise the autumn of 1944, to say nothing of 1945, might well have seen London as shattered as Berlin.

For the same period the Germans had prepared a new U-boat fleet and novel tactics which, though we should have eventually destroyed them, might well have carried anti-U-boat warfare back to the high peak days of 1942. Therefore we must rejoice and give thanks, not only for our preservation when we were all alone, but for our timely deliverance from new suffering, new perils not easily to be measured.

I wish I could tell you tonight that all our toils and troubles were over. Then indeed I could end my five years' service happily, and if you thought that you had had enough of me and that I ought to be put out to grass, I tell you I would take it with the best of grace. But, on the contrary, I must warn you, as I did when I began this five years' task – and no one knew then that it would last so long – that there is still a lot to do, and that you must be prepared for further efforts of mind and body and further sacrifices to great causes if you are not to fall back into the rut of inertia, the confusion of aim, and the craven fear of being great. You must not weaken in any way in your alert and vigilant frame of mind. Though holiday rejoicing is necessary to the human spirit, yet it must add to the strength and resilience with which every man and woman turns again to the work they have to do, and also to the outlook and watch they have to keep on public affairs.

On the continent of Europe we have yet to make sure that the simple and honourable purposes for which we entered the war are not brushed aside or overlooked in the months following our success, and that the words 'freedom', 'democracy', and 'liberation' are not distorted from their true meaning as we have understood them. There would be little use in punishing the Hitlerites for their crimes if law and justice did not rule, and if totalitarian or police Governments were to take the place of the German invaders. We seek nothing for ourselves. But we must make sure that those causes which we fought for find recognition at the peace table in facts as well as words, and above all we must labour that the world organisation which the United Nations are creating at San Francisco does not become an idle name, does not become a shield for the strong and a mockery for the weak. It is the victors who must

311

search their hearts in their glowing hours, and be worthy by their nobility of the immense forces that they wield.

We must never forget that beyond all lurks Japan, harassed and failing but still a people of a hundred millions, for whose warriors death has few terrors. I cannot tell you tonight how much time or what exertions will be required to compel the Japanese to make amends for their odious treachery and cruelty. We – like China, so long undaunted – have received horrible injuries from them ourselves, and we are bound by the ties of honour and fraternal loyalty to the United States to fight this great war at the other end of the world at their side without flagging or failing. We must remember that Australia and New Zealand and Canada were and are all directly menaced by this evil Power. They came to our aid in our dark times, and we must not leave unfinished any task which concerns their safety and their future. I told you hard things at the beginning of these last five years; you did not shrink, and I should be unworthy of your confidence and generosity if I did not still cry: Forward, unflinching, unswerving, indomitable, till the whole task is done and the whole world is safe and clean.

A TRIBUTE TO EISENHOWER

A SPEECH AT THE MANSION HOUSE WHEN GENERAL EISENHOWER, SUPREME COMMANDER, RECEIVED THE FREEDOM OF THE CITY OF LONDON, JUNE 12, 1945

I have been brought very closely in contact with General Eisenhower since the day early in 1942 when we first met at the White House after the attack on Pearl Harbour, and all the grave matters of the direction of the armies to the landings in French North Africa and all the great efforts which were called for a year ago had to be discussed and examined, and I had the opportunity of seeing at close quarters General

'Ike' – for that is what I call him – in action. I saw him at all sorts of times, because in war things do not always go as we wish. Another will breaks in, and there is a clash, and questions arise. Never have I seen a man so staunch in pursuing the purpose in hand, so ready to accept responsibility for misfortune, or so generous in victory.

There is one moment I would dwell on. It was just about a little more than a year ago that he had to decide whether to go across the Channel or put it off for, it might be, eleven days. It was a terrible decision. The Army had gathered. A million men in the front line had gathered, and thousands of craft and tens of thousands of aircraft, and the great ships were all arranged. You could not hold it. It was like trying to hold an avalanche in leash. Should it be launched or should it not be launched?

There were a great many people who had a chance of expressing their opinions. I was not one of them, because it was purely a technical matter. A great many generals and admirals were gathered in the High Command to express their opinions and views, but there was only one man on whom the awful brunt fell of saying 'Go' and 'Stay'. To say 'Stay' meant keeping hundreds of thousands of men cooped up in wired enclosures so that the plans they had been told of might not leak out. It meant the problem of hundreds of thousands of men on board ship who had to be provided for and found accommodation: It might have meant that the air could not cover the landing or that the water was too rough for the many boats that were needed.

It was one of the most terrible decisions, and this decision was taken by this man – this very great man [prolonged applause].

It was one of many decisions he has taken. Had he not said 'Go', and eleven days had passed, the weather would have smiled, and all the groups of meteorologists would have been happy. The expedition would have started; and two days later the worst gale for forty years at that season of the year fell upon the beaches in Normandy. Not only did he take the risk and arrive at the fence, he cleared it in magnificent style.

There are many occasions when that kind of decision falls on the supreme commander. Many fearful tales come from the front line. A great deal of anxiety is felt by populations at home. Do we go forward? Do we fight in this area? Are we to push on? These decisions all resolved themselves into an 'Aye' or a 'No', and all I can say about our guest is that in very many most important decisions, history will acclaim his decisions as right, and that the bias, the natural bias, that moved him in these matters was very much more in favour of 'Aye' than of 'No'.

I could go on for a very long time about your guest. There is no doubt whatever that we have among us today one of the greatest Americans who have reached our shores and dwelt a considerable time among us. We honour him very much for his invariable consideration of the British point of view, for his impartial treatment of all the officers under his command. I know he will tell you when he rises that he never gave an order to a British officer which he could not immediately obey.

We also have made our contribution to the battles on the Continent, and I am quite sure that the influence he will wield in the world will be one always of bringing our countries together in the much more difficult task of peace in the same way as he brought them together in the grim and awful cataclysm of war. I have had personal acquaintance with him now for three years. It is not much, but three years of this sort may seem five-and-twenty. I feel we have here a great creative, constructive and combining genius, one from our sister nation across the ocean, one who will never speak evil but will always cherish his contact with the British people, and to whom I feel we should at this moment give the most cordial testimony in our power, of our admiration, of our affection, and of our heartfelt good wishes for everything that may happen to him in the future.

THE SUPREME TRIUMPH

MR CHURCHILL'S FINAL REVIEW OF THE WAR AND HIS
FIRST MAJOR SPEECH AS LEADER OF THE OPPOSITION
IN THE HOUSE OF COMMONS, AUGUST 16, 1945

Our duty is to congratulate His Majesty's Government on the very great improvement in our prospects at home, which comes from the complete victory gained over Japan and the establishment of peace throughout the world. Only a month ago it was necessary to continue at full speed and at enormous cost all preparations for a long and bloody campaign in the Far East. In the first days of the Potsdam Conference, President Truman and I approved the plans submitted to us by the Combined Chiefs of Staff for a series of great battles and landings in Malaya, in the Netherlands East Indies, and in the homeland of Japan itself. These operations involved an effort not surpassed in Europe, and no one could measure the cost in British and American life and treasure they would require. Still less could it be known how long the stamping-out of the resistance of Japan in the many territories she had conquered, and especially in her homeland, would take. All the while the whole process of turning the world from war to peace would be hampered and delayed. Every form of peace activity was half strangled by the overriding priorities of war. No clear-cut decisions could be taken in the presence of this harsh dominating uncertainty.

During the last three months an element of baffling dualism has complicated every problem of policy and administration. We had to plan for peace and war at the same time. Immense armies were being demobilised; another powerful army was being prepared and dispatched to the other side of the globe. All the personal stresses among millions of men eager to return to civil life, and hundreds of thousands of men who would have to be sent to new and severe campaigns in the Far East, presented themselves with growing tension. This dualism affected also every aspect of our economic and financial life. How to set people free to use their activities in reviving the life of Britain, and at the same time to meet the stern demands of the war against Japan, constituted one of the most perplexing and distressing puzzles that in a long lifetime of experience I have ever faced.

I confess it was with great anxiety that I surveyed this prospect a month ago. Since then I have been relieved of the burden. At the same time that burden, heavy though it still remains, has been immeasurably lightened. On July 17 there came to us at Potsdam the eagerly-awaited news of the trial of the atomic bomb in the Mexican desert. Success beyond all dreams crowned this sombre, magnificent venture of our American Allies. The detailed reports of the Mexican desert experiment, which were brought to us a few days later by air, could leave no doubt in the minds of the very few who were informed, that we were in the presence of a new factor in human affairs, and possessed of powers which were irresistible. Great Britain had a right to be consulted in accordance with Anglo-American agreements. The decision to use the atomic bomb was taken by President Truman and myself at Potsdam, and we approved the military plans to unchain the dread, pent-up forces.

From that moment our outlook on the future was transformed. In preparation for the results of this experiment, the statements of the President and of Mr Stimson and my own statement, which by the courtesy of the Prime Minister was subsequently read out on the broadcast, were framed in common agreement. Marshal Stalin was informed by President Truman that we contemplated using an explosive of incomparable power against Japan, and action proceeded in the way we all now know. It is to this atomic bomb more than to any other factor that we may ascribe the sudden and speedy ending of the war against Japan.

Before using it, it was necessary first of all to send a message in the form of an ultimatum to the Japanese which would apprise them of what unconditional surrender meant. This document was published on July 26 — the same day that another event, differently viewed on each side of the House, occurred. [Note: The result of the General Election and the resignation of Mr Churchill from the Premiership.] The assurances given to Japan about her future after her unconditional surrender had been made were generous in the extreme. When we remember the cruel and treacherous nature of the utterly unprovoked attack made by the Japanese warlords upon the United States and Great Britain, these assurances must be considered magnanimous in a high degree. In a nutshell, they implied 'Japan for the Japanese', and even access to raw materials, apart from their control, was not denied to their densely-populated homeland. We felt that in view of the new and fearful agencies of war-power about to be employed, every inducement to surrender, compatible with our declared policy, should be set before them. This we owed to our consciences before using this awful weapon.

Secondly, by repeated warnings, emphasised by heavy bombing attacks, an endeavour was made to procure the general exodus of the civil population from the threatened cities. Thus everything in human power, prior to using the atomic bomb, was done to spare the civil population of Japan. There are voices which assert that the bomb should never have been used at all. I cannot associate myself with such ideas. Six years of total war have convinced most people that had the Germans or Japanese discovered this new weapon, they would have used it upon us to our complete destruction with the utmost alacrity. I am surprised that very worthy people, but people who in most cases had no intention of proceeding to the Japanese front themselves, should adopt the position that rather than throw this bomb, we should have sacrificed a million American, and a quarter of a million British lives in the desperate battles and massacres of an invasion of Japan. Future generations will judge these dire decisions, and I believe that if they find themselves dwelling in a happier world from which war has been banished, and where freedom reigns, they will not condemn those who struggled for their benefit amid the horrors and miseries of this gruesome and ferocious epoch.

The bomb brought peace, but men alone can keep that peace, and henceforward they will keep it under penalties which threaten the survival, not only of civilisation but of humanity itself. I may say that I am entire agreement with the President that the secrets of the atomic bomb should so far as possible not be imparted at the present time to any other country in the world. This is in no design or wish for arbitrary power, but for the common safety of the world. Nothing can stop the progress of research and experiment in every country, but although research will no doubt proceed in many places, the construction of the immense plants necessary to transform theory into action cannot be improvised in any country.

For this and many other reasons the United States stand at this moment at the summit of the world. I rejoice that this should be so. Let them act up to the level of their power and their responsibility, not for themselves but for others, for all men in all lands, and then a brighter day may dawn upon human history. So far as we know, there are at least three and perhaps four years before the concrete progress made in the United States can be overtaken. In these three years we must remould the relationships of all men, wherever they dwell, in all the nations. We must remould them in such a way that these men do not wish or dare to fall upon each other for the sake of vulgar and out-dated ambitions or for passionate differences in ideology, and that international bodies of supreme authority may give peace on earth and degree justice among men. Our pilgrimage has brought us to the sublime moment in the history of the world. From the least to the greatest, all must strive to be worthy of these supreme opportunities. There is not an hour to be wasted; there is not a day to be lost.

It would in my opinion be a mistake to suggest that the Russian declaration of war upon Japan was hastened by the use of the atomic bomb. My understanding with Marshal Stalin in the talks which I had with him had been, for a considerable time past, that Russia would declare war upon Japan within three months of the surrender of the German armies. The reason for the delay of three months was, of course, the need to move over the trans-Siberian Railway the large re-inforcements necessary to convert the Russian-Manchurian army from a defensive to an offensive strength. Three months was the time mentioned, and the fact that the German armies surrendered on May 8, and the Russians declared war on Japan on August 8, is no mere coincidence, but another example of the fidelity and punctuality with which Marshal Stalin and his valiant armies always keep their military engagements.

I now turn to the results of the Potsdam Conference so far as they have been made public in the agreed communiqué and in President Truman's very remarkable speech of a little more than a week ago. There has been general approval of the arrangements proposed for the administration of Germany by the Allied Control Commission during the provisional period of military government. This regime is both transitional and indefinite. The character of Hitler's Nazi party was such as to destroy almost all independent elements in the German people. The struggle was fought to the bitter end. The mass of the people were forced to drain the cup of defeat to the dregs. A headless Germany has fallen into the hands of the conquerors. It may be many years before any structure of German national life will be possible, and there will be plenty of time for the victors to consider how the interests of world peace are affected thereby.

In the meanwhile, it is in my view of the utmost importance that responsibility should be effectively assumed by German local bodies for carrying on under Allied supervision all the processes of production and of administration necessary to maintain the life of a vast population. It is not possible for the Allies to bear responsibility by themselves. We cannot have the German masses lying down upon our hands and expecting to be fed, organised and educated over a period of years by the Allies. We must do our best to help to avert the tragedy of famine. But it would be in vain for us in our small island, which still needs to import half its food, to imagine that we can make any further appreciable contribution in that respect. The rationing of this country cannot be made more severe without endangering the life and physical strength of our people, all of which will be needed for the immense tasks we have to do. I, therefore, most strongly advise the encouragement of the assumption of responsibility by trustworthy German local bodies in proportion as they can be brought into existence.

The Council which was set up at Potsdam of the Foreign Secretaries of the three, four or five Powers, meeting in various combinations as occasion served, affords a new and flexible machinery for the continuous further study of the immense problems that lie before us in Europe and Asia. I am very glad that the request that I made to the conference that the seat of the Council's permanent Secretariat should be London, was granted. I must say that the late Foreign Secretary (Mr Anthony Eden), who has, over a long period, gained an increasing measure of confidence from the Foreign Secretaries of Russia and the United States, and who through the European Advisory Committee which is located in London has always gained the feeling that things could be settled in a friendly and easy way, deserves some of the credit for the fact that these great Powers willingly accorded us the seat in London of the permanent Secretariat. It is high time that the place of London, one of the controlling centres of international world affairs, should at last be recognised. It is the oldest, the largest, the most battered capital, the capital which was first in the war, and the time is certainly overdue when we should have our recognition.

I am glad also that a beginning is to be made with the evacuation of Persia by the British and Russian armed forces, in accordance with the triple treaty which we made with each other and with Persia in 1941. Although it does not appear in the communiqué, we have since seen it announced that the first stage in the process, namely the withdrawal of Russian and British troops from Teheran, has already begun or is about to begin. There are various other matters arising out of this conference which should be noted as satisfactory. We should not, however, delude ourselves into supposing that the results of this first conference of the victors were free from disappointment or anxiety, or that the most serious questions before us were brought to good solutions. Those which proved incapable of agreement at the conference have been relegated to the Foreign Secretaries' Council, which, though most capable of relieving difficulties, is essentially one gifted with far less-reaching powers. Other grave questions are left for the final peace settlement, by which time many of them may have settled themselves, not necessarily in the best way.

It would be at once wrong and impossible to conceal the divergences of view which exist inevitably between the victors about the state of affairs in Eastern and Middle Europe. I do not at all blame the Prime Minister or the new Foreign Secretary, whose task it was to finish up the discussions which we had begun. I am sure they did their best. We have to realise that no one of the three leading Powers can impose its solutions upon others, and that the only solutions possible are those which are in the nature of compromise. We British have had very early and increasingly to recognise the limitations of our own power and influence, great though it be, in the gaunt world arising from the ruins of this hideous war. It is not in the power of any British Government to bring home solutions which would be regarded as perfect by the great majority of Members of this House, wherever they may sit. I must put on record my own opinion that the provisional western frontier agreed upon for Poland, running from Stetin on the Baltic, along the Oder and its tributary, the Western Neisse, comprising as it does one quarter of the arable land of all Germany, is not a good augury for the future map of Europe. We always had in the Coalition Government a desire that Poland should receive ample compensation in the west for the territory ceded to Russia east of the Curzon Line. But here I think a mistake has been made, in which the Provisional Government of Poland have been an ardent partner, by going far beyond what necessity or equity required. There are few virtues that the

Poles do not possess – and there are few mistakes they have ever avoided.

I am particularly concerned, at this moment, with the reports reaching us of the conditions under which the expulsion and exodus of Germans from the new Poland are being carried out. Between eight and nine million persons dwelt in those regions before the war. The Polish Government say that there are still 1,500,000 of these, not yet expelled, within their new frontiers. Other millions must have taken refuge behind the British and American lines, thus increasing the food stringency in our sector. But enormous numbers are utterly unaccounted for. Where are they gone, and what has been their fate? The same conditions may reproduce themselves in a modified form in the expulsion of great numbers of Sudeten and other Germans from Czechoslovakia. Sparse and guarded accounts of what has happened and is happening have filtered through, but it is not impossible that tragedy on a prodigious scale is unfolding itself behind the iron curtain which at the moment divides Europe in twain. I should welcome any statement which the Prime Minister can make which would relieve, or at least inform us upon this very anxious and grievous matter.

There is another sphere of anxiety. I remember that a fortnight or so before the last war, the Kaiser's friend Herr Ballin, the great shipping magnate, told me that he had heard Bismarck say towards the end of his life, 'If there is ever another war in Europe, it will come out of some damned silly thing in the Balkans.' The murder of the Archduke at Sarajevo in 1914 set the signal for the first world war. I cannot conceive that the elements for a new conflict do not exist in the Balkans today. I am not using the language of Bismarck, but nevertheless not many Members of the new House of Commons will be content with the new situation that prevails in those mountainous, turbulent, ill-organised and warlike regions. I do not intend to particularise. I am very glad to see the new Foreign Secretary (Mr Ernest Bevin) sitting on the Front Bench opposite. I should like to say with what gratification I learned that he had taken on this high and most profoundly difficult office, and we

322

are sure he will do his best to preserve the great causes for which we have so long pulled together. But as I say, not many Members will be content with the situation in that region to which I have referred, for almost everywhere Communist forces have obtained, or are in process of obtaining, dictatorial powers. It does not mean that the Communist system is everywhere being established, nor does it mean that Soviet Russia seeks to reduce all those independent States to provinces of the Soviet Union. Marshal Stalin is a very wise man, and I would set no limits to the immense contributions that he and his associates have to make to the future.

In those countries, torn and convulsed by war, there may be, for some months to come, the need of authoritarian government. The alternative would be anarchy. Therefore it would be unreasonable to ask or expect that liberal government – as spelt with a small 'l' – and British or United States democratic conditions, should be instituted immediately. They take their politics very seriously in those countries. A friend of mine, an officer, was in Zagreb when the results of the late General Election came in. An old lady said to him, 'Poor Mr Churchill! I suppose now he will be shot.' My friend was able to reassure her. He said the sentence might be mitigated to one of the various forms of hard labour which are always open to His Majesty's subjects. Nevertheless we must know where we stand, and we must make clear where we stand, in these affairs of the Balkans and of Eastern Europe, and indeed of any country which comes into this field. Our ideal is government of the people by the people, for the people – the people being free without duress to express, by secret ballot without intimidation, their deep-seated wish as to the form and conditions of the Government under which they are to live.

At the present time – I trust a very fleeting time – 'police governments' rule over a great number of countries. It is a case of the odious 18B, carried to a horrible excess. The family is gathered round the fireside to enjoy the scanty fruits of their toil and to recruit their exhausted strength by the little food that they have been able to gather. There they sit. Suddenly there is a knock at the door, and a heavily-armed policeman appears. He is not, of course, one who resembled in any way those functionaries whom we honour and obey in the London streets. It may be that the father or son, or a friend sitting in the cottage, is called out and taken off into the dark, and no one knows whether he will ever come back again, or what his fate has been. All they know is that they had better not inquire. There are millions of humble homes in Europe at the moment, in Poland, in Czechoslovakia, in Austria, in Hungary, in Yugoslavia, in Rumania, in Bulgaria – where this fear is the main preoccupation of the family life. President Roosevelt laid down the four freedoms, and these are expressed in the Atlantic Charter which we agreed together. 'Freedom from fear' – but this has been interpreted as if it were only freedom from fear of invasion from a foreign country. That is the least of the fears of the common man. His patriotism arms him to withstand invasion or go down fighting; but that is not the fear of the ordinary family in Europe tonight. Their fear is of the policeman's knock. It is not fear for the country, for all men can unite in comradeship for the defence of their native soil. It is for the life and liberty of the individual, for the fundamental rights of man, now menaced and precarious in so many lands, that peoples tremble.

Surely we can agree in this new Parliament, or the great majority of us, wherever we sit – there are naturally and rightly differences and cleavages of thought – but surely we can agree in this new Parliament, which will either fail the world or once again play a part in saving it, that it is the will of the people freely expressed by secret ballot, in universal suffrage elections, as to the form of their government and as to the laws which shall prevail, which is the first solution and safeguard. Let us then march steadily along that plain and simple line. I avow my faith in democracy, whatever course or view it may take with individuals and parties. They may make their mistakes, and they may profit from their mistakes. Democracy is now on trial as it never was before, and in these islands we must uphold it, as we upheld it in the dark days of 1940 and 1941, with all our hearts, with all our vigilance, and with all our enduring and inexhaustible strength. While the war was

on and all the Allies were fighting for victory, the word
'democracy', like many people, had to work overtime, but now
that peace has come we must search for more precise defini-
tions. Elections have been proposed in some of these Balkan
countries where only one set of candidates is allowed to
appear, and where, if other parties are to express their opinion,
it has to be arranged beforehand that the governing party,
armed with its political police and all its propaganda, is the
only one which has the slightest chance. Chance, did I say? It
is a certainty.

Now is the time for Britons to speak out. It is odious to us
that Governments should seek to maintain their rule otherwise
than by free unfettered elections by the mass of the people.
Governments derive their just powers from the consent of the
governed, says the Constitution of the United States. This must
not evaporate in swindles and lies propped up by servitude
and murder. In our foreign policy let us strike continually the
notes of freedom and fair play as we understood them in these
islands. Then you will find there will be an overwhelming
measure of agreement between us, and we shall in this House
march forward on an honourable theme having within it all
that invests human life with dignity and happiness. In saying
all this, I have been trying to gather together and present in a
direct form the things which, I believe, are dear to the great
majority of us. I rejoiced to read them expressed in
golden words by the President of the United States when he
said:

'Our victory in Europe was more than a victory of arms. It
was a victory of one way of life over another. It was a victory
of an ideal founded on the right of the common man, on the
dignity of the human being, and on the conception of the
State as the servant, not the master, of its people.'

I think there is not such great disagreement between us.
Emphasis may be cast this way and that in particular incidents,
but surely this is what the new Parliament on the whole
means. This is what in our heart and conscience, in foreign
affairs and world issues, we desire. Just as in the baleful glare
of 1940, as now, when calmer lights shine, let us be united

upon these resurgent principles and impulses of the good and generous hearts of men. Thus to all the material strength we possess and the honoured position we have acquired, we shall add those moral forces which glorify mankind and make even the weakest equals of the strong.

I now turn to the domestic sphere. I have already spoken of the enormous easement in their task which the new Government have obtained through the swift and sudden ending of the Japanese war. What thousands of millions of pounds sterling are saved from the waste of war, what scores and hundreds of thousands of lives are saved, what vast numbers of ships are set free to carry the soldiers home to all their lands, to carry about the world the food and raw materials vital to industry! What noble opportunities have the new Government inherited! Let them be worthy of their fortune, which is also the fortune of us all. To release and liberate the vital springs of British energy and inventiveness, to let the honest earnings of the nation fructify in the pockets of the people, to spread well-being and security against accident and misfortune throughout the whole nation, to plan, wherever State planning is imperative, and to guide into fertile and healthy channels the native British genius for comprehension and good will – all these are open to them, and all these ought to be open to all of us now. I hope we may go forward together, not only abroad but also at home, in all matters so far as we possibly can.

During the period of the 'Caretaker Government', while we still had to contemplate eighteen months of strenuous war with Japan, we reviewed the plans for demobilisation in such a way as to make a very great acceleration in the whole process of releasing men and women from the armed forces and from compulsory industrial employment. Now, all that is overtaken by the world-wide end of the war. I must say at once that the paragraph of the Gracious Speech [The King's speech outlining the new Government's policy] referring to demobilisation and to the plans which were made in the autumn of 1944 – with which I am in entire agreement in principle – gives a somewhat chilling impression. Now that we have had this wonderful windfall, I am surprised that any Government should imagine that language of this kind is still appropriate or equal to the new situation. I see that in the United States the President has said that all the American troops that the American ships can carry home in the next year will be brought home and set free. Are His Majesty's Government now able to make any statement of that kind about our armed forces abroad? Or what statement can they make? I do not want to harass them unduly, but perhaps some time next week some statement could be made. No doubt the Prime Minister will think of that. Great hopes have been raised in the electoral campaign, and from those hopes has sprung their great political victory. Time will show whether those hopes are well founded, as we deeply trust they may be. But many decisions can be taken now, in the completely altered circumstances in which we find ourselves. The duty of the Government is to fix the minimum numbers who must be retained in the next six or twelve months' period in all the foreign theatres, and to bring the rest home with the utmost speed that our immensely expanded shipping resources will permit.

Even more is this releasing process important in the de-mobilisation of the home establishment. I quite agree that the feeling of the Class A men must ever be the dominant factor, but short of that the most extreme efforts should be made to release people who are standing about doing nothing. I hope the Public Expenditure Committee will be at once reconstituted, and that they will travel about the country examining home establishments and reporting frequently to the House. Now that the war is over, there is no ground of military secrecy which should prevent the publication of the exact numerical ration strengths of our Army, Navy and Air Force in every theatre and at home, and we should certainly have weekly, or at least monthly figures of the progressive demobilisation effected. It is an opportunity for the new Government to win distinction. At the end of the last war, when I was in charge of the Army and Air Force, I published periodically very precise information. I agree with the words used by the Foreign Secretary when he was Minister of Labour in my

327

Administration, namely, that the tremendous winding-up process of the war must be followed by a methodical and regulated unwinding. We agree that if the process is to be pressed forward with the utmost speed it is necessary for the Government to wield exceptional powers for the time being, and so long as they use those powers to achieve the great administrative and executive tasks imposed upon them, we shall not attack them. It is only if, and in so far as, those powers are used to bring about by a side-wind a state of controlled society agreeable to Socialist doctrinaires, but which we deem odious to British freedom, that we shall be forced to resist them. So long as the exceptional powers are used as part of the war emergency, His Majesty's Government may consider us as helpers and not as opponents, as friend and not as foes.

To say this in no way relieves the Government of their duty to set the nation free as soon as possible, to bring home the soldiers in accordance with the scheme with the utmost rapidity, and to enable the mass of the people to resume their normal lives and employment in the best, easiest and speediest manner. There ought not to be a long-dragged-out period of many months when hundreds of thousands of Service men and women are kept waiting about under discipline, doing useless tasks at the public expense, and other tens of thousands, more highly paid, finding them sterile work to do. What we desire is freedom; what we need is abundance. Freedom and abundance – these must be our aims. The production of new wealth is far more beneficial, and on an incomparably larger scale, than class and party fights about the liquidation of old wealth. We must try to share blessings and not miseries.

The production of new wealth must precede common wealth, otherwise there will only be common poverty. I am sorry these simple truisms should excite the hon Member opposite – whom I watched so often during the course of the last Parliament and whose many agreeable qualities I have often admired – as if they had some sense of novelty for him.

We do not propose to join issue immediately about the

legislative proposals in the Gracious Speech. We do not know what is meant by the control of investment – but apparently it is a subject for mirth. Evidently, in war you may do one thing, and in peace perhaps another must be considered. Allowance must also be made for the transitional period through which we are passing. The Debate on the Address should probe and elicit the Government's intentions in this matter. The same is true of the proposal to nationalise the coal mines. If that is really the best way of securing a larger supply of coal at a cheaper price, and at an earlier moment than is now in view, I, for one, should approach the plan in a sympathetic spirit. It is by results that the Government will be judged, and it is by results that this policy must be judged. The national ownership of the Bank of England does not in my opinion raise any matter of principle. I give my opinion – anybody else may give his own. There are important examples in the United States and in our Dominions of central banking institutions, but what matters is the use to be made of this public ownership. On this we must await the detailed statement by the Chancellor of the Exchequer, who, I am glad to say, has pledged himself to resist inflation. Meanwhile it may be helpful for me to express the opinion, as Leader of the Opposition, that foreign countries need not be alarmed by the language of the Gracious Speech on this subject, and that British credit will be resolutely upheld.

Then there is the Trade Disputes Act. We are told that this is to be repealed. Personally, I feel that we owe an inestimable debt to the trade unions for all they have done for the country in the long struggle against the foreign foe. But they would surely be unwise to reinstitute the political levy on the old basis. It would also be very odd if they wished to regain full facilities for legalising and organising a general strike. It does not say much for the confidence with which the Trades Union Council view the brave new world, or for what they think about the progressive nationalisation of our industries, that they should deem it necessary on what an hon and gallant Gentleman called 'the D-Day of the new Britain' to restore and sharpen the general strike weapon, at this particular time of all others. Apparently nationalisation is not regarded by them as any security against conditions which would render a general strike imperative and justified in the interests of the workers. We are, I understand, after nationalising the coal-mines, to deal with the railways, electricity and transport. Yet at the same time the trade unions feel it necessary to be heavily re-armed against State Socialism. Apparently the new age is not to be so happy for the wage-earners as we have been asked to believe. At any rate, there seems to be a fundamental incongruity in these conceptions to which the attention of the Socialist intelligentsia should speedily be directed. Perhaps it may be said that these powers will only be needed if the Tories come into office. Surely these are early days to get frightened. I will ask the Prime Minister if he will just tell us broadly what is meant by the word 'repeal'.

I have offered these comments to the House, and I do not wish to end on a sombre or even slightly controversial note. As to the situation which exists today, it is evident that not only are the two Parties in the House agreed in the main essentials of foreign policy and in our moral outlook on world affairs, but we also have an immense programme, prepared by our joint exertions during the Coalition, which requires to be brought into law and made an inherent part of the life of the people. Here and there there may be differences of emphasis and view, but in the main no Parliament ever assembled with such a mass of agreed legislation as lies before us this after-noon. I have great hopes of this Parliament, and I shall do my utmost to make its work fruitful. It may heal the wounds of war, and turn to good account the new conceptions and powers which we have gathered amid the storm. I do not underrate the difficult and intricate complications of the task which lies before us; I know too much about it to cherish vain illusions; but the morrow of such a victory as we have gained is a splendid moment both in our small lives and in our great history. It is a time not only of rejoicing but even more of resolve. When we look back on all the perils through which we have passed and at the mighty foes we have laid low and all the dark and deadly designs we have frustrated, why should we fear for our future? We have come safely through the worst.

> 'Home is the sailor, home from the sea,
> And the hunter home from the hill.'

THE END

NOTES

NOTES

NOTES

NOTES

NOTES